Changes and Challenges for the
Human Resource Professional

Changes and Challenges for the Human Resource Professional

RONALD R. SIMS AND SERBRENIA J. SIMS

Q

QUORUM BOOKS
Westport, Connecticut • London

HF5549
.S5924
1994

Library of Congress Cataloging-in-Publication Data

Sims, Ronald R.
   Changes and challenges for the human resource professional /
Ronald R. Sims and Serbrenia J. Sims.
       p.   cm.
   Includes bibliographical references and index.
   ISBN 0–89930–885–6 (alk. paper)
   1. Personnel management. I. Sims, Serbrenia J. II. Title.
HF5549.S5924 1994
658.3—dc20   94–15876

British Library Cataloguing in Publication Data is available.

Library of Congress Catalog Card Number: 94–15876
ISBN 0–89930–885–6

First published in 1994

Quorum Books, 88 Post Road West, Westport, CT 06881
An imprint of Greenwood Publishing Group, Inc.

Printed in the United States of America

The paper used in this book complies with the
Permanent Paper Standard issued by the National
Information Standards Organization (Z39.48–1984).
10 9 8 7 6 5 4 3 2 1

To Ronald, Jr., Marchet, Vellice, Shelley, Sharisse,
Nandi, Dangaia, and Sieya

Contents

Preface

The management of people at work is one of the primary keys to organizational success. Yet, a backlog of problems has caused too little attention to the management of human resources in the past. Finance, general management, marketing, production, and research and development all received much more attention than human resources management (HRM). Awareness of inadequacies of HRM has come as we compared our success in this area with that of organizations in other countries where human resources were considered critical to success. Organizations in the United States have considerable catching up to do.

In efforts to catch up, it is not enough to stay on top of the latest developments within a rapidly changing discipline. Increasingly, managers in some organizations recognize that people are human resources to be managed effectively, just like money and other organizational resources. In addition, these same organizations and managers have discovered that better management of human resources can be a major source of productivity improvement and growth. These companies' corporate public relations documents often refer to people as the most important or valuable resources in an organization.

In response to the recognition given to human resources, organizations have recently elevated the importance of their HRM function as a major organizational component in their efforts to be successful and remain competitive. Despite the elevation of the HRM function to date, it is the contention of this book that as HRM professionals increasingly receive more responsibilities, they will be confronted by a number of challenges (for example, in the areas of compensation and benefits, training, and so forth) and changes. And by helping their organizations successfully address these challenges and changes,

HRM professionals will become equal strategic partners in their organizations.

Because we believe that the impact of future challenges and issues on organizations in general, and the role of HRM in particular, require a more indepth discussion, a major goal of this book is to help HRM professionals better address what we see as the more prominent and complex HRM challenges and issues in the coming years. A major focus of the book will be first to acknowledge that in today's organizations, HRM issues are replacing capital resource issues as the guiding force of organizations. That is, employees are becoming the most important resources of the organization. Thus, this rise to prominence of human resources is caused by the combined effect of two events: a backlog of unsolved problems in HRM and a dramatic increase in knowledge of human resources. With this focus as a backdrop, the book is organized as follows:

Chapter 1, "The Changing Role of Human Resources Management" discusses the changing environment of HRM and the changing role of HRM professionals. Chapter 2, "The Role of Human Resources Management and Changing Employee Expectations," suggests that the success of HRM professionals in meeting the challenges associated with changing expectations may be the way to many organizations' continued success. Chapter 3, "Human Resources Management and the Challenges of a Diverse Workforce: Including the Disabled in the Diversity Equation," presents several challenges related to increasing diversity in organizations for HRM professionals as they wrestle with the competing demands of changing employee expectations as highlighted in the previous chapter and the demands of legislation like the American with Disabilities Act. In Chapters 4 and 5, "Employee Compensation and Human Resources Management" and "Benefits and Human Resources Management," the discussion turns to the need for HRM professionals to understand the ever changing challenges that accompany the development of a comprehensive, yet flexible and responsive, compensation system that must meet both the organizations and employee's needs.

Chapter 6, "Human Resource Information Systems and Human Resources Management," examines the increasing importance of computers and accompanying challenges to HRM professionals in their efforts to provide more efficient services for the organization and its employees so that they can both be more productive. Chapter 7, "Human Resources Management and Employee Training and Development," addresses the human resource development challenges associated with organizational efforts to respond to an increasingly volatile internal and external environment. Chapter 8, "Downsizing and Human Resources Management," discusses the HRM challenges accompanying organizational efforts in the form of downsizing to respond to slower growth and the need to streamline their operations to become more competitive in the global marketplace. Chapter 9, "Ethics and the Role of Human Resources Management," argues that as a strategic resource for management to achieve its organizational goals, HRM will play an increasingly important role in the design and execution of an ethics strategy. Chapter 10, the concluding chapter, "Human Resources Management: A Review and Preview," returns to a discussion of the mission and activities of the HRM department by highlighting the importance of HRM as a strategic partner and concludes with a look at some of the continuing changes and challenges for HRM professionals.

Acknowledgments

A special thanks goes to Herrington Bryce of the College of William and Mary, who, as always, continues to expect us to stretch ourselves to take on new challenges. The administrative support of Al Page, Dean of the School of Business Administration, is also acknowledged. A special thanks goes to Julie Heck, Nancy Smith, and Phyllis Viandis for their assistance in this project. And finally, Vellice, Nandi, Dangaia, and Sieya are always there to remind us to that we need to keep raising the bar.

Changes and Challenges for the Human Resource Professional

1

The Changing Role of Human Resources Management

An increasing number of organizations are recognizing the critical role that human resources and the field of personnel or human resources management (HRM) can play in corporate success or failure. The HRM function is concerned with helping their organization to effectively use the assets of human resources for the attainment of organizational goals and the continued viability and success of the organization.

HRM activities include such things as recruiting and selecting qualified individuals, training them, and finding ways to motivate them through such things as performance appraisal and pay systems, thereby creating work environments that are responsive to both the needs of the employees and the organization, and ensuring that all of the HRM and organizational activities are performed within the requirements of the United States and international legal systems.

We begin this chapter with a look at the evolution of HRM and at the challenges and demands it currently faces. Then we offer suggestions on how the HRM function and the HRM professional need to change to add more value to the organization.

A HISTORICAL PERSPECTIVE OF HRM

To understand the present HRM function in the United States, one first needs to understand its historical evolution. This evolution can best be characterized as a constant struggle for recognition as a legitimate organizational function. However, with each successive generation, HRM has been perceived and treated as a weak stepsister, a necessary evil that must be dealt with while HRM professionals have sought to justify their existence in a variety of ways.

During the 1800s, the U.S. economy depended primarily on agriculture and small family businesses. HRM activities were conducted by the most senior employees of the organization. Employees new to the organization learned their jobs through serving as an apprentice to a more experienced employee. Relatives and friends of the senior members of the companies or farm were given priority for new jobs. Compensation often included a small wage, food, and housing.

The first formal HRM practices developed as a result of the Industrial Revolution. Factories required large numbers of employees with specific skills to operate machines that performed specialized operations. As a result, managers who specialized in human resources were needed to train and schedule workers.

The development of scientific management in 1911 emphasized the importance of identifying employees who had the appropriate skills and abilities for performing each job, providing wage incentives to employees for increased productivity, providing employees with rest breaks, and carefully studying jobs to identify the best method for performing the job. Most organizations were bureaucratic organizations. That is, positions were organized into a hierarchy of authority, with each position given specific responsibilities. Employees made decisions about how work was to be done and provided suggestions to improve products only if management assigned these responsibilities to them. From 1911 to 1930, HRM practices were primarily conducted by what was known as the personnel department.

Early institutional roles were based on bureaucratic and legal aspects of dealing with employees. The personnel department's major role was to ensure that employment records were accurate. These records included basic information about employees such as the date of their hire, their position, health information, and performance reviews. The personnel department also ensured that people were paid, they interviewed job applicants, and terminated poorly performing employees.

Industrial expansion and the emergence of labor unions, which characterized the early 1900s, necessitated an organizational function designed to deal with the union environment. Personnel departments emphasized welfare capitalism as a means of convincing employees that unions were unnecessary. The next few decades saw added responsibilities for the HRM function.

The personnel department often reported to an accounting department or to someone in charge of administration. As new procedures were developed for making administrative decisions about employees, the HRM function gained some power in its own right, and it began to play a role in making sure that administrative decisions were made appropriately and fairly.

Combined with the existence of a tight labor market during World War I and the work of several industrial psychologists (Munstberg,

1913), the HRM function began to engage in such activities as employment testing, training, and performance appraisal. Past activities, by contrast, had focused most often on keeping unions out or negotiating with existing unions over wages, hours, and the terms and conditions of employment. The HRM activities engaged in during this time provided a more proactive orientation aimed at promoting higher levels of productivity, and with the work of Mayo and Roethlisberger came an awareness of social factors on employee satisfaction and productivity (Roethlisberger & Dickson, 1939). In a sense, this resulted in a revival of welfare capitalism, now resurfacing under a new name — the human relations movement. This movement's basic assumption was that a satisfied employee was a productive employee. The human relations movement, which saw an unprecedented amount of government-sponsored research into personnel-related areas, such as groups, motivation, morale, and leadership, flourished from World War II until the 1960s.

Between 1930 and 1970, organizations began to recognize the relationship between employee participation in decision making, employee job satisfaction, and employee absenteeism, turnover, and unionization efforts. This was a result of a new management philosophy that suggested that employees will contribute to company goals if they are given the opportunity to participate in decisions concerning their job and to take responsibility for their work.

The rise of the union movement, particularly during the 1930s and 1940s, meant that someone in the organization was needed to counter the union's efforts to organize the company and, when these efforts failed, to deal effectively with the union. The personnel department typically took on these roles, and in many cases the labor-relations people who were more responsible for them gained considerable power and prestige within corporations. They positioned themselves as the only ones who could deal effectively with unions and developed special relationships and knowledge with regard to unions and their leadership.

During this time, major advances in employee selection techniques were made. World War II sparked the development of psychological tests that could quickly and accurately identify individuals' interests, skills, and abilities. These tests were increasingly used for selecting new employees and placing them in appropriate jobs. HRM departments also became responsible for ensuring that companies' human resource practices were in compliance with legislation such as the Civil Rights Act of 1964, which made it illegal for employment decisions to be made on the basis of gender, religion, race, color, or national origin.

As an increasing amount of research began to cast doubt on the idea that job satisfaction and productivity are strongly related, the role of the HRM function was again questioned. However, a major change in this situation of HRM departments occurred because of the civil rights movement and the discrimination legislation of the 1960s and 1970s.

The civil rights movement produced a good deal of legislation bearing on the employment relationship, such as the Equal Pay Act of 1963, which forbade pay discrimination based on sex, and the Civil Rights Act of 1964, which made it illegal to discriminate in any employment decision on the basis of race, religion, color, sex, or national origin. Because of the large penalties and disruptions that lawsuits could cause for organizations, employment practices became increasingly important in organizations. The increase in discrimination-based litigation during the 1970s significantly increased the legitimacy of the HRM function in organizations.

It has only been in the last ten years that organizations have viewed HRM practices as a means to enhance the operations of the other functions of the business and to contribute directly to the organization's profitability. This has occurred because chief executive officers (CEOs), line managers, and HRM managers increasingly recognize that HRM practices play a key role in determining organizations' success in gaining a competitive advantage.

Although all of the previous developments added status to the HRM function in the United States, it is the rise of international competition in a global market that may finally raise the function above that of second-class status. As U.S. companies suffered more and more defeats in the global business arena, the critical need for using employees as a competitive resource has become increasingly evident. As a result of such things as international competition, HRM has begun to move from a specialized, stand-alone function to a broad corporate competency in which HRM professionals and line managers can build partnerships to gain competitive advantage and achieve overall organizational goals.

Changes in the reporting relationships of HRM managers also emphasize the increased importance and greater role that HRM is beginning to play in many organizations. HRM managers sit on high-level committees that are given the task of shaping the strategic direction of the company; they report directly to the CEO, president, or board of directors; and they are being asked to propose solutions to the challenges that the firm is facing (Bailey, 1991; Flipowski, 1991).

CHANGING ENVIRONMENT OF
HUMAN RESOURCES MANAGEMENT

As important as HRM is now, it is our contention that its importance will grow in the future. This is because changes are occurring today in the environment of HRM — changes that are requiring HRM to play an even more crucial role in their organizations. Some of these changes are highlighted in the following section.

Demographic Trends Impacting
Human Resources Management

Just when it is becoming important to hire and train an effective front-line workforce, the rate of growth of the nation's workforce is projected to drop over the next five years. For example, the nation's labor force will expand by about 21 million people (or 18 percent) in the 1990s. This marks a dramatic slowdown in labor-force growth, which between 1972 and 1986 grew by almost 31 million people (or 35 percent). This will make the HRM professional's job more difficult in terms of recruiting, screening, and training employees.

At the same time, the composition of the workforce has and will continue to change dramatically. For one thing, it will include more minorities and women. For example, between now and the year 2000, the white labor force is projected to increase less than 15 percent, while the black labor force will grow by nearly 29 percent, and the Hispanic labor force by more than 74 percent. Also, women are projected to account for about 64 percent of the net increase in the labor force in the 1990s. Related to this, about two-thirds of all single mothers (separated, divorced, widowed, or never married) are in the labor force today, as are almost 45 percent of mothers with children under three. The HRM department will increasingly be called upon to help companies accommodate these new employees, with new child care and maternity leave provisions, for example, and with basic skills training where such training is required.

Along with the shift from manufacturing to services, as highlighted later in this chapter, five occupational groups are projected to expand faster than average over the next ten years. Technicians, service workers, professional workers, sales workers, and executive and management employees will all experience faster than average employment growth between now and the year 2000. Increasingly, jobs will require at least one year of college, while the share of jobs requiring a high school diploma will decline slightly. There will be a sharp decline in the share of jobs for which less than a high school education is sufficient to perform the job. New jobs will thus increasingly require a higher level of education, while the workers available for these jobs will increasingly come from minority groups who are less likely to have the requisite skills and education. Basic skills training, selection on the basis of training potential, and programs to encourage continuing education will thus take an added importance over the next few years.

The Challenge of Globalization

A long-term trend with profound and far-reaching implications for HRM professionals is that of a global economy. The marketplace is marked by increased competition from all over the globe: a new European economy, expanding Asian markets, the restructuring of the Soviet Union and Central Europe, and a developing South America. Opportunities are also available for U.S. businesses as a result of the provisions of the North American Freed Trade Agreement. Thus, some forecasters predict that by the end of the 1990s, the European Common Market and markets of countries in the Pacific Rim will be equal to the North American market (Marciariello, Burke, & Tilley, 1989). The new global economies have brought competitive changes unequaled in U.S. history.

Many U.S. organizations already have substantial foreign operations. Of the 50 largest multinational companies, 21 received at least 40 percent of their total operating profits from foreign operations (Forbes, 1987). For example, to gain access to European markets, General Electric (GE) recently purchased Tungstram, a Budapest, Hungary, light bulb maker (O'Reilly, 1992). Other U.S. organizations are beginning to penetrate foreign markets. For example, Ferro Corporation, a $1 billion manufacturer of coatings, plastics, and specialty chemicals, has recently reorganized its corporate structure to focus its products and businesses toward overseas markets (Brandt, 1991).

As a result of increased globalization, a fundamental shift is also underway in where works gets done. The key to this change is the emergence of a truly global labor force (O'Reilly, 1992). Examples of work, new plants, and facilities located outside the United States are common. 3M makes tapes in Bangalore, India; Hewlett-Packard Company assembles computers and designs memory boards in Guadalajara, Mexico. After GE purchased Tungstram, the workforce turned out to be the best in the world at designing and making advanced lighting. The Hungarian plant is GE's center for lighting research and is a source of lighting for Europe and Japan. This is not an isolated example of highly educated and motivated workers. All across Ireland, dozens of offices are devoted to handling complex service work for U.S. firms (O'Reilly, 1992).

Implications for Human Resources Management

It is clear that there is a vast realignment underway. Work appears to be flowing to the countries best suited to perform it. The implication is that managers must scan globally to find sources of talent and analyze relative labor costs and productivity. Global information about skills available is also going to be required. At the minimum, employees at facilities in other countries must be managed in a style consistent with the cultural, social, and legal conditions of their countries.

Increasing Competition

There is a growing belief, which we share, that effective management of an organization's human resources will be the basis for gaining competitive advantage in the foreseeable future. Throughout the 1980s, organizations began to seriously make efforts to improve their competitive advantage by launching initiatives in productivity, total quality, and customer service. In most instances, a senior manager was put in charge of such initiatives. Despite making some progress, organizations have been disappointed with the result most of the time. Very often, progress has led to survival, rather than to any competitive advantage; productivity, quality, and customer service are competitive necessities, not competitive advantages, because most organizations have launched initiatives and made some progress. Today's organization gets a competitive advantage only if it is early in adopting the next strategic initiative or if it is much better than others at executing it.

Chaparral Steel's success illustrated that the management of human resources plays a key role in determining the effectiveness and competitiveness of U.S. businesses in the next decade (Forward, Beach, Gray & Quick, 1991).

A Texas steel company, Chaparral Steel, produces steel products used in the construction of mobile homes, automobiles, and appliances. Chaparral Steel has been able to increase sales, profit margins, and labor productivity. For example, labor productivity is over two times that of other U.S. steel-making firms. How has Chaparral Steel achieved such success in an industry dominated by Japanese and German steel companies? Its success is the result both of technological innovativeness and of the way the company has used its human resources to meet competitive challenges.

Chaparral Steel's human resources policies and managerial practices motivate employees to use their talents to design and implement equipment and process improvements. One such practice is the company's compensation policy. Every employee is salaried and shares in the profits. A participative approach to performance management gives employees the opportunity to increase their levels of knowledge and expertise.

Performance is measured against the employee's goals and objectives rather than job requirements or a job description. The goals and objectives are established jointly between supervisors and employees. Employees are free to use whatever means possible to reach their goals.

The company also uses training and education to gain competitive advantage. To ensure that employees are prepared to deal with advances in steel-producing technology, each employee receives approximately 120 hours of classroom training each year. The company encourages employees to become familiar with other operations through cross-training, thereby developing a workforce that has multiple skills. This provides the company with the ability to quickly change manufacturing processes and adopt new technology to meet customer needs.

Competitiveness refers to the company's ability to maintain and gain market share in its industry. Chaparral Steel's HRM practices have given the company a competitive advantage over U.S. and foreign competitors. That is, Chaparral Steel's HRM practices have helped the company create products that are valued by their customers. The value of a product is determined by its quality and how closely the product fits customer needs.

The competitive pressure on today's organizations is probably one of the strongest forces on HRM. The challenge of the continued search for competitive advantage has affected the role of HRM professionals and led to demands that they reorganize and in many instances refocus their efforts. HRM professionals are being asked to be part of the organization's response to competition. Today, the more focused an organization is on competition, the more central HRM becomes to organizational effectiveness and success.

Two ways that HRM is being asked to respond to competition are by cost cutting and increasingly finding ways to add value. In many ways, it appears that the most immediate challenge for HRM departments is cost pressure. Particularly, HRM departments must justify their cost structures on a competitive basis. Increased attention is being paid to headcount comparisons among organizations to check the ratio of employees to members of the HRM department (that is, increasingly using benchmarking to make staffing and other decisions). In addition, questions on the value added by HRM is a question that is being asked more and more often by senior management in organizations. In reality, HRM departments are being asked to justify why they are necessary and what they add to the organization's efforts to get the product out the door or meet their service requirements.

While cost pressures are not new, in most organizations they have come and gone over the years according to the economy and particular organizations. What is new, however, is the strength of the pressures, the strong emphasis on competitive benchmarking, an increasing emphasis on quality, and the implications of competition that accompanies a more global marketplace. Together, these have created a set of cost pressures that are stronger and more difficult for HRM professionals to respond to.

HRM practices contribute to a company's competitiveness in many ways. For example, HRM practices contribute to the delivery of the organization's products and services by selecting employees who will be innovative, creative, and successful in performing their jobs; preparing employees to work with new manufacturing and service technologies; and rewarding good performance (Tsui & Gomez-Mejia, 1988). Effective HRM practices also contribute to customer and employee satisfaction and retention, and the development of a favorable reputation in the community in which the organization is located. However, the potential role of HRM in organizational effectiveness has only recently been recognized.

Shift from a Manufacturing to a Service Economy

A dramatic shift from manufacturing to services has taken place in North America and Western Europe. For example, today, nearly two-thirds of the U.S. workforce is employed in producing and delivering services. In fact, during the 1980s, the manufacturing workforce declined over 12 percent. And of all the 21 million or so new jobs added by the U.S. economy in the 1990s, virtually all will be in services, in industries like retailing, consulting, teaching, fast foods, and legal work.

Albrecht and Zemke (1985) point out that the change to a service economy is important to HRM because in service businesses critical incidents can make you or break you and that what they term "the last four feet" can mean success or failure for an organization. In discussing a retail furniture chain, for instance, they relate how "much of the enormous investment evaporated at the moment when a customer walked into the store and encountered a nonsupportive psychological environment" (p. 99). All of those dollars spent on advertising were effective, in terms of getting the customers to walk in the front door. But once they are in the door, "it's up to the people in the store to take over at the last four feet." And, here, if an organization's customers are confronted by a salesperson who is tactless or unprepared to discuss the pros and cons of different products or (even worse) discourteous, all of the organization's efforts will have been for naught. The service organization has little else to sell but their service, and that makes them uniquely dependent on their employees' attitudes, aptitudes, and motivation (Dessler, 1994).

Some specific examples of the role HRM professionals play in service companies follow.

Service and Quality of Work Life

To get the best from its employees, an organization requires that the organization's culture and morale and the employee's work environment be positive. That is, efforts must be made to ensure that the organization creates and maintains a work environment that is sensitive to the needs of its employees. Quality of work life, according to one expert, involves at least the following factors: a job worth doing, safe and secure working conditions, adequate pay and benefits, job security, competent supervision, feedback and job performance, opportunities to learn and grow in the job, a chance to get ahead on merit, positive social climate, and justice and fair pay (Albrecht, 1988).

HRM professionals are normally charged with designing and implementing the systems to improve many of these factors. For example, job design helps ensure that the job is worth doing, and employee safety and health programs are aimed at ensuring safe and secure working conditions. Similarly, pay and benefits, promotions based on merit, and feedback on job performance (performance appraisal) are all essentially HRM responsibilities. An effective HRM department thus helps to create the organization's quality of work life (the overall fabric within which service employees can be motivated to do their jobs).

Service and Employee Selection

In many respects, effective employee selection is the first line of defense for a service organization or any other type of organization. It has been noted, for instance, that there are "quite a few who lack the temperament, maturity, social skills, and tolerance for frequent human contact" and that the first step in avoiding this problem is screening and selection (Albrecht & Zemke, 1985, p. 101). Yet, ironically, many of the front-line jobs in service organizations are often minimum wage positions with relatively little career potential. As a result, the employee selection job is complicated by the fact that there is often a relatively limited work history for HRM professionals to go by when hiring into these entry-level positions. As a result, such things as employee screening and testing performed by the HRM department take on a critical importance in service organizations.

Service and Employee Training and Development

Poorly trained or untrained front-line service employees usually have no choice but to improvise whatever methods they can in order to help them do their jobs; this can, in turn, have a corrosive effect on service performance (Albrecht & Zemke, 1985). Many employees in service organizations are front-line employees who deal with customers every day. Unlike errors made by some back office or production workers, errors made on the front line normally cannot be easily detected by inspectors. As a result, training and development efforts conducted by the HRM department are important in service organizations.

Service and Performance Appraisal

The fact that front-line service employees often fill positions that are not subject to traditional types of inspection demands an effective way to measure and evaluate their performance. Therefore, the design, implementation, and evaluation of a performance appraisal process with the help of the HRM department is important in service organizations.

The vast majority of employees today are in service jobs, working for a variety of service organizations. And as a result of the movement from a manufacturing to a service economy, where organizations rely so heavily on committed front-line employees, the role of HRM takes on a new significance (Dessler, 1994).

NEW WAYS OF ORGANIZING: THE CHALLENGE TO HUMAN RESOURCES MANAGEMENT

One change and challenge that confronts the HRM professional has been the emergence of new ways of organizing the workplace. The concept of the U.S. corporation has been evolving for some time. The traditional design of U.S. companies emphasizes efficiency, decision making by managers, and dissemination of information from the top of the company to lower levels. As a result, by the early 1980s, a consensus had developed around the different types of corporations and how they should be organized. As the 1980s came to a close, that consensus had all but unraveled when many organizational leaders began to recognize that the traditionally accepted structure would not be effective in the contemporary work environment (that is, in which personal computers increasingly give employees immediate access to information needed to complete customer orders or modify product lines).

Until Chandler's (1962) historical study of U.S. enterprises, managers debated the pros and cons of functional versus product organizations. Chandler showed that organizations in a single business used a functional organization. When the company diversified into several businesses, the multidivisional profit-center organization was created. Chandler's work established the concept that different strategies lead to different organizations. Both the functional and the product organization were appropriate for their respective strategies.

The 1970s saw the rise of the conglomerates. Instead of using internally generated business opportunities, as Procter and Gamble and GE did, companies like Litton, ITT, Teledyne, and Textron used acquisition to diversify into new business areas. These firms bought and sold companies and came to administer portfolios of unrelated businesses through holding companies. While other types of organizations were suggested, a consensus developed around the following three classical models (Galbraith, 1993):

single business (strategy) → internal (growth) → functional (structure);

related diversification (strategy) → internal (growth) → divisional (structure);

unrelated diversification (strategy) → acquisition (growth) → holding company (structure).

The expansion of structure to the concept of organization also resulted in an increased appreciation of the interaction between organization and HRM practices like compensation policies and career paths. That is, it was recognized that human resource policies also varied with a company's portfolio strategy. For example, compensation policies vary, from company-based salary structures for single-business and divisionalized companies to industry-based compensation for the divisions of a holding company. Galbraith (1993) notes that managers in different divisions of a related business company receive the same salary for the same level of job. Managers in a holding company receive salaries defined by the industry in which the division competes, rather than a company-defined salary. Managers working in the divisions of a holding company receive much higher amounts of variable compensation than managers do in divisionalized companies. Divisionalized managers of a holding company may receive 50 percent of their take-home pay in the form of bonuses. Managers of a divisionalized company may only receive 10 to 30 percent of salary as bonuses. If managers in functional and divisionalized companies do receive bonuses, they are usually based on company profits rather than on divisional profitability.

The implications of new ways of organizing for HRM practices are also evident in the performance measures on which salaries and promotions are granted. That is, the performance measures on which salaries are granted increase in objectivity depending upon the organizational structure (for example, the manager of a division holding company is measured strictly on meeting financial goals. The manager of a cost center in a single business is measured on budgetary performance but may also be judged on other characteristics of performance (such as cooperation) as well as on personal goals. HRM professionals must be cognizant of the implications of different ways of organizing and of their impact on HRM activities like career and management development.

A number of concepts represent the emergence of new ways of organizing the workplace as highlighted in the remainder of this section. The modern organization is made up of a complex set of units and relationships among them. Many organizations, such as Levi Strauss, Xerox, and Apple Computer, have recognized the need to move to an adaptive, high-involvement organization (Kavanaugh, Guetal, & Tannenbaum, 1990). In the adaptive organizational structure, employees are in a constant state of learning and performance improvement. Employees are free to move wherever they are needed in the company. The adaptive organization is characterized by a core set of values or vital vision that drives all organizational efforts (Peters, 1988). Previously established boundaries between managers and employees, employees and customers, employees and vendors, and the various functions within the company are abandoned. Employees, managers, vendors, customers, and suppliers work together to improve service and product quality and to create new products and services. Line employees are trained in multiple jobs, communicate directly with suppliers and customers, and interact frequently with engineers, quality experts, and employees from other functions.

The concept of the shamrock organization represents one new way of organizing in the contemporary environment. A shamrock has three leaves per stem; Handy (1990) believes it aptly symbolizes how some organizations are evolving as they adapt to changing environments. Each leaf represents a different group of people. Leaf 1 is a core group of workers made up of permanent, full-time employees with critical skills who follow standard career paths. This is a relatively small group, perhaps the group that remains after major downsizing of a more traditional organization. Leaf 2 is a group of outside operators who are engaged on contracts by the core group to perform a variety of jobs essential to the daily functioning of the organization. Many of these jobs would be performed by full-time staff in a more traditional organization. Leaf 3 is a group of part-timers who can be hired temporarily by the core group as the needs of the business grow and who can just as easily be let go when business fails. The essential work is done in leaf 1; the remainder is contracted out or done part-time by leaves 2 and 3. Naturally, this type of organization has profound implications for workers of tomorrow — workers, Handy (1990) believes, who must plan and manage their career with a full understanding that they must be prepared to succeed in leaves 2 and 3. This issue, along with other career planning and development issues, poses new challenges for not only the worker but also the HRM professional.

Another, perhaps even more futuristic, description of new organizing directions is the virtual corporation (Davidlow & Malone, 1993). This is an organization that exists only as a temporary network or alliance of otherwise independent companies who are jointly pursuing a particular business interest. The network is created via collaboration to make it possible to pursue good ideas by expanding the resources available and facilitating quick adaptation to shifting business conditions. Members of a typical network consist of independent suppliers, customers, and even competitors, who link up with the latest electronic information technologies and share such things as skills, costs, and access to global markets. *Business Week* (1993) describes the virtual corporation as follows:

Technology — Virtual partnerships are based on electronic linkages among companies and entrepreneurs otherwise separated by great distances.

Excellence — Virtual partnerships draw upon the core competencies of each member to create a best everything world-class organization.

Opportunism — Virtual partnerships are temporary and opportunity focused; they disband once the opportunity no longer exists.

Trust — Virtual partnerships require trust among members whose fates are highly interdependent.

No Borders — Virtual partnerships, with their complex networks of relationships, make it hard to identify the boundaries of any one organization.

The notions of partnership and collaboration are central to the virtual corporation. This idea relates to the trend toward more strategic business alliances, about which Corning CEO James R. Houghton says, "More companies are waking up to the fact that alliances are critical to the future" (*Business Week*, 1993, p. 98). In concept, however, the virtual corporation takes this point even further. A true virtual corporation of the future will be a shifting mass of alliances that are formed, utilized, and disbanded with ease, and in quick response to business opportunities. This organization of the future has endless applications in small and large businesses operating in services or manufacturing as highlighted in the following examples.

Former Apple CEO, John Sculley, believes that the steps toward virtual corporations are just beginning. Assessing today's popularity of alliances and outsourcing agreements, Sculley says: "Tens of thousands of virtual corporations may come of this" (*Business Week*, 1993, p. 100). For its own part, Apple has been actively involved in this trend. The organization formed an alliance with Sony to manufacture its low-cost version of the PowerBook, overcoming its own limited manufacturing capacity at the time. More than 100,000 units sold the first year, after which Apple discontinued the agreement. It had served its purpose: A new product was brought to market more quickly than otherwise possible, given the initial limits on manufacturing.

Intersolve, a management consulting firm based in Dallas, consists of four major partners. The firm mobilizes just-in-time talent to deal with the specific needs of various clients. An assignment for First Interstate involved 4 teams and 26 experts and only 1 Intersolve partner. A client vice president says: "The advantage is that you get specialists to work on your problems" (Schermerhorn, Hunt, & Osborn, 1993, p. 43). Intersolve partner Edward R. McPherson says: "One of the founding principles of our firm is that we would assemble and disassemble teams for work. . . . We don't have to warehouse staff or specialists" (p. 43).

Many new ways of organizing are a response to the recognition that the contributions of people are essential to the success of all organizations. And, in the new workplace, a common theme is the creation of work settings in which people have the freedom and opportunity to use their talents to their best advantage. As HRM professionals work with nonstaff managers in these settings to examine different organizing approaches, their focus is often on bringing people and technology together to create high-performance systems. Today's HRM and other managers are experimenting with production and service operations that emphasize teamwork and group-based tasks, performance-based incentives and reward systems, intense training and development of employees, continuous learning and improvement for the organization as a whole, reduced external supervision and increased individual responsibilities, fewer levels of management, fewer numbers of staff personnel, and greater emphasis on organizational adaptation, innovation, and performance.

HRM professionals have a major responsibility to see that their organizations' managers are informed about such developments and that they are willing and able to participate fully in the new workplaces they represent. It may well be, for example, that the 1990s will become known as the decade that fundamentally changed the way people work. Consider the upside-down pyramid perspective that reflects the emerging view of managers as helpers, coaches, and supporters. It emphasizes a customer orientation and the need to unlock the full potential of every employee to serve both the customer's and the organization's interests. And, like the shamrock organization and virtual corporation, this perspective also exemplifies the dynamic and promising setting of organization and management into which tomorrow's HRM professionals will most likely step.

DEALING WITH THE INEVITABLE: MANAGING CHANGE

For today's organizations to develop a competitive advantage, they have had to recognize the importance of the need to respond to such things as the movement from a manufacturing to a service economy. To effectively develop organizational responses to increased international competition and movement to a more service economy requires more than just using the old practices in a better way. It means fundamental change in the way organizations operate. Therefore, if an organization is to survive and thrive today and tomorrow, its managers must be able to handle change positively — to alter policies, structure, and products in time to meet new conditions — and do it with a minimum of resistance and disruption.

Because many organizational change efforts are moving in the direction of changing individual behaviors in the form of new management styles and trying to increase employee participation in the form of team-based work initiatives, the HRM department is faced with major change agendas itself. First and foremost, HRM must change many of its operating systems in order to respond to the new organizational changes. Most often, what is needed is a well-coordinated HRM support system (that is, training, compensation, selection, and performance appraisal systems) that will enable organizations and their people to successfully mount ambitious change projects with potential for high payoff.

Ulrich (1989) also notes that the opportunity exists for the HRM department to be major consultants to the rest of the organization on how it can change the way it does business. This is particularly true with respect to new forms of organizing, management style, and change programs to name a few. The key to acceptance of change is effective communication. That involves intensive efforts to promote trust and ensure that managers, for example, share information honestly and on a timely basis with employees. And that is where the HRM department also comes in. When change causes resistance in an organization, as it inevitably will, the HRM function must be capable of stepping in and guiding other managers and staffers, as well as senior executives, in developing strategies and teaching the skills needed to integrate the change.

The effective HRM function of today and tomorrow will need to share with line and other functional managers responsibility for creating and maintaining a climate in which change can be accepted rather than resisted. In their own departments, and with respect to the HRM function in other elements of the organization, they are increasingly responsible for introducing and evaluating change; they must develop detailed plans for making change happen. In addition, HRM professionals have another significant responsibility: They must help other members of the organization (particularly managers and staffers) to effect changes of their own, primarily by training.

As a result of the increased emphasis on managing change in organizations, the most effective strategy involves building an organizational climate for change, protecting employees from adverse effects, improving communication, encouraging participation in decision making, using consulting and negotiating tactics, sharing benefits derived from the change, avoiding trivial change, making change tentative and gradual, and providing training for all levels of employees. In order to better help their organizations respond to and effectively manage change in the future, HRM professionals must:

get themselves ready for change,

establish realistic and attainable goals and objectives that are HRM-sensitive,

help the organization select and train a team of change agents,

help to formulate and implement an overall organizational and HRM support system change plan,

be proactive in helping to manage the ongoing change process, and

actively participate in the evaluation of results and revision of the change plan as needed.

As evidenced by the discussion to this point, the role of HRM is changing, and it is our belief that it will continue to change and evolve as suggested in the next section.

THE CHANGING ROLE OF HUMAN RESOURCES MANAGEMENT PROFESSIONALS

As noted thus far in this chapter, several external and internal factors are key to shaping the HRM functions in all types of organizations and have significant effects on operations. They span social, economic, political, and technological developments and many types of changes in the size and composition of the workforce. Each one of these factors has helped organizations in the 1990s to begin to recognize that human resources are the most critical resources for organizations. More specifically, the reasons for this pivotal position are changing demographics, the change in the composition and size of the workforce, increasing occupational obsolescence, and increasing recognition of the HRM function as the key element in helping organizations meet their organizational goals and objectives. Thus, the predominant role played by HRM in the recruitment, selection, training, and development of human resources will give HRM professionals greater responsibilities for maximizing the use of human resources by their organizations.

In the coming years, several factors that are and will continue to impact the role of HRM professionals and their organizations' workforces are:

the changing profile of the entry-level worker;

the changing size and nature of the population;

increased generational, gender, ethnic, and cultural conflict and confrontation;

mismatches between the supply and demand for specific job skills;

changing lifestyles, value systems, and expectations;

less acceptance of the traditional work ethic;

rapid growth of technology, especially in the areas of information, communication, and automation;

increased competition for domestic and foreign markets;

the change from a production- to a service-centered economy;

increased participation of employees in managing organizations;

uncertainty about the role of unions; and

increased participation of employees in managing organizations.

These items have important implications for every area of organizational and HRM thought and activity. These factors will create more requirements for employee services, modifications to compensation and benefits programs, career planning, employee training and retraining, management development, and organizational development and change, to name but a few. A number of the most profound changes for the HRM function follow.

As a result of increased involvement in the overall strategic operations of the organization, HRM professionals will become more professional and more competent in the eyes of top management and their line management. HRM professionals will continually be faced with the challenge of meeting corporate strategic goals; translating the higher expectations of the new workforce into productive, safe, and cost-effective work environments; and providing more tailored and integrated employee services in a timely, coordinated, cost-effective manner based on a thorough knowledge of organizational culture, politics, and financial resources and changing employee needs, wants, and various expectations.

The HRM department and professionals will become even more visible and will be more widely recognized as a key factor in organizational viability and profitability. As a consequence, there may be a shift to investing more resources in human capital investments than in plant and equipment. In addition, HRM departments will take on the form of profit centers, selling their products and services both inside and outside the organization. HRM professionals will be more like entrepreneurs, and HRM managers will run the HRM function as a business within a business.

There will be general acceptance of the fact that everything that happens in the organization is in some way influenced by its human resources and that human resources go far beyond the traditional HRM functions; that, in fact, they are central to the operation of the organization, and, thus, human resources must be integrated with overall organizational planning, both strategic and tactical.

Much more will be expected of HRM managers and staff. They will be expected to be more action-oriented and must:

participate as full partners in corporate strategic planning;

objectively determine accomplishments and results;

focus on managing results — bottom-line outcomes;

perform as leaders;

effectively utilize managerial skills and behavior;

demonstrate and promote innovation and creativity;

build an organizational atmosphere of openness, trust, and respect;

implement programs, services, and activities that are effective in helping to change attitudes, behavior, and performance in ways that benefit the employee and organization;

communicate accomplishments to all levels of the organization; and

identify and communicate barriers to accomplishments and significant problems to individual, group and organizational efficiency, effectiveness, and productivity.

As a result of the dwindling pool of highly qualified people, small organizations will compete intensively to attract and retain highly qualified employees (for example, top executives, middle managers, scientists, engineers, and technicians). Larger organizations will concentrate on developing their own executives, managers, and supervisors. Regardless of size, smart organizations will pool their resources and collaborate with other organizations to meet their employee training and development needs.

The projected shortage of opportunities for advancement will create a need for realistic career expectations and increased emphasis on the potential rewards of lateral transfers and the enrichment of current jobs. The concept of lifelong learning will continue to grow and prosper. There will be an increased emphasis on self-directed learning and learner-centered training and education. In addition, there will be a greater need for accelerated learning strategies. That is, shorter knowledge and skill modules will make use of advances in learning technologies. The focal point of such efforts will be objectives such as learning how to learn, problem sensing and problem solving, and working as a member of a team.

The way organizations are structured will have a greater impact on employee training and management development than it has in the past. Decentralized organizations will require long-range training — often in the form of self-instructional programs while centralized organizations will require corporate training centers and an emphasis on team building.

All organizational members will have to learn the dos and don'ts of behavior while doing business in foreign cultures both within and outside the United States. Thus, there will be an increased need for language, intercultural, and cross-cultural training for managers, engineers, technicians, and scientists so that they can develop cultural knowledge and empathy.

As a result of the growth of technology, particularly in the areas of computers, robotics, and telecommunications, there will be an increased demand for more broadly trained and better-trained employees who are able to deal with such subjects as electronics, computer programming, hydraulics, and mechanics. Training will be customized to meet the specific needs of groups of employees. It will focus on specific results, in terms of knowledge and skills, and on measurable objectives that relate to improved efficiency and productivity. In addition, the value of training will be determined by the degree to which behavior, performance, and work attitudes have been changed by the programs offered.

There is likely to be a dramatic increase in the number of organizations offering parental and family-leave policies and programs, designed to enable parents to care for newly arrived and sick or disabled children. In addition, organizations are likely to increase the number of benefits they offer to meet the demands of working women for high-quality, accessible, affordable, and safe child care. The underlying reasons are the high percentage of women in the workforce, including those in managerial positions, intense competition for the recruitment and retention of high-potential and high-performance employees, comparatively lower costs for such programs than for hiring replacements, and increased federal and state legislation (for example, the Family Medical and Leave Act) supporting such programs.

Across-the-board pay raises and automatic increases in benefits will become a thing of the past; they will be replaced by a system that rewards exceptional performance or shortage-area value-based skills. More incentives will be offered to gain organizational loyalty and long-term commitment. Variable, cafeteria-style compensation and benefits packages will become more common: schedules of bonuses, incentives, pension, and savings plans to allow individual employees to choose the combination that best suits their needs.

The costs of health care for employees and retirees will continue to rise, due to cost-shifting by the federal government and insurance companies and the high incidence rate of a number of health-related problems (for example, the high incidence of substance abuse and AIDS). The continued growth in the number of drug and alcohol users and abusers in the workforce will raise problems relating to policies about drug testing, treatment, and the establishment or expansion of employee assistance programs. As a result, HRM professionals will need to help their organizations develop clear and firm policies with respect to testing, treatment, nondiscrimination, and provisions for the education and training of employees and supervisors.

A large part of changes in the role of HRM professionals in organizations rests in the HRM professionals' skills — in technology and marketing sensitivity, in finding fresh and innovative approaches, in moving from a research-technology–product orientation to a marketing and customer-oriented stance, providing top-notch leadership.

REQUIREMENTS FOR HUMAN RESOURCES MANAGEMENT LEADERSHIP

As suggested earlier in this chapter, a prime characteristic of business today is its intensely competitive climate. There is competition within an organization for resources, and there is competition with other organizations — both in the United States and abroad — for markets. Add the complexity of modern organizations to this level of competitiveness, and one can immediately see why U.S. organizations demand better leadership at all levels. It is our contention that such a demand is of particular importance to HRM professionals, because they are required to take on more leadership and less management roles.

In our view, good management and leadership are not mutually exclusive. Some people have both abilities, and those who do will become essential to their organizations in the highly competitive, complex world of tomorrow. Unfortunately, today's typical HRM manager (and professional) tends to concentrate on managing, thereby neglecting leadership behaviors. In this section, we will examine leadership behavior, particularly in connection with increased calls for leadership from the HRM function.

The functions of a leader, and the skills needed for effectiveness, do not differ radically from one level of HRM to another. Both the HRM manager and other supervisors are concerned with people and with analysis and action. But leadership for HRM professionals has become increasingly complex with increased responsibilities and upward movement in the organization, not simply because of the more complex or large problems the HRM department is involved in, but because new expectations are being placed on HRM professionals.

In today's and tomorrow's organizations, HRM managers in particular have three basic functions:

1. To create and communicate an HRM vision — an image of the HRM department as it should be in terms of the larger organizational culture, climate, the quality of work life, and its performance. That means generating clear and practicable conceptualization, a realistic image of the HRM department, its role and status in the organization, its reputation, accomplishments, and success. It means transmitting the vision to all members of the organization so successfully that they enthusiastically embrace the conceptualization and the way in which it adds value to the achievement of organizational success.

2. To take actions that will result in improved performance of specific jobs and the overall use of the organization's human resources. Actions include setting worthwhile and achievable goals and measurable objectives, developing forward-looking HRM strategic and tactical plans, establishing workable policies, training HRM staff and other employees, and evaluating performance. This also includes specific initiatives that will provide people with purpose, direction, and motivation.

3. To take actions that contribute to the improvement of organizational and human relationships. Examples are encouraging risk taking, providing assistance and encouragement, developing and implementing fair and equitable compensation and benefits programs, developing people, rewarding outstanding performance, resolving conflicts and differences, building teams, and improving working conditions and the quality of worklife.

To perform these three functions well in the future, HRM leaders need a particular skill set and a package of behaviors recognized as leader, bolstered by certain personal characteristics. All leaders need these qualities, but HRM managers and professionals are probably in a much better position to provide leadership than managers of many other departments simply because their jobs require them to pay special attention to such skills as communicating, listening, coaching, counseling, and negotiating. Of particular importance to the development of such skills by HRM professionals is increased self-knowledge and recognition of the leadership challenges that will confront them.

One thing that is crucial to effective leadership by the HRM professional is that of increased self-knowledge or awareness (the realistic assessment of one's strengths and weaknesses). Increased self-awareness is especially important as situations increasingly require HRM professionals to develop skills in understanding other people's perspectives, empowering others, and taking risks and absorbing failures. Such self-awareness is even more important for HRM professionals since they have an increasing responsibility in the development of their organization's leaders. Bennis has emphasized the importance of self-knowledge as one of the crucial characteristics of the successful leader. He concludes: "Nothing is truly yours until you understand it — not even yourself. Our feelings are raw, unadultered truth, but until we understand why we are happy or angry or anxious, the truth is useless to us" (1989, p. 61).

The idea that one must understand himself to be effective with others is, of course, not new. Thus, it should be no surprise that if HRM professionals are going to be able to be more effective leaders by influencing others through their own actions, they must recognize the importance of self-awareness. For HRM professionals, self-awareness is crucial to knowing their own limits, knowing what they really want to do and what they are willing to sacrifice to get it, taking responsibility for their own and their department's growth, and being prepared to take on additional organizational responsibilities while also seizing opportunities when they appear.

To be successful leaders in their organizations, HRM professionals must know themselves — their strengths, weaknesses, prejudices, and biases. They must also know people and what motivates and activates them. They must understand the criticality of trust among department and organization peers and other employees. And they must know how to build cohesive teams through example.

LEADERSHIP CHALLENGES FOR THE HUMAN RESOURCES MANAGEMENT PROFESSIONAL

The leadership challenges facing HRM professionals in today's organization are unprecedented. Unless HRM professionals are able to cope with these problems, they will lose more than their credibility — they may just as well forfeit their jobs.

Earn Top Management Respect

Although the HRM function and professional have come a long way in many organizations in recent years, there is still a good distance to travel to earn full recognition and respect. HRM professionals must find ways to get top management to understand the value-added role of the HRM department in the organizational scheme of things.

Integrate with Strategic Plans

HRM professionals must successfully link their goals, objectives, plans, and programs with the organization's strategic plan. An HRM department can be justified only on the basis of the value it adds to the overall organization (that is, by hard evidence that it makes a measurable contribution to the overall goals and objectives, such as improving productivity and increasing return on investment). The HRM department must recognize that integrating with the organization's strategic planning efforts is the right and best place for them to start identifying and demonstrating how they add value to the organization.

Deal with Change

The rate and magnitude of change and the impact on people are profound. Consider the challenges of dealing with mergers and acquisitions, planning for downsizing, streamlining, restructuring, and at the same time ensuring the continued viability, efficiency, and profitability of the organization. HRM professionals must deal competently with such changes.

Attracting and Retaining Good People

A part of the HRM department's helping their organization to maintain an advantage in today's highly competitive environment is the ability to get the right people and hold on to them. Adding to the difficulty of attracting and retaining good people are the problems of a reduced labor pool; the growing number of functional illiterates; and inadequate communication, reading, and mathematical skills among job applicants.

Train and Develop People

Employee training and development are primary means that HRM professionals use to help their organizations improve productivity and quality. Today's employees must be trained to compensate for deficiencies in their formal education, retained to keep them employable in the face of advancing technology, and reeducated or retrained to help them meet the requirements of their new positions. A related requirement for the HRM professional is to help create self-directed and effective work teams.

Deal with People Problems

Another facet of the people challenge that HRM professionals must help their organizations deal with is providing for employee wellness, job satisfaction, and self-realization in an era characterized by monumental problems of substance abuse, increased stress, and employee apathy and lack of commitment. Getting managers to deal sensitively, compassionately, and successfully with those problems and their consequences in on-the-job performance is an enormous challenge for the HRM professionals and their organizations.

Develop Managerial and Leadership Potential

From the standpoint of organizational viability, there are other challenges that HRM professionals must help their organizations address. One is to identify earlier and more reliably those who have the potential to make good managers and executives. Another is to help managers develop an understanding of what leadership means in both domestic and international settings and help them develop strong cross-cultural perspectives. A related challenge involves sensitizing managers to the ethical dimensions of behavior and teaching them to deal with the many ethical challenges that confront them.

Overcome Obstacles to the Success of Human Resources Management Professionals and Their Departments

In our view, over the years, HRM professionals and their departments have not seized the opportunity to take on more leadership responsibilities in their organizations. In many instances, a number of reasons might be offered for such behavior: the organization culture prevented it; the organization climate was never right; they feared failure; they lacked the necessary skills; they never took the time to figure out or understand what the leadership role involves in their organization; they never took the initiative; or they had a mistaken view that HRM professionals cannot be leaders in their organizations.

CONCLUSION

In this chapter we have discussed a number of challenges and issues that are increasing the value of HRM professionals in the organization and requiring proactive efforts to change the role of the HRM department and professionals in their organizations. It has been our contention that the management of human resources will play an even more important role in determining organizational success in meeting a variety of internal and external challenges. Traditionally, HRM practices have not been seen as adding economic value to the organization. Economic value is usually associated with facilities, equipment, and technology (Cascio, 1991). Compensation, staffing, training and development, performance management, and other HRM activities are investments. These investments directly affect employees' motivation and ability to provide products and services that are valued by customers. Research has shown that organizations that attempt to increase their competitiveness by investing in new technology and becoming involved in the quality movement also make investments in state-of-the-art staffing, training, and compensation practices (Snell & Dean, 1992).

One of the most comprehensive studies ever conducted regarding HRM was done by IBM and Towers Perrin consulting firm. They solicited the opinions of approximately 3,000 human resources professionals, managers, and consultants from 12 countries. The goals of this project were to determine HRM's role in gaining a competitive advantage and identifying the key priorities of organizational decision makers (HRM executives, consultants, chief operating officers) who influence HRM activities. The study found that:

Globalization of businesses, a reduction in the number of persons entering the workforce, and changing characteristics of the workforce were the environmental factors most likely to influence the competitiveness of American companies from 1991 to 2000.

Line managers and HR managers agreed that high productivity, quality, customer satisfaction, and linking HRM to the company's business strategy were the most important goals for both 1991 and the year 2000.

The single biggest challenge for HR managers is to shift their focus from current operation to strategies for the future.

HRM should focus on quality, customer service, productivity, employee involvement, teamwork, and creating a flexible workforce.

HRM needs to be responsive to the competitive marketplace.

HRM activities should be jointly developed and implemented by human resource and line managers (Towers Perrin, 1992).

The report concludes that "human resources is being transformed from a specialized, stand-alone function to a broad corporate competency in which human resources and line managers build partnerships to gain competitive advantage and achieve overall business goals" (Towers Perrin, 1992, p. 6).

In addition to opinions and beliefs, changes in reporting relationships of managers emphasize the increased importance and greater role that HRM is beginning to play in many organizations. Managers in charge of the HRM function sit on high-level committees that are given the task of shaping the strategic direction of the company; they report directly to the CEO, president, or board of directors; and they are being asked to propose solutions to the challenges that the firm is facing (Bailey, 1991).

In closing, the increasing responsibilities of HRM professionals will continue to the extent that HRM professionals are successful in helping their organizations develop competitive advantage in today's and tomorrow's constantly changing environment. It is hoped that the ideas presented in the remainder of this book can increase the likelihood that HRM professionals will be able to continue to make the necessary changes to address the inevitable challenges that will accompany their increased responsibilities.

REFERENCES

Albrecht, K. 1988. *At America's service*. Homewood, IL: Dow Jones-Irwin.

Albrecht, K., & Zemke, R. 1985. *Service America!* Homewood, IL: Dow Jones-Irwin.

Bailey, B. 1991. Ask what HR can do for itself. *Personnel Journal 70*(7): 35–39.

Bennis, W. 1989. *On becoming a leader*. Reading, MA: Addison-Wesley.

Brandt, E. 1991. Global HR. *Personnel Journal 70*: 38–44.

Business Week. 1993, February 8. The virtual corporation. 98–103.

Cascio, W. F. 1991. *Costing human resources: The financial impact of behavior in organizations* (3rd ed.). Boston: PWS-Kent.

Chandler, A. D. 1962. *Strategy and structure: Chapters in the history of the American industrial enterprise*. Cambridge, MA: MIT Press.

Davidlow, W. H. & Malone, M. S. 1993. *The virtual corporation: Structuring and revitalizing the corporation of the 21st century*. New York: Harper Business.

Dessler, G. 1994. *Human resource management* (6th ed.). Englewood Cliffs, NJ: Prentice-Hall.

Flipowski, D. 1991, June. Life after HR. *Personnel Journal*: 64–71.

Forbes. 1987, July 27: 152–54.

Forward, G. E., Beach, D. E., Gray, D. A., & Quick, J. C. 1991. Mentofacturing: A vision for American industrial excellence. *Academy of Management Executive 5*(3): 32–44.

Galbraith, J. R. 1993. The value-adding corporation: Matching structure with strategy. In Galbraith, J. R., Lawler E. E., III, and Associates. *Organizing for the future: The new logic for managing complex organizations*. pp. 15–42.

Handy, C. 1990. *The age of unreason*. Boston: Harvard Business School Press.

Kavanaugh, M. J., Guétal, H. G., & Tannenbaum, S. I. 1990. *Human resource information systems: Development and application*. Boston: PWS-Kent.

Marciariello, J. A., Burke, J. W., & Tilley, D. 1989. Improving American competitiveness: A management systems perspective. *Academy of Management Executive 3*(4): 294–303.

Munstberg, H. 1913. *The psychology of industrial efficiency*. Boston: Houghton Mifflin.

O'Reilly, B. 1992, December 14. Your new global workforce. *Fortune*: 52–63.

Peters, T. 1988. Restoring American competitiveness: Looking for new models of organizations. *The Executive 2*:103–10.

Roethlisberger, F. & Dickson, W. 1939. *Management and the worker*. Cambridge, MA: Harvard University Press.

Schermerhorn, J. R., Jr., Hunt, J. G., & Osborn, R. N. 1993. *Managing organizational behavior* (5th ed.). New York: John Wiley & Sons, Inc.

Snell, S. A., & Dean, J. W. 1992. Integrated manufacturing and human resource management: A human capital perspective. *Academy of Management Journal* 35: 467–504.

Towers Perrin. 1992. *Priorities for competitive advantage: An IBM study conducted by Towers Perrin.*

Tsui, A. S., & Gomez-Mejia, L. R. 1988. Evaluating human resource effectiveness. In L. Dyer (ed.) *Human resource management evolving rules and responsibilities.* Washington, DC: BNA Books, pp. 1187–1227.

Ulrich, D. 1989. Tie the corporate knot: Gaining complete customer commitment. *Sloan Management Review* 30(4): 19–27.

2

The Role of Human Resources Management and Changing Employee Expectations

In today's global marketplace, U.S. organizations will have to find new ways of managing. This is especially important since U.S. firms entering the global marketplace are finding that people make the difference. Raw material, technology, and systems are available to everyone. A critical factor of U.S. business survival and profitability will be understanding and managing changing employee expectations.

During this time of restructuring — mergers, acquisitions, and the struggle to regain competitiveness — the corporate structure has changed radically. It used to be that peer groups would move up the ranks together. Now people of all ages, business backgrounds, and experience must work together without benefit of the old hierarchy. Managers are experiencing the new generation gap as they try to manage very diverse groups where no one seems to understand each other.

This chapter will discuss the major issues driving employees' changing expectations as well as the manner in which many companies are striving to meet these changing expectations. The chapter will particularly emphasize the role of human resource management (HRM) professionals in helping their organizations recognize that their organizations will be constantly challenged throughout the coming years as they strive to meet these changing expectations in a manner that will also benefit the company. It is the contention of this chapter that the success of HRM professionals in meeting the challenges associated with changing expectations will be a contributing factor to the continued financial success of organizations.

ORIGINS OF CHANGING EXPECTATIONS

Employee and employer expectations have varied greatly throughout the years. Companies in the United States from 1950 to 1980 enjoyed prosperity and world leadership. It was not unusual for many employees and their children to spend their entire working lives at one organization. Organizations invested considerable time and money in employee training and management development, and employees in turn embraced the corporate culture. Firing of long-term employees was an unheard of practice, often resulting in a family-like atmosphere in many organizations. As a result, employees and management believed in a cradle-to-grave employee and employer contract (psychological contract): hard work and loyalty would be rewarded with job security and steady rewards (financial and promotional).

Traditional psychological contracts existed in organizations where there was stability, predictability, and growth. Organizations expected steady increases in revenue and the number of employees. Organizations saw their workforce as permanent and tried to build loyalty among its employees by making financial investments in training and by providing guaranteed long-term employment. Employees were committed to the organization and expected steady advancement up the corporate ladder. On the climb up the corporate ladder, the symbols of success were visible: vertical job growth (career paths were linear, job preparation generally meant one-time learning, and education and professional training were usually job-specific), steady salary increases, employee recognition plans, and perks like cars and country clubs for managers. Pensions, life insurance, and health care plans that addressed long-term needs were funded by the organization.

Today, there is change, uncertainty, and continuous cuts in human resources in organizations. Reorganizations, downsizings, mergers, and acquisitions threaten job security and career paths. An organization's workforce is flexible, employees are recruited, hired, and retained for their particular skills for the short run as organizations focus less and less on long-term performance. Opportunities for advancement are limited by slower growth and leaner organizational structures with fewer levels of management. Dwindling career opportunities and greater emphasis on economy has forced managers to reexamine their reliance on this definition as a motivator of performance. In addition, employees have learned that good performance is no longer a guarantee, even of job security. Not only have the tangible symbols of success become less available, but the entire strata of career positions have been obliterated in corporate downsizing. More and more employees recognize that they can expect multiple careers, have more responsibility for assessing and designing their own careers, must seek new definitions of success, and need to put more emphasis on life-long learning to avoid obsolescence of job skills.

The changing psychological contract also has implications for the organization. For example, with more and more well-qualified workers competing for a shrinking number of managerial jobs, the problem for organizations has changed from coaching employees with skill deficiencies to finding ways to motivate bright people with the carrot of promotion (Morin, 1992). In addition, old-style management techniques no longer apply and familiar incentives have evaporated, which make the management of a brave new workforce considerably more challenging. The unilateral cancellation of the implied contract (that is, from downsizings and so forth) profoundly affects the surviving employees as well. Some of their most basic tenets — beliefs in fairness, equity, and justice — have been violated. Their sense of security has been destroyed; their identity and self-esteem are threatened; and organizations must be concerned about the implications that employees feel they can no longer trust management or the organization to look out for their welfare or to be truthful to them (that is, the contract has become null and void). It is not surprising that company loyalty is quickly becoming extinct.

Employees are increasingly looking to employers for help in their family, financial, and professional lives through benefits packages, work environment changes, and even workplace changes. One of the leading issues driving employee expectations in the workplace is the family. With the divorce rate now approaching 50 percent, larger numbers of families that are intact having two parents working and the increase in health care costs, employees are looking to employers for help to cope with these issues as the U.S. family continues to change.

Another issue that is driving the changes in employee expectations is the growing diversity in the workplace. Women are entering the workforce in record numbers and the workplace is becoming both ethnically and culturally diverse. Gender and ethnic diversification bring varied expectations on the part of the workers. Women may require additional time off from work in small increments to take care of children and family matters. People of different religions may require time off to celebrate holidays that are different from those celebrated by the rest of the employees. Even the food served by the cafeteria may be the subject of changing expectations by a more diverse workforce.

A third issue driving employee expectations is corporate downsizing. Fewer and fewer employees are staying with the same company for their entire work experience. In the past, employees could rely on a large company to provide them with a steady paycheck, a health care and pension plan, and long-term job security. With companies as large as IBM and General Motors laying off large numbers of workers, the mentality of a job-for-life is increasingly beginning to change. Employees are expecting empowering options from their employers that enable them to take control of their own future.

As employees' expectations change, HRM professionals and their organizations must be prepared to help their employees meet their changing personal, financial, and professional goals in a manner that will also benefit the company. If not, they will lose good employees to companies that do meet the employees' shifting demands or decrease their own companies' bottom line.

CHALLENGES OF CHANGING EMPLOYEE EXPECTATIONS FOR HUMAN RESOURCES MANAGEMENT

Changing employee expectations pose several different challenges for HRM professionals. In order to retain good employees and keep them happy and productive, these challenges must be successfully met. One of the first challenges changing employee expectations pose for the HRM professional is simply identifying what the organization's employees need from the company and how the company is most able to meet these needs. Organizations may develop a human resource policy, such as a child-care center, utilizing thousands or even millions of dollars only to find the center under utilized or the benefit not taken advantage of. In short, the HRM department may think they know what the employees need, and sometimes give it to them without consulting the employees themselves. HRM professionals are then left to wonder what went wrong with their policy. Weyerhauser Co., of Federal Way, Washington, had one such experience in their company. The company thought that their employees did not have enough children to warrant a child-care program. Operating under this assumption, the company failed to offer any type of child-care benefits. When employees Mary Larson and Kim Johnson learned of the company's assumptions, they disagreed and decided to conduct their own employee survey to confirm their hypothesis. The survey received an overwhelming response, reinforcing their beliefs in a need for a child-care policy at Weyerhauser (Haupt, 1993).

In some cases, employee expectations may be different in different areas of the country. If a company has many different office locations, the needs of the employees may differ among the various locations. This may be due to ethnic or regional differences, the availability and price of services, such as child care, or health care, in the area or different emphases on what the employees may need. What works in Charlotte may not be suitable for the office in Tulsa. HRM professionals may be faced with the additional challenge of gauging not only what is needed for the employees but also how these needs may differ from region to region in order to fashion a human resources plan that will meet the needs of employees around the country.

The second challenge that changing employee expectations pose for HRM professionals is fashioning a plan to meet the needs of the employees after the employees' expectations have been learned. It is not enough to come up with grand benefit schemes for every potential employee's needs; these solutions must also be cost-effective for the company when implemented. Once the expectations of the employees are discerned, the HRM department must plan the way in which they will address the problem. For instance, the Weyerhauser example listed above can be addressed in a number of ways. The company can build a child-care center for its employees, it could negotiate a deal with local child-care providers for its employees, or it may simply allow a voucher to be used at the child-care facility of the parent's choice. All of these alternatives have the potential to solve the problem, but research must be done into which will provide the best choice for both the employees and the employer. An in-house child-care center may be convenient for the parents, but it also removes the option for the parent to send the child to the care provider of their choice. For the employer, a child-care facility can be very costly, and there are other concerns, such as liability of the company in providing a service that must be taken into consideration. Negotiating with local health care providers also poses many cost and benefit questions. Again, the local child-care provider option may serve to limit the option of the parent to send their child to the child-care provider of their choice, but it may also serve to lower the cost to both the parent and the company. The company again may be concerned about liability issues if they become involved in negotiating a deal with the child-care provider. Also, will costs escalate over the next few years? Are there enough local child-care providers in each area where they have offices? All these questions must be considered before proceeding.

The voucher option also leaves many questions to be considered. The company must look at how much they can afford to give each employee toward child care, how much it costs their employees for this service, and the possibility of costs severely escalating in the near future. For the employees, the voucher would give them a choice among options in the care of their child. They may choose to hire a babysitter, put their child in a private home, or utilize a child-care provider company or service. Depending upon the options available to them, however, a voucher may not be sufficient to cover the costs of their child's care, making the option of company-provided health care more attractive to them because it may reduce out-of-pocket costs. For the HRM professional, there is much to be considered, and a wrong choice can cost the company thousands or even millions of dollars without solving the problem. While considering the options, the HRM professional must also consider whether the plan will be cost effective for the company. Will these benefits truly help to retain the employees over the long term? Will it make them more productive? Can we afford it? Do the costs outweigh the benefits? Just because the HRM professional has identified a need on the part of the employees does not necessarily mean he or she should rush into action to solve the problem. By answering the questions listed above, the HRM department can decide whether the benefit is in the best interest of the company and how the company can best go about fashioning a plan to meet the needs of its employees.

A third challenge for the HRM professional is coming up with creative ways to meet the employee's changing expectations and overcoming management obstacles in putting some of these plans into place. Issues such as work-at-home schemes, employee empowerment programs, and support groups can sometimes be very hard to sell to a management team that is set in its ways. The challenge for the HRM professional is to show the employer how these plans will achieve the goals of the department by meeting the employee's expectations while helping to maintain or increase the company's bottom line or the employee's productivity. The HRM department must have a clear plan of action for a new or especially inventive proposal in order to convince management of the program's long-term success. The ability of HRM professionals to remain flexible and creative in meeting changing employee expectations, all the while keeping an eye on the corporation's bottom line, will pose a significant challenge in the decades to come. The challenge to the HRM professional is especially difficult because the need of the employees is constantly changing or evolving. The managers that are best able to come up with plans to meet these changes in the manner outlined above are the people whose companies will benefit from the best human capital.

The changing demographics of the U.S. population are leading to diversity of the U.S. workforce, which contributes to the changing employee and employer expectations challenge. The last 30 years have seen dramatic changes in the U.S. labor force. In the 1950s, the labor force was dominated by the white male head of the household, who was the family's wage earner. Since the 1960s, more women have entered the workforce. Dual-income families are becoming the norm and not the exception, while the number of single head of households and single parents is increasing. The population growth has been the slowest since the 1930s, resulting in an aging workforce and a shortage of young entry level workers. Minorities comprise a larger portion of the new entrants in the labor market, while immigrants compose the largest share of the workforce since World War I (Goddard, 1989). By the end of the century, the population will have a completely different profile. One in three U.S. citizens will be nonwhite; 85 percent of the new workforce entrants will be women, minorities, or immigrants; and more than one-third of the population will be 65 years or older (Wagel & Levine, 1990). These new employees are bringing their own set of values, norms, and styles as well as talents, skills, and knowledge to the workplace.

It is difficult to address changing employee expectations without addressing the challenges associated with the diversification of the U.S. workforce. As the workforce diversifies, each subgroup brings its own job expectations to the workplace. To meet this challenge firms are creating workforce diversity programs that address gender, lifestyle, age, and ethnic background.

With an increase in diversity comes changing employee expectations and changes in the psychological contract between employees and their organizations. The challenge facing corporate America is how to manage this diversity to develop a stronger, more productive, and competitive workforce. In the past, the employee-employer contract was easy to understand: Happy employees were those who accepted the terms of the employer and unhappy employees were free to leave. With the shrinking of entrants to the labor force and the changing demographics, these terms are changing. Smart employers are paying attention to their employees' concerns. They realize that understanding the changing expectations of the employee is the key to recruiting the best candidates, keeping the best employees, and removing barriers to greater productivity.

THE ROLE OF HUMAN RESOURCES MANAGEMENT AND CHANGING EXPECTATIONS

The role of HRM is changing as a result of such things as changing employee and employer expectations. No longer are employee relations HRM's primary function. Top management is realizing that their company's competitive edge in today's marketplace resides in its people and are turning to HRM for help to lead the company into the future. More companies are linking HRM to corporate strategy by having their HRM professionals directly report to the chief executive officer and by including them in major strategic decisions (Kaplan, 1991). Increasingly, top management will expect HRM professionals to predict and facilitate change by opening the lines of communications (Wagel & Levine, 1990). One way HRM can facilitate change is by making management sensitive to the impact of possible changes. This way, management can take a pro-active, not a reactive, stance.

Understanding the changing expectations of the employees is the key to developing a pro-active stance. Companies need to identify ways to tap the diversity of their employees to improve productivity and increase retention. The more diverse age range of the workforce, coupled with the structural upheavals, has brought the generation gaps to the workplace. This area needs to be addressed. Before a company can do that, it must first make sure it has a strategic plan. A strategic plan should consist of four primary steps. First, the company needs to define its mission and objectives, so it knows what its business is and what makes it unique. Second, it needs to analyze both the internal and external factors in the business environment. This includes evaluating the company's strengths, weaknesses, opportunities, challenges, and threats. Included in this step should be an assessment of the company's current labor resources: its skills, educational background, and knowledge (also, those of the workforce as a whole). The next step is to consider strategic alternatives and anticipate their potential impact on the workforce. The last step is having each department consider what needs to be done, by whom, when, and with what resource (Anthony & Norton, 1991). For a strategic plan to be effective, it must be reevaluated regularly and adjusted as necessary. It is difficult to develop a company culture without strategic objectives and direction.

Once a company knows where it is going, it can then determine what kinds of people it needs in terms of: skills, knowledge, and abilities; personal characteristics; background and job experience; and their workforce demographics. It is up to HRM to identify ways in which the organization can recruit the best candidates, keep the valued employees, and help remove productivity barriers. To achieve this, HRM must understand employees' attitudes toward work, what motivates them, and what gives them job satisfaction. A 1989 Gallup Poll Survey reported that generation (age), not income, was the major factor in job satisfaction and attitudes toward work (Society, 1989).

With advances in health and increasing life spans, more people are working longer. Coupling this with the aging of the baby boomers, the workforce is becoming older. What impact is age having in the workplace? Now there are three generations with different values and expectations in the workplace. These generations have been given a variety of names: Radio Babies (birth dates: 1925 to 1942), TV Babies (birth dates: 1943 to 1960), and Computer Babies (birth dates: 1961 to 1979) (Murphy, 1991); World War II Generation (1925–45), Baby-Boom Generation (1946–64), and Twentysomething Generation (1965–75) (*The Futurist*, 1992); Non-Baby Boomers (before 1946); Baby Boomers (1946–64); and Baby Busters (born after 1964) (Chanick, 1992). This chapter will address the generations as follows: Pre-Boomers (those born before 1946), Baby Boomers (born between 1946 and 1964), and Baby Busters (born after 1964).

The massive restructuring of the last decade displaced many Pre-Boomers workers who were in their fifties and sixties. Many of these workers entered new industries and found their bosses and co-workers were often younger. This mixing and matching of business background and experience has the potential to increase an organization's competitiveness. "But it can also create a clash of cultures the likes of which managers have rarely dealt with before," comments Murphy (1991, p. 43). These groups are bringing fundamentally different views of the world to the workplace, each having its own set of values, perceptions, experiences, and anxieties.

The HRM department's first step toward blending the generations is to understand why they are so different. What were the influencing social and economical factors? Pre-Boomers are products of the Great Depression. The traditional Protestant work-ethic that stresses hard work, sacrifice, and delayed gratification is their creed. Mostly male, this group steadily worked itself up the ladder believing in hard work and paying one's dues. They value structure and have some problem adapting to the new organizational trends. As a group, they are politically and financially conservative. Loyalty is important to them. They work hard to get a job done because it is good for the organization. The job is viewed as a way to earn a living and support a family, not something meant to be enjoyed. They often define themselves through their work (Chanick, 1992). If asked to talk about themselves, they might say, "I am a controller for XYZ Company in Chicago."

Then there are the Baby Boomers, who grew up with television. Products of the 1960s and the Vietnam War, they have turned the Protestant work ethic on its head (Braus, 1992). They are hard workers, but the focus is on self-fulfillment and not on organizational loyalty. Dual-wage-earner families comprise this group. They are looking for a better world and to make a difference. As this group ages, it finds itself struggling to balance family and careers. They are not afraid to take risks, viewing them as the only way to make change happen. They seek and expect more control over their work. Their paycheck is viewed as this generation's report card — the more the better — and they want it to reflect individual productivity (Braus, 1992). Having grown up as part of the electronic revolution, this group easily adapts to the changing workplace. They want the workplace to be warm and fuzzy and do not mind getting emotionally involved with fellow employees (Murphy, 1991). They define themselves in more rounded terms than the older group. When asked to talk about themselves, they might say "I live in Larkspur. I have been married for 20 years and have 2 children, Christian and Megan. I work for XYZ Company."

The Baby Busters are the youngest generation. They are the products of the dual-wage-earner family and the television babysitter. Some social scientists have dubbed this the "Why bother?" generation (*The Futurist*, 1992). They lack the idealism of the Baby Boomers having grown up under nuclear threat and having inherited a world full of economic and social problems. They are very self-oriented; "What's in it for me?" could be their creed. Having spent much time outside the home in child care, they are independent and accustomed to being on their own. Job autonomy is important to them. Money, power, and status drive this generation. Authority is viewed as something to question, not to defer to. This generation is slow to commit and less loyal to employers than older generations. Having fun is their top priority. They are postponing moving into adult roles, extending their adolescence, by taking longer to complete school and leave home. Quantity time is more important to them than quality time (*The Futurist*, 1992). Interest in a project motivates them to work hard, not because they want to be good soldiers. "They are naturals when it comes to the new focus on quality and customer satisfaction. 'To them, satisfying the customer makes more sense than satisfying the boss'" (Murphy, 1991, p. 44).

The HRM department's next step is deciding how to best motivate and satisfy this diverse group. No longer is there just one set of rules on how to motivate and create job satisfaction. Flexibility is the name of the game, being different things to different people. This can be done in several ways. When possible, offer choices to get the best match between motivator and employee. Encouraging mentor-protege relationships helps to break down the generation gap and to build harmonious teams. Open the lines of communication by freely discussing age differences at meetings. Provide manageable challenges; employees like to be stretched but not too far. Allow for control so the employee will feel he is participating in decisions. Develop the sense of belonging through nurturing and setting boundaries; it is important for people to feel supported and connected to others. Create a sense of purpose through communication.

ORGANIZATIONAL RESPONSES TO CHANGING EMPLOYEE EXPECTATIONS

Organizations are beginning to listen more to their employees. This dialogue is taking place at the bargaining table, in the workplace, and through HRM channels. Employers are asking employees to express their concerns and needs through surveys and informal discussion groups. More companies are finding out like the United Services Automobile Association (USAA) has, that a friendlier workplace that meets employees' needs is more productive. In an effort to attract and retain women, who now comprise 70 percent of its workforce, USAA made changes that address the home and work conflict issues. The company went to a 4-day work week, added van pools to reduce commuting hassles, and provided shopping facilities. There is a cafe that provides inexpensive whole meals to take home as well as a bakery. The company store carries a wide variety of items from fresh flowers to children's clothes. A clinic is available for routine shots and wellness screening. Chairman Robert McDermott is the driving force behind USAA's success. He believes it is important to nurture "talent within the ranks through training and education" (Brophy, 1989, p. 51). To encourage this development, USAA pays for night courses taught by local colleges and professional organizations. Job rotation is encouraged as a means of providing new job challenges.

The corporate pyramid is getting smaller at the top as companies downsize, restructure, and streamline their operations. Competition among the Baby Boomers is high as they vie for those decreasing top management positions. Employees are leaving companies for better opportunities or to start their own businesses. This exodus of experience and talent is hurting companies. In an attempt to stem this outflow of valuable resources, organizations are looking for innovative and cost-effective ways to motivate and satisfy their employees.

National Semiconductor developed a dual career path as mechanism for professional growth of both the individual contributor and managers. An individual contributor is described by Milan Moravec, human resources manager at National Semiconductor, as "a person with innovative ideas, technical aptitude and entrepreneurial spirit. Not a 'company person'" but someone who wants to make a personal contribution to the company's competitiveness and success (Wagel & Levine, 1990, p. 18). To be effective, dual career paths must be truly comparable in terms of required competence, responsibility, and influence. They must also have distinctive levels and guide employees to positions with greater responsibility, influence, risk, and compensation. Other companies, such as Southern California Gas Co., are offering employees lateral transfers, allowing them to learn new areas of the business.

Key motivators, such as control, compensation, and flexibility, are being looked at for ways to recruit and retrain employees. Baby Boomers and Baby Busters seek and expect more control over their work. They want their pay directly linked to productivity. The job is considered only a component of their lives, so free time is important.

Companies are looking at ways to move accountability down to the workplace. Quality circles are being used by Allstate, Honeywell, Lockheed, General Dynamics, Westinghouse, and over 500 other companies to identify, investigate, and solve production problems. Ford, General Motors, General Electric (GE), and Continental Group are among those who have formed quality-of-worklife committees tasked with improving the organization (Goddard & Bernard, 1989). Companies like Southern California Edison are broadening the levels of decision making by pushing it down to lower levels (Black, 1991). Digital Equipment Corporation, 3M, Emerson Electric, Exxon, Union Pacific Railroad, and others have empowered their employees through ad hoc teams, which are formed to solve specific problems and then are dissolved (Chanick, 1992; Goddard & Bernard, 1989). The Associated Group took a more radical approach and restructured its organization so the decision-making process was decentralized (Chanick, 1992). General Foods, Kaiser Aluminum, Proctor & Gamble, and GE have encouraged bottom-up management by setting up self-managed factories or divisions.

Flexibility is becoming the key word in management. Flexible compensation packages and flex policies are ways to contain costs and to give employees maximum control over their life and changing needs. The workforce spans a wide age range with a wider span of changing needs. Health and retirement issues concern the Pre-Boomers, Baby Boomers are concerned with balancing family and work; while Baby Busters are interested in money and leisure time. Xerox, 3M, Steelcase Inc., and others offer variable hours, part-time work, job sharing, and benefits (Cohn, 1988; Black, 1991). Steelcase, the number one office-furniture maker, is a pioneer in flex policies. Both managers and workers attribute the company's success to the flex policies that include flexible pay, flexible hours, and flexible benefits (Cohn, 1988).

Employee fulfillment and individual performance are other areas being addressed in the struggle to build a competitive workforce. Companies like IBM, Dana Corporation, Walt Disney Productions, and McDonald's are investing in employee training and education. Career planning programs have been set up by Gulf Oil, IBM, GE, Xerox, TRW, and General Motors to help employees select and achieve meaningful goals and objectives. Mars, Inc. recognized individual performance by giving each employee a weekly 10 percent bonus just for showing up on time each day (Goddard & Bernard, 1989).

A number of progressive organizations and managers are successfully addressing the problem of changing employee expectations by listening to their employees. They realize their number one resource is people. Unfortunately, many organizations still view the employee as a disposable commodity, not a valuable resource. This kind of attitude leads to disgruntled workers who are less productive and loyal. During uncertain economic times, employees are less likely to jeopardize their jobs by voicing their discontent, but when the economy turns around, they will be asking for more or moving on to new jobs. More companies are finding out that it is cheaper to satisfy a key employee's needs than it is to replace him. When a company loses a key employee, they lose not only a person but also a wealth of valuable knowledge and expertise.

The joke in many companies is, "What's today's management style?" Often, managers will jump onto the latest bandwagon with little thought or commitment. They embrace the latest change for the sake of change, not for what it can do for the organization. If management does not believe in a program, or will not support it, then it is doomed to failure. Programs fail most often because they have been put in place without proper preparation or thought given to employee impact.

Some HRM professionals have recognized that, while benefit programs are very important, just providing the programs is sometimes not enough. Take, for example, the case of Manor Care, a Silver Spring, Maryland, holding company that owns Choice Hotels International and Manor Health Care Corporation. Both businesses are heavily dependent upon low-paid front-line workers. The turnover rate for these employees is extremely high, sometimes approaching 100 percent. Manor Care wanted to increase their quality of service by retaining their front-line workers. A cursory look at their benefits programs showed the company had a 401(k) plan and health care plans that included an indemnity plan and a Preferred Provider Organization as well as Health Maintenance Organizations at several locations. Upon further investigation, however, the company found that participation was very low — 15 percent in the Preferred Provider Organization and among employees making $12,000 a year or less and 20 percent in the 401(k) program. The reason for the lack of participation in the programs was that the costs, while relatively low, were still too high for the front-line workers. They needed all additional money for food, clothes, and other necessities and could not afford the extra money to buy into benefits programs. The company decided they would meet the employees' needs in order to increase their standard of service. They devised a benefit plan that would compensate employees based upon length of service, and lower-paid employees were paid benefits on a larger portion of their salaries than higher-paid employees. For example, the indemnity plan now was based upon salary. Lower-paid employees had a lower deductible, and higher-paid employees had a larger deductible. The company also reduced the contribution amount for all employees based upon length of service. A similar scheme was devised for the pension plan. Lower-paid employees received a contribution that was a larger percentage of their salary than higher-paid employees. In addition to the above, employees can cash-out of the plan by using money for medical plans for other benefits or to increase their pay. Eighty-five percent of the employees polled indicated that their benefits had improved as a result of the plan's implementation. Adjusting the plan slightly for some of the higher-paid workers who had some objections, the company is now well on its way to achieving its goals. Turnover at Manor Care is down 12 percent overall, and among front-line employees, turnover has decreased 25 percent from October 1991. Customer satisfaction surveys had also increased in the past year, a result of higher retention rates and happier employees (Gunsch, 1993).

The above examples give a good picture of how many companies are drastically changing various programs through consultation with their workers and to meet changing worker's expectations. The change does not necessarily have to be so drastic, however. Sometimes, minor issues need fine-tuning to accomplish corporate goals and meet changing expectations. A good example is employee relocation. Although the recession and lack of job security have made some employees less resistant to moving, a full 35 percent of companies in a 1992 Relocation Trends Survey reported reluctance on their employees' part to take the transfer. Many families now require two parents to work in order to maintain an acceptable standard of living. Moving requires the spouse of the employee also to find a new job opportunity. Additionally, cost of living increases are feared in new communities as well as the prospects of giving up a favorable mortgage rate. Companies are combatting these needs by taking employee relocations on a case-by-case basis. Whereas in the past, HRM professionals had written guidelines for what moving expenses the company would and would not pay, today the company may look at many different relocation-help plans. Assistance might include increased living allowances while the employee accumulates a down payment, subsidized mortgage assistance for the first few years, help for spouses to find a new job, spousal assistance, and counseling to help the family with their relocations. As factors such as the housing market, interest rates and cost-of-living change so do the needs of the employee being relocated. Although it may be a small adjustment in the total human resources plan, relocation considerations are among the examples of how human resources departments must adjust to meet changing employee situations (Caudron, 1993).

Changing employee expectations sometimes force HRM professionals to be creative in developing plans to meet these changing demands. Sometimes these plans are unorthodox and seem to go against the grain of the corporate structure, but a successful plan can pay big dividends for the company that implements it. Take, for example, the growing trend in telecommuting. When employees first bring up the idea of telecommuting, the first reaction of most employers is that the employee will lose touch with his or her fellow employees, job performance and productivity will suffer, and he or she will be unable to monitor employee performance. With careful planning, however, telecommuting can become a great success. In a telecommuting program that AT&T started in Arizona, 80 percent of the supervisors reported that telecommuting increased employee productivity, and 67 percent reported an increase in the overall efficiency of the department. It seems that the largest barrier to increased telecommuting options is the mindset of managers. Many managers still feel the need to monitor an employee's progress on a constant basis. Unless the employee is in front of them working, they feel there is no work getting done. When properly planned and monitored, telecommuting can be a way to increase management skills. Telecommuting forces managers to set clear goals for their employees and to monitor progress. The emphasis is less on activity than on results. Many managers report increased communication with their telecommuting employees. Managers find they get more done and, more importantly, are happier with their work arrangements. The Travelers Companies in Hartford have been able to see great results from their telecommuting programs. Increased productivity, reduced absenteeism, and the ability to attract and retain top talent are some of the results. Although telecommuting is not for every employee, the advent of personal computers, E-Mail and proliferation of fax machines has given human resources departments the ability to meet some changing employee expectations while also helping to improve the company's performance. The electronics age will no doubt produce many additional opportunities for creative human resources managers and progressive companies to adjust to a changing work environment as well as to help their companies compete.

A final example of a company's HRM department utilizing creative ideas to meet employees' changing expectations is Pearle Vision, a nationwide chain that provides eye-wear products and services in the retail market (Laabs, 1993). Pearle has over 1,000 stores around the country, about half of which are corporate owned. By 1991, data from the company's stores showed that the franchise stores were consistently outperforming the corporate-owned stores. The company began to look for reasons why this was occurring. What they found was that their store managers were not given the ability to act like entrepreneurs. They were not allowed to manage bills or employees, develop marketing strategies, or make decisions on their own without corporate involvement. The company's rules were not allowing managers to best serve their customers' needs or to use any innovative management techniques. Pearle then came up with a program that would operate more like the franchise stores. Dubbed the Optipreneur program, a seven-month test was undertaken. The program gave store managers sweeping control over almost every aspect of the store's business. Bonuses for the managers were no longer capped, but tied to the controllable profits of the store. Of course, the managers were also graded on customer service and quality of work. The test program exceeded human resources and corporate expectations. Stores that had never been profitable were suddenly turning a profit. Sales for stores increased and store managers were pleased with the program. The new system gave the managers the opportunity to own their own store with no capital investment and they were paid based on performance, as if they actually owned the store. The program has now been introduced on a company-wide basis and early results are very promising. It will be many years before the full effects of the program are felt, but senior management believes the chances for success are very high. One of the most difficult parts of the program's implementation was selling it to senior management. The plan called for sweeping changes in the corporate system and empowering the employees. Luckily for Pearle, the plan prevailed and both the employees and management are reaping the benefits.

A GLIMPSE OF THE FUTURE

The coming decade will continue to pose significant challenges for HRM professionals and organizations in meeting their employees' changing expectations. Some areas such as health care and child care are seeing costs rise and insurance becoming out of reach for some small businesses. A referral service program probably will not be sufficient if an employer is going to retain a worker with a small child to care for. New options other than blanket medical coverage should be explored if companies are to pay for health insurance and remain profitable. Tele-commuting on a two-day basis may become permanent if productivity continues to increase and child care is impossible to obtain. No one can predict the future. Employees' expectations will change as circumstances and events in our society change. Many of the current benefit packages will become outdated or obsolete as time goes on. One trend we can easily see occurring is the advent of corporate downsizing. Corporations are becoming leaner, smaller, and, hopefully, smarter. Under these circumstances, employees become even more important and the retention of key employees essential. How employers keep their employees is very important. In most of the examples listed above, the needed change came as a result of years of neglect in certain cases or an event that made the company aware of the human resources problem in others. In the coming decade, employees may not have the luxury of reacting to festering problems after they have come to a head. Good employees will be able to find greener pastures at a company that has already addressed the problem and remedied it. If companies are to continue to compete in the coming decade, simply coming up with plans for existing problems may be too little, too late.

The largest problem still in need of answers with respect to changing employee expectations is how the company can identify these changing needs before they become serious retention problems, resulting in business setback or failure. Organizations must assess the needs of the employees at an earlier stage and address the needs where applicable. A cafeteria-style benefit plan, where the employee can choose among different benefits according to his or her needs, is one solution touted to meet the needs of changing employee expectations. While this option seems attractive because of its flexibility, the employee cannot choose benefits that the company does not provide. In short, there may be no applicable benefit for an employee's need. Of course, not every employee expectation can or should be met by the cafeteria-style benefit plan, but who will continue to monitor the program for additions or deletions? How can the company and its HRM department add to the programs before they become a problem for the company, and how can costs be controlled? The answers to these questions are the key to an organization remaining profitable while keeping its employees in the coming decades. Meeting the changing expectations in a cost effective manner is the key to the company's success. How this goal will be accomplished remains to be seen.

If the HRM professional is to stay on top of changing employee expectations, he or she must have good, vital information from the organization's employees. As seen above, some problems are not always what they seem. A simple, insurmountable problem can sometimes be fixed very easily with a little ingenuity. Weyerhauser was on the right track when they formed a child-care task force. In like manner, HRM professionals should form task forces made up of employees on a rotating basis to address the concerns of changing employee expectations. Since the employees are closest to their fellow workers, they have the best knowledge of the needs of their fellow employees as well as their own. If the company has a cafeteria-style plan, the options should be reviewed frequently, with low participation options dropped as new programs are developed. The employees should be polled more frequently for their opinions on the company benefit package and on which plans should be added, retained, or dropped. When a consensus begins to develop on a new program, the various options available should be researched, always keeping an eye on productivity and costs. The program options can then be put before the benefits committee and upper management, or the employees themselves, to decide which option to choose. As evidenced earlier, what the human resources department sees as a solution to a problem may not always be the same option the employees want or participate in. By constantly monitoring the company's benefits program, keeping frequent contact with employee needs changes through surveys and participation in the employee benefits committee, HRM professionals should be able to identify potential needs of their employees and develop cost-effective programs for meeting those needs before they become problems. The very nature of the problem requires constant monitoring in the workplace. Exit surveys should be scrutinized to see why employees are leaving and if an item is frequently cited, why this is a problem and how it can be remedied. HRM professionals must also keep abreast of changes in technology that may enable additional flexibility in meeting the needs of their employees and have the ability to show senior management how these new programs can benefit the company through increased productivity, quality, or performance. In an ever-changing world and work environment, the companies that are in touch with their employees' needs and have plans to address them in a cost-effective manner are the companies that will prosper with their human capital.

The issue of changing expectations is just beginning to be addressed. Many organizations have developed aggressive programs to deal with the issue, but most of the business community does not recognize the problem and how it will affect them. Traditionally, they have taken a reactive stance to change. With the globalization of the marketplace, the U.S. business community needs to be pro-active when it comes to changes. To do this, HRM needs to anticipate the future of today's issues as well as manage them.

Today's U.S. workforce is the best educated ever, and, because of this, they are demanding opportunities to become more actively involved in the workplace. To meet these demands, companies are going to have to restructure so they can decentralize the decision-making process, putting it into the hands of the workers. Employers will have to consider redesigning jobs to meet individual employee needs for recognition, autonomy, and personal growth. Tomorrow's worker will seek jobs in which he or she can use and be recognized for their individual skills, talents, and knowledge. Our current reward system is based on time at the job, not on skills and knowledge used and work performed. It will have to be replaced with one that rewards an individual's skills, knowledge, and results. With increased competition and the emergence of a world marketplace, the job of matching employee skills with appropriate jobs will become increasingly difficult. HRM professionals will need to take job skills inventories and match them against projected required skills so they design ongoing training to meet future demands.

HRM professionals are going to have to become more aware of what is happening in the business world. No longer can they just function as personnel managers making sure policy is being followed. They must understand their company's business and take an active part in developing its strategy.

The issue of worker compensation will be one of the most critical areas of the future. As the labor force becomes more diverse, entrants decline, and the economy tightens, employers will need to develop compensation packages that are tailored to individual workers' needs, while trying to control labor costs. Based on current compensation trends, the package of the future will be more flexible. The major components of the future package will include basic and supplemental pay, comprehensive paid leave, cafeteria-style benefit plans to cover insurance, retirement, and savings with defined contribution plans and built-in portability, and legally required benefits.

CONCLUSION

No one can anticipate the specific changes that will arise in employee expectations in the coming years. A company can be prepared for most changes, however, if it makes a commitment to remain flexible. Empowerment of employees, telecommuting, and flex-time are just a few of the recent innovations in HRM. All were developed to meet employees' changing expectations in the workplace in order to spend additional time with families, take more power over their own destiny, or just be more comfortable when working. Whatever the new issue, companies should look at each plan to address the need on a cost and benefit basis. Employers should not fear new innovations but seize them as opportunities to make their employees happier and more productive and their company more profitable. The decade will pose many challenges to employees, employers, and HRM professionals. By working together with employers and remaining flexible and tolerant of new ideas and technologies, organizations will be able to meet the changing expectations of their employees and, quite possibly, see their company benefit from it.

When companies pay attention to the development, clarification, and management of changing employee-organization relationships, they create progressive organizational cultures that capitalize on the psychological contract. HRM professionals can, and should, play an active role in the development of such a culture. More than ever, HRM professionals must ensure that their management devotes time to staying in touch with its employees. Through the use of meetings, surveys, and informational videos HRM professionals can put management in contact with its employees. In addition, HRM professionals must see to it that talking and listening to employees are requirements included in a company's management development efforts. Today's psychological contract requires an emphasis on talking with people, not at people.

A number of progressive organizations and managers are successfully addressing the changing psychological contract by listening to their employees. These companies have established career planning programs through their HRM departments to address employee fulfillment and enhance individual and organizational performance. The dialogue between the employee and employer is taking place at the bargaining table, in the workplace, and through HRM channels. Employers are asking employees to express their concerns and needs through surveys and informal discussion groups.

HRM professionals have a responsibility to ensure that their organization recognizes that each employee has unique needs that may be different from those of top- and middle-level managers. By ensuring that their organizations hold regular meetings to exchange ideas, express needs, and debate goals, HRM professionals improve the potential success of the new psychological contract. For example, CEOs and other managers benefit from meetings because they learn that what others feel is important. The employees learn from meetings how the chief executive officer views them, the organization, ethical issues, and the progress of the firm.

HRM professionals will be challenged throughout the coming years as they strive to assist their organizations in reshaping the new psychological contract by implementing innovative employment strategies. Such strategies as flexible compensation packages and flex policies can contain costs and maximize employees' control over their lives and changing needs. The current workforce spans a wide age range with a wider span of needs that affect the psychological contract with its employers. Health and retirement issues concern the Pre-Boomers (those born before 1946); Baby Boomers (people born between 1946 and 1964) are concerned with balancing family and work; and Baby Busters (those born after 1964) are interested in money and leisure time. Steelcase, the number one office-furniture maker, is a pioneer in flex policies. Both managers and employees attribute the company's success to the flex policies that include flexible pay, flexible hours, and flexible benefits (Cohn, 1988).

HRM professionals also must ensure that performance standards and objectives are clearly stated and are timely. Performance management, including appraisals, must become a continuous process rather than an intermittent effort. And because of the increased emphasis on work in teams, newer performance management approaches must be used to address the psychological considerations of receiving feedback and rewards based on team performance. Rewards must be related more realistically to continuing performance, which is adjusted to the needs and concerns of both the employee and the organization. HRM professionals are vital to reshaping the new psychological contract when they provide a comprehensive and systematic basis for recruiting, retaining, and laying off employees.

This chapter has looked at HRM and changing employee expectations. The impact of the changing demographics of the labor force on employees' expectations was covered along with other related challenges. Special focus was placed on the generation gaps in the labor force, their needs, and impact on the workplace. Some examples on how employers are trying to meet the diverse expectations of the employee were given. And finally, a brief look at what the HRM's role will be in the future.

REFERENCES

Anthony, P. & Norton, L. A. 1991, April. Link HR to corporate strategy. *Personnel Journal*: 75–86.

Black, K. S. 1991, October. How to hold onto a staff when . . . , *Working Woman*: 15–16.

Braus, P. 1992, August. What workers want. *American Demographics*: 30–37.

Brophy, B. 1989, April. You're in the office of the future now; at USAA, adding amenities to the workplace has boosted output along with morale. *U.S. News & World Report*: 50–53.

Caudron, S. 1993, March. Options alleviate employee qualms about relocating. *Personnel Journal*: 35–40.

Chanick, R. 1992, January. Career growth for baby boomers. *Personnel Journal*: 40–44.

Cohn, B. 1988, August 1. A glimpse of the 'flex' future; at Steelcase, offering variable hours, pay and perks benefits the firm and its workers. *Newsweek*, 38–39.

Goddard, R. W. 1989, February. Work Force 2000. *Personnel Journal*: 64–71.

Goddard, R. W. & Bernard, J. 1989, April. How to reward the '80's employee. *Public Management*: 7–10.

Gunsch, D. 1993, February. Benefits program helps retain frontline workers. *Personnel Journal*: 88–94.

Haupt, J. 1993, February. Employee action prompts management to respond to work-and-family needs. *Personnel Journal*: 96–107.

Kaplan, G. 1991, July. Renaissance HR: A perspective for the '90s. *Personnel Journal*: 15–16.

Laabs, J. J. 1993, January. Pearle Vision's managers think like entrepreneurs. *Personnel Journal*: 41–46.

Murphy, T. 1991, July. Boomers, busters and 50-plussers: Managing the new generation gaps. Working Woman: 41–46.

Morin, W. J. 1992. Redefining success. *Executive Excellence*, 9(8), 9–10.

Society. 1989, November/December. Job satisfaction based on generation, not class: 2.

The Futurist. 1992, May/June. Baby busters enter the workforce: 52–53.

Wagel, W. H. & Levine, H. Z. 1990, June. HR '90: Challenges and opportunities. Personnel: 18–42.

3

Human Resources Management and the Challenges of a Diverse Workforce: Including the Disabled in the Diversity Equation

The challenges of assembling and managing a workforce that reflects the population it serves — in terms of age, race, gender, educational experience, etc. — is complex now and will become more so as the nation diversifies further. As a result of the transformation to a more diverse workforce, organizations will need to develop competencies in effectively managing such a diverse workforce.

While past efforts to assimilate a culturally diverse workforce have sprung from legal pressure or moral concerns over fairness, those efforts must now be viewed in light of bottom-line issues. Consider, for example, a diaper manufacturer with an all-male product development team, "How close to the customer is the male team likely to get? How innovative will team members be?" (Loden & Roesner, 1991, p. 9).

Successful organizations will react to diversity as the important business issue it is by implementing proactive, strategic human resources planning. Short-term strategies designed to circumvent the situation will keep an organization from effectively positioning itself in tomorrow's world of cultural, gender, and lifestyle diversity (Foster, 1988). Today, and in the coming years, top management, in conjunction with their HRM departments, will need to emphasize to line managers two goals of diversity competence: productivity growth and market share expansion, both domestically and internationally.

More than ever before, HRM professionals and their organizations must find ways of including a variety of individuals from very diverse backgrounds and experiences throughout the innerworkings of the organization if they are to survive and thrive in the coming years. However, the phenomenon of inclusiveness and diversity of workforces is not new; HRM professionals have had to diversify workforces in response to gender, race, and age legislation for years.

Working under the same general premises of existing legislation, HRM departments must now add yet another variable to their diversity efforts and the employment process (that is, selection, recruitment, development and termination — the inclusion of disabled individuals). The inclusion of the disabled should serve as a welcomed invitation to their open participation in the existing organization. This change in the status quo of most organizations requires new attitudes and behaviors on the part of all organizational members in order to be successfully implemented.

It is the contention of this chapter that the HRM department will continue to serve as the guiding force for this needed change. Thus, HRM departments must be aware of the issues and possible implications that are associated with implementing Americans with Disabilities Act of 1990 (ADA) legislation; and must issue organizational specific guidelines for their institutionalization. Other organizational leaders and departments should give great care to abiding by the guidelines established by the HRM department once they are issued. This chapter is intended to aid the process by presenting an overview of challenges and issues presented by changing demographics that HRM departments must be aware of as they assist their organizations in managing diversity in the coming years. More specifically, this chapter will first, briefly, introduce several challenges related to increasing diversity in organizations for HRM professionals. The chapter will then discuss how the ADA and its requirements for inclusion of the disabled pose a challenge for HRM professionals in their diversity initiatives. In addition, the chapter will identify possible conflicts in legislation and regulatory guidelines governing HRM practices sensitive to race, age, gender, and disability. The chapter will conclude with a look at the importance of the role of HRM professionals in getting their organizations to look within to find ways to anticipate and respond to the needs and wants of members of society that have previously received secondary attention.

DIVERSITY CHALLENGES FOR
HUMAN RESOURCES MANAGEMENT

Several authors have recently outlined some of the challenges a more diverse workforce poses for organizations in general and HRM professionals in particular (Loden & Roesner, 1991). Management must be able to:

communicate effectively with employees from diverse cultural backgrounds;

coach and develop people who are diverse along many dimensions, including age, education, ethnicity, gender, physical ability, race, sexual/affectional orientation, and so on;

provide objective performance feedback that is based on substance rather than on style;

help create organizational climates that nurture and utilize the rich array of talents and perspectives that diversity can offer.

These guidelines illustrate the need for organizations to recognize that for too long they have focused on recruitment of female and minority candidates without putting in place the training, mentoring, and communication programs that will ensure everyone has the opportunity to be successful. HRM professionals and other managers must understand that the workplace remains heavily influenced by the values of the dominant white male culture. Many evaluation systems reflect this bias, and supervisors must be trained not to mistake differences for problems.

Organizations cannot sit back and expect diverse people to assimilate automatically, but rather they should take steps to incorporate all people into the business and use their different perspectives to strengthen it. In recent years, HRM professionals have focused on several key areas in response to the challenges that accompany increasing and managing diversity, like those presented above, in the following ways:

Recruitment — Exert a concerted effort to find quality minority hires by improved college relations programs.

Career development — Expose those minority employees with high potential to the same key developmental jobs that have led traditionally to senior positions for their white, male counterparts.

Diversity training for managers — Address stereotypes and cultural differences that interfere with the full participation of all employees in the workplace.

Diversity training for employees — Help employees understand the corporate culture requirements for success in the firm, and career choices open to them.

Upward mobility — Break the invisible or glass ceiling and increase the number of minorities in upper management through mentors and executive appointment.

Diverse input and feedbak — Ask minority employees themselves what they need rather than ask managers what they think minorities need.

Self-help — Encourage networking and support groups among minorities.

Accountability — Hold managers accountable for developing their diverse workforces.

Systems accommodation — develop respect and support for cultural diversity through recognition of different cultural and religious holidays, diet restrictions, and so forth.

Outreach — support minority organizations and programs, thus developing a reputation as a multicultural leader (Copeland, 1988; Dastmalchian, Blyton, & Adamson, 1991).

There is every indication that focus on the above areas will improve the likelihood of more successfully including diverse individuals in the organization. However, it appears that, with continued legal requirements and court decisions, there will be a never-ending expectation that HRM professionals find ways to include more and more diverse individuals into their organizations. A clear example of such legislation is the ADA. And more particularly, there is the need to respond to the demands of the ADA while also meeting the requirements of previous legislation.

AMERICANS WITH DISABILITIES ACT OF 1990 AND ITS EXISTENCE WITH OTHER LEGISLATION

With the introduction of the ADA, HRM professionals will be challenged to continue to find ways to meet the demands of the ADA while coexisting with several other important pieces of legislation designed to increase underrepresented groups in organizations. The need to understand how the ADA coexists with existing legislation can serve as a useful starting point in recognizing how potential conflicts may arise as HRM professionals and their organizations attempt to meet the needs of the different protected groups and a more diverse workforce. The following review of other diversity-related legislation can help to determine what, if any, conflicts may result between the various legislation as HRM professionals and their organizations work to achieve their own and legislative-mandated diversity initiatives.

The Equal Pay Act of 1963

The Equal Pay Act, an amendment to the Fair Labor Standards Act, requires that men and women in the same organization who are doing equal work must be paid equally. The act defines "equal" in terms of skill, effort, responsibility, and working conditions. However, the act allows for reasons why men and women performing the same job might be paid differently. If the pay differences are the result of differences in seniority, merit, quantity or quality of production, or any factor other than sex (for example, shift differentials or training programs), then differences are legally allowable.

The Civil Rights Act of 1964

The Civil Rights Act of 1964 is the cornerstone of legislation designed to increase diversity within organizations and to reduce discriminatory practices in employment and promotion. It is divided into sections called titles and applies to organizations that are involved in interstate commerce, state and local governments, employment agencies, and labor organizations with 15 or more employees who work a minimum of 20 weeks a year. Title VII is the major legislation regulating equal employment opportunity in the United States and is of primary importance to HRM departments. Title VII forbids employment discrimination based on race, color, religion, sex, or national origin. Specifically it states that it is illegal for an employer to

(1) fail or refuse to hire or discharge any individual, or otherwise discriminate against any individual with respect to his compensation, terms, conditions, or privileges of employment because of such individual's race, color, religion, sex, or national origin, or (2) to limit, segregate, or classify his employees or applicants for employment in any way that would deprive or tend to deprive any individual employment opportunities or otherwise adversely affect status as an employee because of such individual's race, color, religion, sex, or national origin.

Title VII stipulates that organizations must go beyond simply discontinuing employment discrimination but should engage in the active recruitment of minority group members. In addition, these organizations are expected to give preferential treatment to minority group members. This action is referred to as affirmative action (DeCenzo & Robbins, 1994).

The Age Discrimination in Employment Act of 1967

Passed in 1967 and amended in 1986, the Age Discrimination in Employment Act of 1967 (ADEA) prohibits discrimination against employees over the age of 40. The act almost exactly mirrors Title VII in terms of its substantive provisions and the procedures to be followed in pursuing a case. The ADEA was designed to protect older employees when a firm reduces its workforce through layoffs. By targeting older employees who tend to have higher pay, a firm can substantially cut their labor costs. The ADEA applies to employers that are involved in interstate commerce; federal, state, and local governments; employment agencies; and labor organizations with 15 or more employees working 20 or more weeks a year. On October 16, 1990, the Older Workers Benefit Protection Act (Older Workers Act), substantially revised the provisions of the ADEA. The Older Workers Act codified both the equal-benefit-or-equal-cost rule and the benefit-by-benefit testing rule already found in the Equal Employment Opportunity Commission (EEOC) regulations.

The Vietnam Era Veteran's Readjustment Act of 1974

Similar to the Rehabilitation Act, this act requires federal contractors and subcontractors to take affirmative action steps toward employing Vietnam veterans (those serving between August 5, 1964, and May 7, 1975).

The Vocational Rehabilitation Act of 1973

This act requires executive agencies and contractors and subcontractors that receive $2,500 or more annually in federal contracts to actively recruit, employ, and promote all qualified disabled individuals through affirmative action measures. However, despite this act and numerous related state and local regulations, almost 15 million workers with disabilities in the private sector still lacked protection against employment discrimination. The ADA was enacted to fill this gap in coverage (Kohl & Greelaw, 1992).

The Pregnancy Discrimination Act of 1979

The Pregnancy Discrimination Act of 1979 (PDA) prohibits employment discrimination based on pregnancy. It requires that pregnant women be treated as other employees based on their ability or inability to do the job. The law also stipulates that organizations may not terminate the employment of a female for being pregnant or for having an abortion, refuse to make an employment decision based on one's pregnancy, or deny insurance coverage for the individual. The law also requires organizations to offer the employee a reasonable period of time off from work. At the end of this leave period, the worker is entitled to return to work. If an exact job is not available, a similar one in pay, benefits, and status must be provided.

The Civil Rights Act of 1991

The Civil Rights Act of 1991 was passed in an effort to reverse the effects of five Supreme Court decisions in 1989 that served to diminish the effects of the Civil Rights Act of 1964. These cases were: *Wards Cove* v. *Antonio*; *Martin* v. *Wilks*; *Hopkins* v. *Price Waterhouse*; *Patterson* v. *McClean Credit Union*, and *Lorance* v. *AT&T Technologies*. One of the major changes to the Civil Rights Act of 1991 is that now employees can receive compensatory and punitive damages in cases of discrimination under Title VII of the Civil Rights Act of 1964. Prior to the passage of the Civil Rights Act of 1991, damage claims were limited to equitable relief such as back pay, lost benefits, front pay, and attorney's fees. Compensatory damages include such things as future pecuniary loss, emotional pain, suffering, and loss of the enjoyment of life. Likewise, punitive damages are meant to discourage employers from discriminating by providing payment to the plaintiffs beyond the actual damages suffered. The amount of these charges, however, will be prorated based on the number of employees in the organization.

Also included in the Civil Rights Act of 1991 is the Glass Ceiling Act of 1991. The purpose of this act is to establish a Glass Ceiling commission to study the manner in which businesses fill management and decision-making positions, the developmental and skill-enhancing practices used to foster the necessary qualifications for advancement to such positions, and the compensation programs and reward structures currently utilized in the workplace. It also established an annual reward for excellence in promoting a more diverse skilled workforce at the management and decision-making levels in business.

Americans with Disabilities Act of 1990

The ADA, intended to grant equal employment opportunities to the disabled, is a far-reaching law that will require employers to reexamine and perhaps change virtually every aspect of their employment and HRM procedures. It will affect practices and decisions in areas ranging from hiring to promotion, to health and pension benefits, to the company picnic.

ADA goes one step farther than the traditional civil rights laws that prohibit employment discrimination on the grounds of race, sex, age, or other conditions. It is not sufficient under ADA that an employer simply not discriminate; as an employer, the organization must also take positive steps to make reasonable accommodation for people with disabilities.

Yet, ADA is not an affirmative action law. Organizations are not required to seek out disabled people to hire or to promote disabled employees ahead of others. And it has a distinctly anti-paternalistic stance, with employers prohibited from suggesting that disabled employees might need accommodations, from protecting disabled employees from supposed ill effects of working, or from generalizing about the limitations of a certain disability or disease.

ADA provides no clear-cut rules for how to deal with a given employee situation or disability. Instead, it requires that an organization make case-by-case decisions on whether an action could be discriminatory and how best to accommodate each employee. As a result, many of the requirements of the law are still vague and may not be clarified until precedent-setting cases are resolved in court. The act covers employers with 25 or more employees and will be expanded to cover employers with 15 or more employees as of July 26, 1994.

The Family and Medical Leave Act

The Family and Medical Leave Act (FMLA) requires covered employers to grant full-time employees a maximum of 12 weeks of unpaid, job-protected leave during a 12-month period for the following reasons:

to care for a newborn child, a newly adopted child or a child placed with an
employee for foster care;

to care for a child, parent or spouse who has a serious health condition; and

for an employee's own serious health condition.

The act, which went into effect on August 5, 1993, applies to any
employer engaged in commerce who employs 50 or more employees.
Special rules apply to employers who have collective-bargain-
ing agreements (CBAs). For companies that had CBAs in effect on
August 5, 1993, the FMLA became effective for the company on
February 5, 1994, or the date that the CBA terminates, whichever date
is earlier.

As a result of the various legislation cited above HRM professionals
must recognize that their organizations' obligations neither begin nor
end with any one piece of legislation. Added to the complexity of the
federal legislation are numerous state and local laws regarding
discrimination. A number of states and some cities have passed fair
employment practice laws prohibiting discrimination on the basis of
race, color, religion, gender, or national origin. Even prior to federal
legislation, several states had anti-discrimination legislation relating to
age and gender. For instance, New York protected individuals between
the ages of 18 and 65 prior to the 1978 and 1986 ADEA amendments,
and California had no upper limit on protected age. However, when
EEOC regulations conflict with state or local civil rights regulations,
the legislation more favorable to women and minorities applies.

The complexity of and the potential for conflict among the various
legislations can best be represented in the following discussion on the
ADA, PDA, FMLA, and the family-leave legislation.

The PDA requires that employers provide leave to employees who
are temporarily and medically disabled because of pregnancy,
childbirth, or related conditions, in a like manner to that provided to
employees who are disabled for other nonwork-related conditions or
injuries. ADA prohibits both public- and private-sector employees from
discrimination against persons with disabilities. It also requires that
employers reasonably accommodate employees and applicants with
disabilities, so long as such accommodation doesn't result in undue
hardship to the employer. Accommodation includes job restructuring,
and permitting part-time or modified work schedules.

An employer may be confronted with a family-leave request by an
individual considered disabled under the ADA or a comparable state
statute. The regulations make clear that the employer must afford an
employee his or her rights provided by the FMLA, and reasonable
accommodation as required by the ADA.

The following examples contained in the FMLA and ADA
regulations illustrate potential areas of conflict that HRM professionals
and their organizations must be concerned with:

1. A reasonable accommodation under the ADA may be accomplished by "providing the employee with a part-time job with no health benefits." The FMLA permits an employee to work a reduced-leave schedule during his or her 12 weeks of leave, and requires the employer to maintain health benefits during this period at its cost. At the end of the leave entitlement, the employer would then be required to reinstate the employee to the same job or to an equivalent position.

However, if the employee were unable to perform the equivalent position because of a disability, and the employee exhausted family-leave entitlements, the ADA "may permit or require the employer to make a reasonable accommodation at that time by placing the employee in a part-time job, with only those benefits provided to part-time employees."

2. Although family-leave statutes may entitle an employee to take leave, the regulations make clear that an employer may not, in lieu of family leave, "require an employee to take a job with a reasonable accommodation. However, the ADA may require that an employer offer an employee the opportunity to take such a position."

3. If an employer requires a health-provider's certification that an employee is fit to return to work as permitted by the FMLA, then the employer "must comply with the ADA requirement that a fitness-for-duty physical be job-related."

The above examples are but one comparison of the complexity and potential for conflicts that HRM professionals are faced with as a result of the ADA legislation. HRM professionals will need to make careful comparisons of the multitude of provisions found in the ADA and other legislation geared to increase the diversity within organizations and develop proactive action plans if they are to successfully meet the legal and societal calls for increased diversity.

Internal Contradictions within the Americans with Disabilities Act of 1990

McKee (1993), identifies two sections of the ADA that are in conflict with each other that could result in employers' confusion and possible legal action against violating organizations. The first section of concern is Section 1630.4. This section bars employers from discriminating against disabled individuals in employment practices, including fringe benefits. More specifically, it states:

Section 1630.4 [Employment] Discrimination Prohibited
It is unlawful for a covered entity to discriminate on the basis of disability against a qualified individual with a disability in regard to: (a) Recruitment, (b) Hiring, (c) Rates of pay, (d) Job assignments, (e) Leaves of absence, and

(f) Fringe benefits available by virtue of employment, whether or not administered by the covered entity.

The second part of the law tells employers, unions, and others sponsoring benefits plans that insurers may set rates based on age, gender, or health conditions of those covered as long as they do not exclude specific disabilities as a cost-cutting measure.

Subpart B—General Requirements
Section 36.212 Insurance
(a) [The ADA] shall not be construed to prohibit or restrict — (1) An insurer . . . or entity that administers benefit plans, or similar organizations from underwriting risks, classifying risks, or administering such risks that are based on or not inconsistent with State law; or
(2) A person or organization covered by [the ADA] from establishing, sponsoring, observing, or administering the terms of a bona fide benefit plan that are based on underwriting risks, classifying risks, or administering such risk that are based on or not inconsistent with State law; or
(3) A person or organization covered by [the ADA] from establishing . . . a benefits plan that is not subject to State laws that regulate insurance.

The discrepancy within the legislation is apparent when looking at differentiations made in health insurance based on illness. However, the EEOC, the enforcement arm for the ADA, has not determined how these two sections of the law are to be reconciled. Legal analysts agree that employers can continue to limit coverage as long as it is imposed without regard to disabilities.

HUMAN RESOURCES MANAGEMENT AND INCLUSION OF THE DISABLED

Disabled employees, like all other employees, depict the common, the different, and the unique aspects of human diversity. We are referring here to the fact that every person is, in certain respects, like all other people (for example, common features of all groups), or like some other people (for example, common aspects of ethnic, class, color, religion, race, age, and so on); and like no other person, each individual manifests differently his or her affiliations with all other humans and with other members of his or her particular group (for example, one of a kind). In reality, the experiences of many disabled employees in and out of organizations have great differences in background and outlook. Too often, there is one constant that stands out: the profound sense of alienation experienced by those who are disabled as they move further into the organizational mainstream. Today, more than ever before, the causes of such alienation along with other barriers that may stifle the inclusion and productivity of the disabled must be understood by HRM professionals and other organizational personnel. How, then, might HRM professionals approach such a task?

As HRM departments and their organizations earnestly work to design, develop, and implement strategies to fully include the disabled, there is a real need to be clear that a primary reason for bringing disabled employees into the organization is to make both the disabled individual and the organization successful. In other words, today's and tomorrow's organizations need to view the disabled employee as a value to the organization. Often, organizations, when addressing issues related to diversity in general (that is, racial heritage, culture, language, gender, age, and so on), and the disabled in particular, begin with the question: How can we develop programs that will aid us to better manage diversity and get others in our organization to accept the disabled?

The driving force with this view in mind is one of us (management or administration) creating a program that will do something to reduce the problem (diversity in the form of the disabled) in order to help them (disabled employees) to try to fit in with us, if they can. It quickly and clearly becomes another chore and another good deed on the part of the organization to help the poor, less fortunate, different them. So often, such efforts either fail before they start or shortly thereafter. Many times, such programs remain as paper programs, which are in the organization but not of the organization. In essence, a program that has no true influence on reducing alienation or promoting/embracing diversity in the form of the disabled serves to promote all the negative attributes of political correctness. To make matters worse, when these programs do not meet the stated goal of helping them become a part of us, the blame is put on them — as in "they just did not try hard enough," "they always isolated themselves from us," and so on.

HRM professionals must understand that when organizations are truly committed to the full inclusion of the disabled into their organizations, then efforts must be made to develop the appropriate support for these employees just as they have for those diverse employees who have preceded them. An organization begins to show this appreciation by giving the disabled employee one straight message at recruitment and throughout the employee's time in the organization: "We are here to assist you in your quest to be a productive member of this organization and we want you here because we believe that what you bring to this organization will add value and make this a better and more productive organization."

The operationalization of this message increasingly calls for HRM professionals to ensure that their organizations are diligent in developing support mechanisms — internally and externally — in order to provide an organizational climate that works to reduce negative alienation, while embracing diversity, and providing for true opportunity for the disabled employee and other employees to meet both their own and the organization's needs. Thus, as HRM departments look for innovative ways to include disabled employees in their organization, they must first look to providing environments where disabled individuals may perform optimally. An important step in developing organizational environments conducive to the inclusion of disabled employees is to widely disseminate the first principle of the ADA: nondiscrimination against people with disabilities. This is the ground floor for the successful implementation of the ADA and should be continuous until the ADA is successfully institutionalized. Other activities that may or may not be conducted by the HRM department are dependent upon the successful communication of this one important point: above all, do not discriminate. Instruments for disseminating this message can include word of mouth, official guidelines, newsletters, posters, bulletin board announcements, or any other avenue that will communicate the message to all employees (Jones, 1993).

Another step that HRM professionals will need to rely on more in the future to successfully change organizational environments so that they are friendlier to disabled individuals is the implementation of attitudinal awareness training. Attitudinal awareness training involves sensitizing all employees to the needs of the disabled where appropriate employees should be exposed to the day to day problems that disabled individuals experience as they face their workday. For example, employees might spend the day in a wheelchair in an effort to understand the barriers encountered by a wheelchair-bound employee. These attitudinal awareness training sessions should be aimed at identifying ways in which misperceptions and discriminatory attitudes can lead to acts of actual discrimination (Jones, 1993).

Still another step in the process — creating and revising forms, policies, and procedures — requires extensive employee involvement and time. That is, HRM professionals will need to continuously reevaluate current HRM policies, procedures, and appropriate forms and adjust them to ensure that they indeed help decrease any barriers that could result in less than a full functioning employee, be they disabled or nondisabled. The development of policies and procedures should also include as much employee involvement as possible.

A key step to the inclusion of disabled employees into an organization is to create an environment in which needs of the disabled, like all other employees, are accepted as paramount to the success of the organization. Today, HRM professionals must work to see that their organizations develop a collective standard for the entire organization to follow when it comes to the disabled as well as other employees. Every employee must know that every one of his or her colleagues adheres to the same standards of valuing the disabled or any other employee.

Several issues are related to the inclusion of disabled individuals that must be addressed by HRM professionals and their organizations.

These issues include fairness, obstacles to promotions, career path mentoring, special needs of the disabled, and altering existing organizational cultures (Brown & Mazza, 1991; Christensen, 1988; Coleman, 1990).

These issues must be addressed by HRM departments under more general guidelines such as optimizing organizational success as related to the ADA; evaluations and promotion criteria and application; and understanding the differences and needs of disabled members of the organizational workforce.

Optimizing Organizational Success

As the workforce in general becomes more diverse with the inclusion of older workers, more women, racial and ethnic minorities, and disabled individuals, the emphasis of HRM departments should be shifted away from simply meeting legal requirements to an educational emphasis focusing on the organization's need to adapt to a more diverse workplace. Educational or training programs should prepare all employees to value diversity and should focus on the overall goal of employee development while at the same time providing an environment in which each employee may perform to their best abilities.

Organizations that only emphasize the legal requirements of legislation such as the ADA will eventually become stagnated by simply trying to comply with the numbers or statistics for employing more disabled individuals. Such an organizational attitude might possibly lead to natural resistance to disabled individuals by employees within the organization, thereby creating environments that are not conducive to the success of disabled employees. On the other hand, organizations that proactively recruit, hire, and accommodate disabled individuals are preparing themselves for success by employing individuals who possess needed skills (Semien, 1990). Valuing diverse human resources is important as organizations approach the challenges of the twenty-first century.

It was predicted by the *Occupational Outlook Handbook* (U.S. Department of Labor, 1992–93 edition), and *Workforce 2000* (Johnston & Packer, 1987) that dramatic changes can be expected in workforce composition over the next 10 to 15 years. These changes include:

White males have historically been the largest component of the labor force. Their percentages have been dropping and will continue to drop from 79 percent in 1990 to 73 percent by 2005.

Women will continue to join the labor force in growing numbers. By the year 2005, women will comprise approximately 47 percent of the labor force.

Blacks, Hispanics, Asians, and other racial groups will account for approximately 35 percent of new entrants into the labor force between 1990 and 2005.

The average age of workforce participants will increase from 36.6 years in
  1990 to 40.6 years by 2005. The percentages of workers between the ages of
  45 and 54 will account for 24 percent of the labor force by the year 2005, up
  from 16 percent in 1990.

It is estimated that the population will increase by 0.75 percent per year with
  employment opportunities increasing by 1.3 percent per year, resulting in
  fewer available employees.

The emphasis on education will continue. It is predicted that well over 50
  percent of new jobs created during the 1990s will require more than a high
  school diploma. Currently, the high school drop-out rate is approaching 50
  percent in some areas of the country. Employment opportunities for high
  school dropouts will be increasingly limited as office and factory
  automation, changes in consumer demand, and substitution of imports for
  domestic products continues.

Although *Workforce 2000* and the *Occupational Outlook Handbook*
are often cited in numerous works, no information or projections are
included on the percentages of disabled individuals expected to enter
the labor market over the next few years. In addition, often when these
two works are cited, they present a biased, pessimistic view about the
future for disabled workers. Hearne (1991) suggests that a careful
review of publications and studies such as these should indicate a
different message. The message is that economic forecasters tell us that
there will be opportunities for increasing the employment of persons
with disabilities, but only if we seize them. Thus, the low birth rate in
the United States since the 1970s, relative to the prior two decades,
means that labor markets will be tighter: more jobs will be available for
fewer workers. At the same time, however, competition from firms in
countries that pay lower wages for comparable work, combined with
cost-cutting pressures at home, are giving employers in the United
States incentives to lay off older workers, who are more expensive in
both pay and benefits. Thus, we add yet another statistic to those listed
above:

According to government estimates cited in the ADA legislation, there are
  currently 43 million Americans with disabilities, of those 43 million, about
  7.5 million are between the ages of 18 and 50, unemployed, and actively
  seeking employment.

Fitz-Enz (1990) suggests that today's organizations and
organizations of the future must be prepared to operate in a volatile
marketplace. Organizations must be prepared to utilize a maze of
workers with varying genders, ages, racial and ethnic backgrounds, as
well as disabilities, in order to be competitive. Once an organization
realizes the necessity to recruit a diverse workforce, attention should be
shifted to personal satisfaction for these individuals. This includes
attention to evaluations and promotion criteria and self satisfaction
inventories.

Evaluations and Promotion Criteria

HRM departments must address the issue of fairness when confronted with affirmative action and equal opportunities as it applies to hiring, training, evaluating, and promoting employees. Legislation such as the ADA and Civil Rights Acts have been interpreted by many employees within an organization as preferential. As a result, organizational efforts to respond to such legislation often causes other protected groups and individuals who are not protected to worry. Such programs have often stimulated a call of reverse discrimination and unfair working advantages accrued by protected groups (Rosen & Lovelace, 1991; Gordon, 1992).

Performance evaluations represent a situation in which decisions are made about individuals (allocation of ratings or rankings and associated rewards) and the potential for misunderstandings and feelings of injustice are great. With the advent of the disabled employee as a new variable in the HRM equation and perceptions of preferential treatment, HRM professionals must recognize that, like other diverse groups, the potential exists for perceptions of unfairness in evaluating the disabled.

Thus, a key diversity issue that HRM professionals must be concerned with in the case of disabled employees in organizations relates to the performance appraisal process and the possible impact of stereotypes and prejudices on evaluations. Evaluations do not occur in a vacuum. They are made based on the observation, attitudes, and judgements of the rater, which may result in some subjective biases being inserted into the process. One of the fundamental purposes for the implementation of the ADA is to bring more physically or emotionally challenged people into the labor force. Many raters, who presently have little experience with those covered by the ADA, will one day be asked to evaluate the job performance of a disabled individual. This can be problematic, because many individuals are probably unaware of the impressions and prejudices they hold toward individuals with disabilities. As a result, such attitudes may unintentionally result in a myriad of problems in the performance appraisal process.

When job restructuring or accommodation occurs, perceptions of inequitable treatment may arise. Employees may perceive that the disabled employee is the recipient of special, unfair treatment. Situations in which a disabled worker has been relieved of marginal job functions may be particularly conducive to feelings of inequitable treatment. Adding to this frustration is the reality that other workers may be required to perform those job duties, as well as their own. In addition, a work schedule modification, which may be required to accommodate a disabled individual, may be an especially problematic issue, as co-workers may covet the work schedule of a disabled individual. These accommodations may result in serious morale problems and a growing feeling among the able-bodied that the disabled worker is getting a free ride (Hodge & Crampton, 1993).

According to a study conducted by the Bureau of National Affairs (*HR Focus*, 1992), 52 percent of the workers surveyed believed it was fair to have their own work schedules or job duties changed in order to accommodate disabled workers. However, 33 percent felt that such accommodation would be unfair, and 16 percent of the respondents indicated that they felt so strongly about the perceived inequity that they would protest the situation. If this survey is a truthful reflection of the feelings of those in the U.S. workforce, it is clear that there will be a significant number of resentful workers that HRM professionals and their organizations will have to deal with when reasonable accommodations are made under the ADA.

Today's and tomorrow's HRM professionals must work to ensure that a very fair and clear evaluation process should be adopted. HRM professionals can combat the potential problems of evaluations (that is, perceptions of preferential treatment to the disabled or any other diverse group or individual) by seeing that fair and consistent standards are applied to all ratees, there is a system by which the ratee can appeal or rebut the evaluation, and, when raters are familiar with a ratee's work, solicit employee input before assigning ratings, provide prompt feedback, and allow two-way communication in the appraisal interview. In addition, evaluation procedures will be more likely to be perceived as fair if employees understand the rating dimensions and the superior's expectations well before the rating takes place. Ideally, HRM professionals should work to see that employees have input into determining the rating criteria.

HRM professionals should work to develop evaluation procedures that meet most of the six rules developed by Folger and Greenberg (1985, p. 146):

1. Consistency Rule: allocation procedures should be consistent across persons and over time;
2. Bias Suppression Rule: personal self-interest in the allocation process should be prevented;
3. Accuracy Rule: decisions must be based on accurate information;
4. Correctability Rule: opportunities must exist to enable decisions to be modified;
5. Representativeness Rule: the allocation process must represent the concerns of all recipients; and
6. Ethicality Rule: allocations must be based on prevailing moral and ethical standards.

The development of such procedures will help to insure that the emotionally-laden process of performance evaluation is seen as fair (regardless of whether it is a disabled or nondisabled employee that is being evaluated), insofar as is humanly possible.

Compounding the problems of affirmative action are issues raised by economic hard times. As has been the case in the past whenever organizations are faced with shrinking revenues, the first department that receives cuts is the HRM department, which in turn leads to cuts in specific HRM functions (for example, training and training programs). Thus, competition for inclusion in limited spaces within training programs become more fierce, resulting in an increase in calls of unfair treatment. To combat this problem in the future, HRM departments must be prepared to justify all inclusions of individuals within training programs by documenting selection and need for training issues or else be prepared to face a climate in which the issue of unfair treatment and feelings of discrimination will abound.

A challenge to valuing diversity in terms of evaluation criteria and promotions is to eliminate perceptual differences in the knowledge, skills, abilities, and behaviors of managerial candidates that can be attributed to gender, minority status, age, or disability. Yet, many organizations still require separate training for women and disabled individuals. Such training tends to foster stereotypes and discourage inclusiveness of all groups in the organization. This action may also tend to discourage positive promotion of all employees into managerial positions.

A recent study conducted by the regional office of a federal agency demonstrated the different realities that may occur for men, women, and minorities despite being in the same work environment. Among the findings were the differences in perceptions of the obstacles for promotion. The survey instrument included the category of "white male culture/network" as a reason for obstacles to promotion. Both women and minorities gave this reason a significantly higher ranking than did white males (Fine, Johnson & Ryan, 1990).

As calls for increasing the diversity in U.S. organizations and new legislation such as the ADA have been introduced, evaluation and promotion criteria must be developed and applied by HRM professionals that are geared to eliminating bias while also placing emphasis on alleviating fears of a quota or preferential system. Consequently, criteria for selection and development of managerial candidates should be based upon skills and abilities relevant to the needs of the organization. Evaluation and promotion criteria should be based on job performance and job requirements. The system must be geared to rewarding performance. Decisions that impact the economic viability of a member of the workforce should reflect evaluation of qualifications and performance, not diversity (Luke, 1990; Lehrer, 1990).

As organizations respond to the call for increased diversity, HRM professionals must continue to recognize that, while women and other diverse groups are receiving additional protection as a result of diversity-related legislation, their white male counterparts may not be getting the chances for employment and promotion that they used to. But what does this mean for the white males? Is the diversity-related legislation preventing the white males from getting jobs or being promoted to a better job? Or is reverse discrimination likely to increase as a result of ADA and similar diversity-related legislation? Such questions are important and point to what may be natural conflicts as a result of legislation like the ADA. The *Bakke* v. *University of California* and the *Weber* v. *Kaiser* cases show the concern of white males and the conflicts that might arise as a result of legislation like Equal Employment Opportunity (EEO) laws and the ADA. These cases will continue to have a significant impact on organizational efforts to diversify.

As noted earlier, Title VII prohibits discrimination based on race and sex, and that includes discrimination against white males. The laws that were originally passed to give better opportunities to women and minorities are now being interpreted as protecting the rights of the majority as well. HRM professionals must identify ways to overcome conflicts that may result from various legislation and maintain the same organizational obligations to all groups: They must not discriminate for or against any race, sex, religion, or minority group. This presents a problem for employers with numerical affirmative action goals. How are goals to be attained without favoring the disadvantaged groups? The answer is to seek other means for satisfying goals that do not in turn discriminate against the advantaged groups. For example, HRM professionals will need to see that their organizations undertake more intensive recruiting efforts for women, minorities, and the disabled as well as eliminating those employment practices that inhibit their hiring and promotion.

In the end, HRM professionals must recognize that conflicts between various diversity-related legislation is inevitable. Although such laws were passed for the benefits of those groups that have historically been the victims of discrimination, these laws do not allow the employer to bestow such benefits voluntarily by depriving those who have traditionally been advantaged (white males or nondisabled) of their rights. In order to eliminate bias, understanding of differences and needs must occur.

Understanding Differences and the Needs of Disabled Employees

As the workforce within organizations becomes more diverse, changes and trends (which will continue to be stimulated in the future by legislation such as the ADA) create new pressures for organizational thinking and behaviors. Human rights, social justice, and diversity are increasingly valued in the workplace, as they are in society at large.

In the future, HRM professionals must work to ensure that their organizations are adept at dealing with these issues.

Pressure for Self-Determination

People seek greater freedom to determine how to do their jobs and when to do them. Pressures for increased worker participation in the forms of job enrichment, autonomous work groups, flexible working hours, and compressed work weeks will grow.

Pressures for Employee Rights

People expect their rights to be respected on the job as well as outside work. These include the rights of individual privacy, due process, free speech, free consent, freedom of conscience, and freedom from sexual harassment.

Pressures for Job Security

People expect their security to be protected. This includes their physical well-being in terms of occupational safety and health matters, and their economic livelihood in terms of guaranteed protection against layoffs and provisions for cost-of-living wage increases.

Pressures for Equal Employment Opportunity

People expect and increasingly demand the right to employment without discrimination on the basis of age, sex, ethnic background, and disability. Among these demands will remain a concern for furthering the modes by dramatic gains made in recent years by the disabled, women, and other minorities in the workplace. Progress will be applauded, but it will not be accepted as a substitute for equality of opportunity.

Pressures for Equity of Earnings

People expect to be compensated for the comparable worth of their work contributions. What began as a concern for earnings differentials between women and men doing the same job has been extended to cross-occupational comparisons. Questions such as why a nurse receives less pay than a carpenter and why a maintenance worker is paid more than a secretary are asked with increasing frequency. They will require answers other than the fact that certain occupational fields have traditionally been dominated by women, whereas others have been dominated by men.

In the future, HRM professionals will continue to have a major responsibility to see that differences in the workforce are identified, understood, and addressed through various HRM activities (for example, sensitivity training programs) in an effort to help leverage such differences and resulting employee needs. Differences, such as redesign of job requirements, to reflect physical limitations of older workers, women, and individuals with physical impairments should be understood by HRM professionals and included in various organizational training sessions. In addition, HRM professionals must recognize that benefits, such as job-sharing and flex-time, are all reflective of businesses that value differences in employees.

Training in the area of valuing differences and recognizing special needs of the disabled and others should focus on attitudes and subtle behaviors that impede individuals from performing work in the best possible manner. New organizational cultures and models must first be examined during new employee orientation training sessions to assess the suitability of the assumption of the new, more inclusive culture to the diverse workforce. Thus, HRM professionals will have to work to help their organizations develop a culture that creates a climate that fosters optimal performance by all members of the workforce.

It should be noted that businesses are taking the diversity issue very seriously. Digital Equipment Corporation has a manager for valuing differences. Honeywell Inc. has a director of workforce diversity, and Avon Products, Inc. has a director of multicultural planning and design (Sims & Sims, 1993). Hewlett-Packard conducts training sessions to teach managers about different cultures and races and about their own gender biases and training needs (Nelson-Horchler, 1988) and Procter & Gamble has implemented valuing diversity programs throughout the company. Equitable Life Assurance encourages minorities and women to form support groups that periodically meet with the chief executive officer to discuss problems in the company pertaining to them (Copeland, 1988). The Principal Financial Group, one of the largest insurance and financial services groups in the United States, has found that finding employment opportunities for the disabled has helped their bottom line by developing the Mainstream Program that recognizes that, with proper rehabilitation, many employees who become disabled are fully able to return to some type of work. From 1990 through 1991, The Principal claims that the Mainstream Program resulted in a total savings of $774,859. In fact, from its inception in 1986, the company has saved over $1 million in disability claims and replacement costs. Thus, The Principal has discovered that keeping employees with disabilities results in increased profits (Tucker, 1992).

DETERMINING THE IMPLICATIONS OF AMERICANS WITH DISABILITIES ACT OF 1990

As the ADA slowly becomes a part of organizations' futures, a coordinated effort must be made by HRM professionals and their organizations, along with the federal government, to aid in the elimination of many of the concerns listed in the form of questions like:

What groups will be adversely affected by increased attention to hiring disabled employees (veterans, minorities, aged, women)?

What are the implications of the ADA for affirmative action versus quotas?

What are the implications of the ADA for reverse discrimination?

How can decreasing HRM budgets adequately meet the demands of the ADA and be equitably distributed to all groups when it is presumed that the disabled will be given preferential treatment?

How can organizations and HRM departments fairly implement the vague, yet complex, provisions of the ADA legislation?

In addition to the ADA, what are the federal, state and local legislations that organizations must address in responding to the ADA and meeting diversity goals?

How do the various pieces of existing legislation differ (that is, what are the key areas of contrast between the various federal, state, and local laws — for example, their effective dates; the purpose for which each legislation is intended)?

How will the organization blend the state and local requirements with those of the federal ADA legislation?

Traditionally, many organizations have passed over the disabled when hiring because of the myths that permeate society about the disabled (for example, that the costs of accommodating the disabled are higher than the nondisabled employee; and, that people with disabilities are more prone to injury [that is, research shows that 98% of the individuals with disabilities have better or similar accident rates compared to able-bodied individuals]) (Kornblau, Soll & Ellexson, 1992). However, in meeting the call for a more diverse workforce and the ADA legislation, HRM professionals must help their employers understand that it is against the law to discriminate against the disabled. Besides, the disabled have proven statistically to be extremely dependable workers.

Some steps that HRM professionals can take in the coming years to help their organizations more effectively include the disabled in the diversity-equation are to:

revamp hiring practices and make a conscious decision to hire the disabled and contact agencies that can help in the matching process;

identify appropriate jobs for the disabled;

take note of the changes necessary to the work environment in order to accommodate the disabled;

consider the redesign of jobs that might more easily accommodate the disabled and make adjustments for individual work habits and preferences;

identify training needs that may be different for the disabled;

establish and maintain a record of disabled employees;

develop ADA expertise in the HRM department;

review health insurance and benefits plans;

plan and implement training programs designed to educate managers about compliance and regard disabled people as potentially valuable employees, not as a group to be grudgingly accommodated simply to avoid lawsuits;

make a good faith approach to ADA compliance through good faith processes for making employment decisions, communicated broadly to all supervisors and managers;

set up a centralized process to handle all ADA issues fairly and consistently, but always with case-by-case decisions.

In the end, HRM professionals must recognize that the ADA will have an impact on nearly every facet of employment practices related to job application procedures, hiring, advancement, discharge, compensation, and job training. HRM professionals will need to review all of their activities in light of ADA requirements and work to make their department a model operation, setting the example for ADA compliance for other departments. HRM professionals must also take responsibility for the development of a plan to help their organization comply with ADA and other diversity-related legislation. In all likelihood, this should include efforts to design training to help the nondisabled employees to understand how disabled workers can contribute.

While ADA will no doubt have its troublesome aspects, with many details yet to be resolved by regulators and the courts, it only reinforces a trend that many employers have already recognized and begun to act upon — the need to attract and retain good employees and improve productivity, even if that requires some adjustments to traditional organizational rules and practices.

Responding to previous legislative efforts to diversify organizations has led many organizations to adopt such things, for example, as efforts to better meet employees' family needs in the form of alternative career patterns, child-care benefits, and flexible work scheduling. Responding to the changing demographics of the workplace has led many organizations to modify their corporate culture to respect and value diversity. Responding to global competition has led many organizations to revise their work processes, putting a greater emphasis on teamwork, minimizing the role of middle management, and making first-line workers responsible for many critical production decisions.

In fact, these changes may have already paved the way for ADA compliance. Proactive HRM professionals and organizations will already have such things as flexible policies, allowing employees to take time off to cope with family emergencies, making it relatively easy to accommodate disabled employees who need time off for medical treatment. If the HRM department is already holding educational sessions for employees and managers to raise their awareness of gender and culture issues within the workforce, the organization has begun to foster a mindset in which disabled employees are accepted.

Indeed, the lessons learned in these efforts may prove instructive in dealing with ADA. The organizations that truly integrate the ideals of diversity into their corporate culture will be more successful than those who merely give lip service. Like other groups that have previously been treated like second-class citizens, equal employment opportunity for the disabled will not automatically come because of passage of the ADA and similar legislation, nor will it come because HRM departments across the country prescribe compliance policies and procedures. It will come when HRM professionals and their organizations understand the complexity and potential conflicts of various legislation, eliminate stereotyped attitudes, and allow all diverse individuals (for example, the disabled) to enter and succeed in the workplace.

CONCLUSION

With the enactment of the Civil Rights Act of 1964, a new era in HRM began. For many managers, the manner in which they previously hired and promoted employees underwent drastic modification. Previously used procedures were scrutinized, and scientific methods were subsequently applied to the development of methods that would accomplish the purposes without illegally discriminating against anyone.

Today's HRM professionals must be aware of the ever-changing rules and regulations governing employment such as the ADA. These continually changing government regulations add new dimensions to the jobs of HRM professionals. They must not only familiarize themselves with the laws presently applicable but also continually monitor and review the constant and complex changes that occur.

Because of the dynamic nature of EEO laws and diversity-related legislation such as the ADA, the focus of this chapter has been but a snapshot of a rapidly changing scene. Nevertheless, several points are important for understanding HRM and diversity in the years to come. First, the diversity legislation issue is here to stay. As long as organizations engage in discriminatory practices that are unfair to protected groups, the enforcement agencies and courts will continue to have an impact on organizations and their HRM policy. The liberalized compensatory and punitive damages that are available under the Civil Rights Act of 1991 will also encourage additional suits against private and public sector organizations.

Second, it is likely that the EEO rights of older employees and the disabled will receive increasing attention. As medical science cushions the adverse effects of age and health-related problems and as technological changes lessen the physical demands of the job, more employment-related decisions in these areas will be challenged. This trend will accelerate as the number of less physically demanding white-collar jobs increases and the labor force participation rate of older employees continues to rise. The passage of the ADA expands EEO protection to a larger number of disabled individuals.

Third, the intense interest in the working rights and conditions of women should continue. The emphasis is clearly on achieving parity between men and women in all facets of employment, as witnessed by the recent legislation on equal pay and comparable worth issues and by the attention given to sexual harassment, employee benefit programs, and pregnancy and employment, among others. At the same time, there is recognition that a conflict may exist between a woman's rights and possible exposure to occupations and industries to toxic substances harmful to the female reproductive system.

Finally, controversy will continue to build regarding sex and racial discrimination in compensation practices (and this will be even further compounded when disability is combined with sex and race, for example). With EEO hearings, professional conferences, and involvement by various special interest groups providing the forum for highlighting various views, the basic tenets of long-accepted job evaluation plans and compensation structures, for example, will be questioned.

Although a number of complex points have been highlighted here, the essence of this chapter is threefold. First, HRM professionals must find ways to anticipate and respond to the needs and wants of the disabled. Second, HRM professionals must be aware of the myriad of EEO laws, administrative regulations, and prominent court decisions. Third, each HRM policy and practice should be evaluated periodically to determine whether it operates unfairly against a specific race, sex, age, disabled, or other protected group. Because of the potential costs in terms of time and money devoted to litigation, back-pay awards, and adverse publicity, diversity-related issues should be approached by HRM professionals in a preventive manner, with emphasis placed on recruiting, selecting, compensating, and treating employees in a way that maximizes the relevance of job performance and minimizes the attention given to factors not directly applicable to the job.

In the years to come, diversity will continue to pose challenges for HRM professionals and their organizations as they attempt to leverage the variety of resources that employees bring to the workplace. Regardless of the steps taken by HRM professionals to include diverse employees in their organizations, they must not lose sight of the parameters established by diversity-related legislation like the ADA.

REFERENCES

Brown, C. R. & Mazza, G. J. 1991, Winter. Peer training strategies for welcoming diversity. *New Directions for Student Services 56*: 39–51.

Christensen, G. 1988, August. Managing workforce diversity: Changing cultures at South Seas Plantation. *The Cornell Hotels and Restaurant Administration Quarterly 29*(2): 30–34.

Coleman, T. L. 1990, October. Managing diversity at work: The new American dilemma. *Public Management 74*(9): 2–5.

Copeland, L. 1988, July. Valuing diversity, Part 2: Pioneers and champions of change. *Personnel*: 48–51.

Dastmalchian, A., Blyton, P., & Adamson, R. 1991. *The climate of workplace relations.* New York: Rutledge.

DeCenzo, D. A. & Robbins, S. P. 1994. *Human resource management* (4th ed.). New York: John Wiley & Sons, Inc.

Fine, M. G., Johnson, F. L., & Ryan, M. S. 1990, Fall. Cultural diversity in the workplace. *Public Personnel Management 19*(3): 305–319.

Fitz-Enz, J. 1990. *Human value management.* San Francisco: Jossey-Bass Publishers.

Folger, R. & Greenberg, J. 1985. Procedural justice: An interpretive analysis of personnel systems. *Research in personnel and human resource management, Vol. 3*, pp: 141–83.

Foster, B. P. 1988, April. Workforce diversity and business. *Training and Development Journal*: 59–61.

Gordon, J. 1992, January. Rethinking diversity. *Training 29*(1): 23–30.

Hearne, P. G. 1991. Employment strategies for people with disabilities: A prescription for change. *Milbank Quarterly 69 Supplements 1, 2.*

Hodge, J. W. & Crampton, S. M. 1993. ADA: Faster said than done. *Supervisory Management 38*: 9–10.

HR Focus. 1992, July. To accommodate workers with disabilities, *69*: 5.

Johnston, W. B. & Packer, A. H. 1987. *Workforce 2000: Work and workers for the twenty-first century.* Indianapolis: The Hudson Institute.

Jones, T. L. 1993. *The Americans with Disabilities Act: A review of best practices.* New York, NY: AMA Membership Publications Division, American Management Association.

Kohl, J. P. & Greelaw, P. S. 1992, Spring. The American with Disabilities Act of 1990: Implication for managers. *Sloan Management Review*, pp. 87–90.

Kornblau, B. L., Soll, M., & Ellexson, M. A. 1992. Insurance options under ADA. *HRMagazine 37*(3): 100–103.

Lehrer, S. 1990, October. EEO program deals management a good hand. *HRMagazine 35*(10): 50–54.

Loden, M. & Roesner, J. B. 1991. *Workforce America! Managing employee diversity as a vital resource.* Homewood, IL: Business One Irwin.

Luke, R. A. 1990, October. Managing the diversity in today's workplace. *Supervisory Management 35*(10): 4.

McKee, B. 1993, April. The disabilities labyrinth. *Nation's Business 81*(4): 18–23.

Nelson-Horchler, J. 1988, April 18. Demographics deliver a warning. *Industry Week*: 58.

Rosen, B. & Lovelace, K. 1991, June. Piecing together the diversity puzzle. *HRMagazine*: 78–82, 84.

Semien, L. J. 1990, July. Opening the utility door for women and minorities. *Public Utilities Forthnightly*, pp. 29–31.

Sims, S. J. & Sims, R. R. 1993. Diversity and difference training in the United States. In R. R. Sims & R. F. Dennehy (eds.). *Diversity and differences in organizations: An agenda for answers and questions*, pp. 73–92. Westport, CT.: Quorum.

Tucker, S. 1992, August. Mainstreaming employees who have disabilities. *Personnel Journal*: 43–49.

U.S. Department of Labor. 1992, May. *Occupational outlook handbook.* (1992–93 ed.). Washington, DC: U.S. Department of Labor, Bureau of Labor Statistics. Bulletin 2400.

4

Employee Compensation and Human Resources Management

Determining employees' compensation is one of the traditional human resources management (HRM) functions. In today's organization, with a number of costly employee wage incentive programs, benefit programs, and structured pay scales, the compensation task is, and will continue to be, even more difficult and challenging for HRM professionals. That difficulty and associated challenges is the focus of this chapter. This chapter will discuss a number of challenges and potential responses organizations can make to effectively design comprehensive compensation systems. In our view, employees' compensation represents the means by which employees are financially compensated for joining organizations, staying in them, and their productivity (that is, accomplishing certain levels of work performance). Although there is no consistent agreement on the degree to which compensation affects productivity, the compensation activity will continue to be a key human resources processing activity, which begins with the planning that occurs before people enter organizations and continues until their departure and beyond.

Employees' need for income and their desire to be fairly treated by the organization make developing the compensation program all the more important for the HRM department. However, the task of developing a compensation system is complicated because there is no exact, objective method of determining compensation for any one job or employee. Employees exchange their labor for financial and nonfinancial rewards. In any case, compensating employees for what they give the organization is to some extent as much an art as a science.

Traditionally, the term "compensation" is often used interchangeably with wage and salary administration; however, compensation actually is a broader concept. Compensation refers not only to extrinsic rewards, such as salary and benefits, but also to intrinsic rewards such as recognition, the chance for promotion, and more challenging job opportunities. Wage and salary administration usually refers to strictly monetary rewards given to employees. Extrinsic rewards can be categorized as direct or indirect compensation. Direct compensation includes the base salary and performance-based pay that an employee receives, while indirect compensation consists of federally- and state-mandated protection programs, private protection programs, paid leave, life cycle benefits, and health care benefits.

Intrinsic or nonfinancial rewards, like praise and self-esteem, although not discussed in this book, are also factors that affect employee satisfaction with the compensation system. Levels of employees' productivity can be related to intrinsic rewards as well. The HRM professional must recognize that a comprehensive compensation system would include an emphasis on nonfinancial rewards in the development and implementation of his or her compensation efforts.

The compensation process is even further complicated, because for a number of organizations, the compensation provided to its employees can account for as much as half of the company's total cash flow and it can account for an even higher percentage in other companies (and in many instances, its percentage of cash flow is still growing). Compensation is also important to the economy. For example, for the past 30 years, salaries and wages have equaled about 60 percent of the gross national product of Canada and the United States.

The compensation equation is complicated further by increased cost pressures and legal challenges associated with compensation. As a result, the compensation equation is increasingly complex and dynamic. In order for organizations to become more competitive and to survive in a global marketplace, HRM professionals are seeking ways to help their organizations reduce costs of programs and activities that do not directly support operations that generate revenue.

OBJECTIVES OF A COMPREHENSIVE COMPENSATION SYSTEM

The objective of a comprehensive compensation system is to develop and implement a system of rewards that is equitable to the organization and its members alike. A comprehensive compensation program is important, because it can serve several major purposes: attract potential job applicants, retain good employees, gain a competitive advantage, motivate employees, administer pay within legal regulations, facilitate organizational strategies, and reinforce and define organizational structure.

All of these objectives are interrelated. When employees are motivated, the organization is more likely to achieve its strategic objectives.

When pay is based on the value of the job, the organization is more likely to accomplish its desired outcome of attracting employees to their organization who are motivated to do a good job for the employer. However, if HRM professionals are to effectively design comprehensive compensation systems for their organizations, they must ensure that all key organizational stakeholders understand those external influences that impact such a system.

EXTERNAL INFLUENCES ON COMPENSATION SYSTEMS

HRM professionals must be concerned about a number of external influences that affect their organization's compensation systems. Among the factors that influence compensation systems outside the organization are the government, union, and economic, and organization conditions.

The Role of Government and Compensation

The government influences pay both directly through laws and regulations and indirectly through its socioeconomic policies. For example, government's monetary policies directly affect demand for goods and services, and subsequently the organization's demand for employees. These actions create economic forces that affect compensation. The government more directly affects compensation through wage controls and guidelines that limit increases in compensation for certain workers at certain times, and laws that regulate wage rates, regulate hours of work, prevent discrimination, and require certain benefits.

Equal employment opportunity laws — especially Title VII of the Civil Rights Act of 1964 and its amendment — prohibits sex- or race-based differences in employment outcomes, such as pay, unless justified by business necessity (for example, pay differences stemming from differences in job performance). There are also a number of laws that HRM professionals must be concerned with that affect the compensation their organizations pay in terms of minimum wages, overtime rates, and benefits. Several of the most important of these laws follow.

Davis-Bacon Act

This act was passed in 1931 and sets wage rates for laborers, who receive more than $2,000, employed by construction contractors working for the federal government. Amendments to the act provide for employee benefits and require contractors or subcontractors to make necessary payment for these benefits. Typically, prevailing wages have been based on relevant union contracts, partly because only 30 percent of the local labor force is required to be used in establishing the prevailing rate.

Walsh-Healy Public Contract Act

This law from 1936 requires minimum wage and working conditions for employees working on any government contract amounting to more than $10,000. The law also requires that time-and-a-half be paid for work over 8 hours a day and 40 hours a week.

Fair Labor Standards Act

This act, originally passed in 1938 and since amended many times, establishes a minimum wage, maximum hours, overtime pay, equal pay, recordkeeping, and child labor provisions covering the majority of U.S. workers — virtually all those engaged in the production and/or sales of goods for interstate and foreign commerce. In addition, agricultural workers and those employed by certain larger retail and service companies are included.

The Fair Labor Standards Act (FLSA) also requires that employees be paid at a rate of one-and-one-half times their hourly rate for each hour of overtime worked beyond 40 hours per week. The hourly rate includes not only the base wage but also other components, such as bonuses and piece-rate payments.

Certain categories of employees are exempt from the act or certain provisions of the act, and particularly from the act's overtime provisions. An employee's exemption depends on the responsibilities, duties, and salary of the job. However, bona fide executive, professional, administrative, and outside sales occupations are generally exempt from FLSA coverage. Nonexempt occupations are covered and include most hourly jobs.

Equal Pay Act

This act is an amendment to the FLSA that requires men and women in the same organization who are doing equal work to be paid equally. The act defines equal in terms of skill, effort, responsibility, and working conditions. However, the act allows for reasons why men and women performing the same job might be paid differently. If the pay differences are the result of differences in seniority, merit, quantity or quality of production, or any factor other than sex (for example, shift differentials or training programs), then differences are legally allowable.

Employee Retirement Income Security Act

The act provides government protection of pensions for all employees with company pension plans. It also regulates vesting rights (employees who leave before retirement may claim compensation from the pension plan). It also covers portability rights (transfer of an employee's vested rights from one organization to another) and contains fiduciary standards to prevent dishonesty in the funding of pension plans.

Other Government Legislation
Affecting Compensation

Various other laws directly or indirectly impact an organization's compensation system. For example, the Tax Reform Act of 1986 affected employee compensation in two ways. The most familiar feature of the law is the reduction of the individual tax rates to just two brackets of 15 percent and 28 percent, which means employees take home more of their wages and salaries. The second feature affects the treatment of employee benefits. Specifically, this feature of the act was intended to increase the benefits coverage for rank-and-file employees while reducing tax-favored benefits that can be provided to highly paid employees.

The Age Discrimination in Employment Act was passed in 1967 and amended in 1986. It prohibits discrimination against employees over the age of 40. The Age Discrimination in Employment Act protected workers with respect to compensation terms, conditions, or privileges of employment. The amendment prohibited employers from requiring retirement at any age.

Each of the 50 states has its own worker's compensation laws, which today cover over 85 million workers. Among other things, the aim of these laws is to provide a prompt, sure, and reasonable income to victims of work-related accidents. The Social Security Act of 1935 has been amended several times. It is aimed at protecting U.S. workers from total economic destitution in the event of termination of employment beyond their control. Employers and employees contribute equally to the benefits provided by this act. This act also provides for unemployment compensation — jobless benefits — for workers unemployed through no fault of their own for up to 26 weeks in duration. The Federal Wage Garnishment Law limits the amount of an employee's earnings that can be garnished in any one week and protects the worker from discharge due to garnishment.

The legal environment in which the compensation activity of HRM professionals and their organizations is conducted is bound by federal legislation. The most basic of these is the FLSA and its amendments, including the Equal Pay Act of 1963, which contains provisions for minimum wage, overtime, and equal pay. However, regardless of the legislation, HRM professionals must ensure that in this context their organization's compensation systems are both attractive and equitable to current and prospective employees.

In addition to the various laws and regulations highlighted above, the government influences compensation in many other ways. If the government is the employer, it can legislate pay levels by setting statutory rates. For example, the pay scale for teachers can be set by law or by edict of the school board, and pay depends on revenues from the current tax base. If taxes decline relative to organizations' revenue streams, no matter how much the organization may wish to pay higher wages, it cannot.

The government affects compensation through its employment-level policy, too. One of the goals of the federal government is full employment of all citizens seeking work. The government may even create jobs for certain categories of workers, thus reducing the supply of workers available and affecting pay rates.

Union Influences on Compensation Systems

Although less than one in five workers are members of unions, it would be a mistake to conclude that their impact on compensation systems is minor. In areas where unionized enterprises exist, unions have an effect on whether the organization's employees are unionized. Unions have tended to be pacesetters in demands for pay, benefits, and improved working conditions. There is reasonable evidence that unions tend to increase pay levels, although this is more likely where an industry has been organized by strong unions. When an organization elects to stay in an area where unions are strong, its compensation policies will be affected.

Frequently, the threat of becoming unionized encourages HRM professionals and the organization's other managers to improve wages, benefits, and other conditions of employment. Specifically, unions influence compensation practices directly through bargaining with employers over hours, wages, and terms and conditions of employment and, in some instances, through threats of strike. They also influence compensation practices indirectly: companies often match union wages in the area to avoid unionization, and benefits bargained by the unionized groups are typically given to unionized employees.

In bargaining activities, unions are likely to increase the compensation of their members when the organization is financially and competitively strong; the union is financially strong enough to support a strike; the union has the support of other unions; and general economic and labor market conditions are such that unemployment is low and the economy is strong (Dickens & Lang, 1986). In bargaining over working conditions and other policies that affect compensation, there is a tendency for unions to prefer fixed pay for each job category or rate ranges that are administered primarily to reflect seniority rather than merit increases. This is true in the private and other sectors. Unions press for time pay rather than merit pay when the amount of performance expected is tied to technology (such as the assembly line). In unionized organizations, the union is one of the main players in designing the direct component (that is, pay) of a compensation system.

Economic Conditions and Compensation Systems

In addition to various legislation and unions, information regarding the external labor market, often supplied through industry or area wage surveys, is necessary for HRM professionals to determine an appropriate pay structure in making individual wage and salary decisions within that structure. Also necessary, is information regarding the internal labor market.

During periods of shortages of qualified employees, pay tends to increase an organization's ability to attract and retain needed workers. In recessions, or when surpluses of qualified employees are available, rates of pay increases are slowed; pay may even decrease.

During times of expanding demand for an organization's products and services, job opportunities expand and employers are more willing and able to increase pay to attract and retain employees with the needed skills and experience.

Increased wages translate into increased production costs that are often passed on to consumers. Passing on production costs is easier to do if there is strong demand for products.

Increased competition also affects compensation decisions. In today's economic environment, HRM professionals must help their organizations control costs to stay in business. So it is not too surprising that increased competition causes an organization's management to think twice about the amount of pay and benefits to offer.

Organizational Influence on Compensation Systems

An organization's compensation policies also influence the wages and benefits the organization will pay, since these policies provide the basic compensation guidelines in several important areas. One is whether the organization wants to be a leader or a follower regarding pay. For example, one organization might have a policy of starting engineers at a wage at least 10 percent above the prevailing market wage. Other important topics usually covered by policies include the basis for salary increases, promotion and demotion policies, overtime pay policy, and policies regarding probationary pay and leaves for military service, jury duty, and holidays. Compensation policies are usually written by HRM professionals in conjunction with top management.

A comprehensive compensation system implies that an organization is being strategic about compensation. That is, HRM professionals and top management develop a compensation system that supports the needs of the organization and are sensitive to anticipated environmental pressures. The development and distribution of the basic elements of the comprehensive compensation system (that is, base pay, incentives, and benefits) is dependent upon an understanding of organizational influences similar to those discussed below.

INTEGRATING COMPENSATION WITH
THE ORGANIZATION'S STRATEGY

In recent years, increasing attention has been given to the relationship between organizational strategy and compensation policies. An organization's strategy defines its business in terms of product line, quality emphasis, market segment, geographical market limits, diversity, and size. Some firms are expanding and diversifying, whereas others are remaining stable, both in size and in terms of product lines. Organizations in declining product markets often elect to retrench by eliminating unprofitable products and reducing their workforce.

Regardless of what the organization is doing, the decision made concerning compensation and business strategy communicates the overall philosophy and strategy of the organization. The implementation of a compensation system can also signal a shift in business strategy or can play a less prominent role during organizational changes.

Internal Pay Structure

The development of a comprehensive compensation system also relates to establishing an internal pay structure that is perceived as fair and equitable. Internal equity refers to the relationship among jobs within a single organization. Employees expect the president of a company to earn more than the executive vice president, who in turn earns more than the plant manager, and so on. Among other things, compensation is presumed to be correlated with the level of knowledge, skill, and experience required to do the job successfully. Internal equity exists when the pay differentials between different jobs within the organization are perceived as fair — neither too large nor too small.

The Consideration of External Equity

From a strategic perspective, external equity refers to positioning an organization's compensation relative to its competitors (for example, the pay received by presidents of various banks). At the most basic level, the options are to lead, lag, or match the pay rates of labor market competitors. Locality matters, as well as industry and company size. In today's competitive environment, external equity has become more complex, with organizations considering the mix of pay forms as well as the risk-return trade off.

Individual Equity

Individual equity refers to comparisons among individuals in the same job with the same organization. In may ways, this is one of the most critical compensation questions. If it is not answered satisfactorily, attention to the integration of compensation with the organization's strategy, and to internal and external equity will have been wasted. For example, suppose the HRM department establishes, through internal and external comparisons, that all engineers should receive between $3,000 and $3,500 per month. The problem now is to determine the pay rate of each engineer. Should long-service engineers be paid more than those who have just been hired? If yes, what is the value of each additional year of service? Should pay differences be based on job performance? If so, how will performance be measured? How will the differences in performance be translated into pay differences? Employees must perceive that these questions are answered fairly in order for individual equity to exist.

Regardless of the influence on an organization's efforts to develop a comprehensive compensation system, HRM professionals must work to ensure that their organizations are able to answer affirmatively the following questions: Is the compensation system attractive? Is it equitable? In addition, HRM professionals must be prepared to address contemporary issues surrounding compensation as discussed in the remainder of this chapter. These issues are: the complexity of the design and implementation of compensation systems; designing globally sensitive systems; and challenges to designing contemporary compensation systems.

COMPLEXITY OF THE DESIGN AND IMPLEMENTATION OF COMPENSATION SYSTEMS

As noted earlier in this chapter, the system that an organization uses to reward its employees can play an important role in the organization's efforts to gain a competitive advantage and to achieve its major objectives. In today's organization, a comprehensive compensation system should attract and retain the talent an organization needs; encourage employees to develop the knowledge, skills, abilities, and attitudes they need; motivate employees; and create the type of team culture in which employees care about the organization's success. Ideally, a comprehensive compensation system should align individual objectives with important strategic goals of the organization, but for most organizations, the reality falls short of this ideal.

The design and implementation of a comprehensive compensation system is one of the most complex activities for which HRM professionals are, and will continue to be, responsible in the years to come. The following are some of the factors that will continue to contribute to this complexity:

One goal of a compensation system is to motivate employees, yet, there is tremendous variation in the value different individuals attached to a specific reward or package of rewards. A single individual's values may also change over time. The importance of values is even more complicated when one recognizes the increased globalization of the marketplace.

With increased emphasis on job enrichment and enlargement, the jobs in most organizations involve an endless variety of knowledge, skills, and abilities, and are performed in situations with a wide range of demands.

Compensation systems consist of many elements in addition to pay for work; these components must be coordinated to work together.

Employee compensation is a major cost of doing business — up to 80 percent for service firms — and can determine the competitiveness of an organization's products or services.

A wide variety of federal and state regulations affect compensation.

The cost of living varies tremendously in different geographic areas, an important consideration for multinational companies.

In most organizations, the compensation system will continue to involve a multifaceted package, not just pay for work and performance. HRM professionals must recognize that factors like those above will affect their ability to design and implement comprehensive compensation systems. An increased emphasis on globalization provides an example of the complexity surrounding compensation.

DESIGNING GLOBALLY SENSITIVE SYSTEMS

The significance of an appropriate compensation and benefit package to attract, retain, and motivate employees in an international organization cannot be overemphasized. Compensation is a crucial link between strategy and its successful implementation — HRM professionals must see that there is a fit between compensation and the goals for which the organization wants its employees (and particularly, its various managers) to aim. So that they will not feel exploited, HRM professionals must work to make sure their employees perceive equity and goodwill in their compensation and benefits (regardless of what country they work in). The premature return of expatriates or the unwillingness of managers to take overseas assignments can often be traced to their knowledge that the assignment is detrimental to them financially.

The design, implementation, and maintenance of an appropriate compensation package is more complex than it would seem because of the need to consider and reconcile parent and host-country financial, legal, and customary practices. For example, while there may be little variation around the world of typical executive salaries at the level of base compensation, there is often a wide variation in net spendable income. While U.S. executives may receive more in cash and stock, they have to spend more for things that foreign companies provide, such as cars, vacations, and entertainment allowances. In addition, the manager's purchasing power with that net income is affected by the relative cost of living. As of 1993, the cost of living is considerably higher in Europe than in the United States.

In order to attract competent employees to carry out overseas assignments, a company must develop an effective expatriate compensation program — one that provides an adequate incentive to encourage people to work outside the country by offsetting the inconvenience and hardship of a new environment and maintaining the U.S. standard of living abroad. The program should also consider that the family and social needs of an expatriate (such as relationships and communication with family, friends, and business associates) must be properly satisfied and maintained.

In designing compensation and benefit packages in the global organization, then, the challenge to HRM professionals is to maintain a standard of living for expatriates equivalent to their colleagues at home, plus compensate them for any additional costs incurred. Teague (1972) has referred to this policy as "keeping the expatriate whole."

HRM professionals must also work to ensure that their organization's expatriates do not lose out through their overseas assignments. There are two common approaches that HRM professionals can use to set up an expatriate compensation program. One is the international cadre approach, which is applied when the organization hires expatriates with the equivalent salaries and benefits of their U.S. counterparts. Another approach is the balance sheet approach. The balance sheet approach is often used by organizations to equalize the standard of living between the host country and the home country and to add some compensation for inconvenience or qualitative loss (Reynolds, 1986). This approach balances all costs of an overseas assignment and obtains an adjustment index. This index is then applied to the expatriate base salary in order to allow the employee to maintain an economic status equivalent to the one the employee would have if he or she had remained in the United States (Firth, 1981). In practice, the balance sheet approach is the most popular approach used by U.S. companies. The components of a compensation program by the balance sheet approach may vary among different companies and even in a single company with multiple multinational operations.

In fairness, the global organization is obliged to make up additional costs that the expatriate would incur for taxes, housing, and goods and services. The tax differential is complex and expensive for the company, and, generally, global organizations use a policy of tax equalization — the company pays any taxes due on any type of additional compensation that the expatriate receives for the assignment and the expatriate pays in taxes only what he or she would be paying at home. The burden of foreign taxes can be lessened, however, by efficient tax planning — a fact often overlooked by small firms. The timing and methods of paying people determine what foreign taxes are incurred; for example, a company can save on taxes by renting an apartment for the employee instead of providing a cash housing allowance (Selz, 1992). All in all, HRM professionals must see to it that their organizations weigh the many aspects of a complete compensation package, especially at high management levels, to effect a tax equalization policy.

Managing compensation in the global organization will continue to be a complex challenge for HRM professionals. Several categories that must be considered by HRM professionals in designing expatriate compensation packages include: salary (home rate/home currency; local rate/local currency; salary adjustments or promotions — home or local standard; bonus — home or local currency, home or local standard; stock options; inducement payment/hardship premium-percentage of salary or lump sum payment, home/local currency; currency protection — discretion or split basis; and global salary and performance structures); taxation (tax protection, tax equalization, other services); benefits (home-country program, local program, social security program); and allowances (cost-of-living allowances, housing standard, education, relocation, perquisites, home leave, shipping and storage) (Dowling & Schuler, 1990).

All components of the compensation package must be considered in light of both home- and host-country legalities and practices. Most important, to be strategically competitive, HRM professionals must work to see that their organization's compensation package is comparatively attractive to the kinds of managers (and other employees) the company wants to hire or relocate.

CHALLENGES TO DESIGNING COMPENSATION SYSTEMS

The Consortium for Alternative Reward Strategies Research (CARS) says organizations should see compensation systems as a tool to develop the value of human assets. This, in turn, will lead to greater motivation, productivity, customer service, quality, and global competitiveness. In fact, the top six objectives when designing and installing a compensation plan are to improve business performance, foster teamwork, improve the performance-reward linkage, improve morale, improve communications, and create an empowering environment. The CARS study reported that of the 1,200 pay plans they studied, half were installed to lead the organization in a new cultural direction (McAdams & Hawk, 1992). For example, many companies are shifting from a high productivity and a low-cost focus to a high quality and an outstanding customer service orientation, and many are using an organizational performance-reward plan to push them down the right path.

The Total Quality Management (TQM) path depends on the continuity of the organization's workers. HRM professionals must devote time and resources to support an environment of long-term cooperation and motivation conducive to constant quality improvements. These plans do not have to solely support other changes that have occurred in the workforce, such as employee empowerment, decentralization, or mergers and acquisitions. They can be used to drive cultural change. And, in today's globally competitive environment, U.S. businesses are realizing that, to be competitive, they must totally revamp their business process. This aggressive reshaping of U.S. organizations is aimed at bringing back the competitive edge.

One movement that is sweeping U.S. organizations is the increase in reliance on the use of teams and employee empowerment. This is basically a commitment-oriented philosophy as opposed to a control approach. To move toward a more involved approach and to increase organizational effectiveness, more and more organizations are turning to teams. Through teams, companies are able to push knowledge, information, and power to lower levels in the organization. HRM professionals must decide what kind of team is appropriate for their organization and what pay systems will be the most motivating and effective.

In thinking about how to design compensation systems, because of the complexity and importance of compensation to the success of an organization, HRM professionals must walk a very thin line. An inappropriately designed system could send the wrong message or promote the wrong values within the organization. More than ever before, HRM professionals must be aware of how compensation systems can affect an organization's overall culture. HRM professionals can proactively change or inadvertently change the culture of the organization through the design, implementation, and management of the compensation system or reward structure. For example, the reward system can highlight the company as a human resources-oriented culture, an entrepreneurial culture, an innovative culture, a participative culture, or a competence-based culture.

HRM professionals must cope with the problem of integrating performance management systems of the past with the cutting edge concepts of the present and future. For example, HRM professionals are struggling with the problem of how to reward individuals for values associated with an organizational TQM focus. Integrating the concepts of TQM with the pervasive principles of compensation will be a tremendous challenge for HRM professionals. How do you reward teamwork, customer satisfaction, and flexibility? (Thornburg, 1992).

Furthermore, many organizations still are struggling with how to change old pay systems to fit new work systems and team setting. It is a challenge to apply pay-for-performance measures to a TQM environment that is increasingly becoming team-oriented. HRM professionals also must deal with the problem of rewarding teams and team members equitably. This is especially difficult when team membership often changes frequently during projects.

It is also much more difficult to administer pay for performance plans rather than simple fixed compensation plans. Pay for performance plans must be continuously monitored, managed, and refined to allow for changing employee needs, market conditions, and organizational objectives.

HRM professionals are also struggling with the problem of how to temper the organizational turmoil associated with radically redesigning an organization. For example, employees may ask, "What is my incentive for reengineering my job?" (Kanin-Lovers & Keilty, 1993). Furthermore, HRM professionals must design a compensation system that will trigger a companywide organizational change rather quickly. The results must be fast so as not to lose competitive advantages.

Another challenge facing HRM professionals is with what to reward employees and groups. "Employee incentives is imprecise, and it takes a lot of thought to give people what they want," says Phil Clark, former national sales promotion manager for General Electric. "You can offer them a single item or 50 different items as rewards, but you may still miss the mark" (Cooper, 1986, p. 26). Moreover, determining what is valued by a group is difficult because of the great variety within the group in terms of culture and perceptions. For example, one group member may value a trip to the ballpark over a chance to meet with the chief executive officer while another member may feel quite different.

Still, another challenge for HRM professionals is overcoming the traditional concepts, methodologies, and competitive culture that place the individual over the group. This is what is so destructive to the concept of TQM. One needs only to turn to Japan for proof. In Japan, cooperation and teamwork are the norm, not competition and individual initiative. In Japan, the nail that sticks up is hammered down. Moreover, base pay is tied to education and to experience with the company, not to individual merit. It is very unlikely that this system could be transplanted to the United States, and one wonders whether it should. However, HRM professionals could learn a great deal from the Japanese and their compensation practices. After all, it was the Japanese who got the idea of TQM from the United States and our quality experts.

Perhaps one of the biggest difficulties concerning compensation facing HRM professionals is designing a total reward strategy that will address the different needs of the employer and the employee. Some compensation experts have noted that companies use rewards to obtain commitment, flexibility, cooperation, loyalty, and productivity. However, employees want security, control, fairness, clear expectations, feedback, and more money (Thornburg, 1992).

Another compensation challenge facing HRM professionals is the traditional adversarial environment in organizations. That is, companies have long thought of employees as a resource to be used, depleted, and replaced, not a resource to be developed. These attitudes are counter-productive in today's economy. In order to be globally competitive, companies must begin to focus on human resources development (McAdams & Hawk, 1992).

ORGANIZATIONAL RESPONSES TO COMPENSATION ISSUES TO DATE

Many companies are experimenting with combinations of individual merit-pay systems and teamwork systems, variable and fixed-pay systems, and gainsharing and individual incentive awards. Such efforts are intended to ensure that the compensation system complements the organization's objectives, values, and present structure. Many organizations have already installed new pay plans, and many more are considering it. Unfortunately, many companies are implementing pay plans with little thought about the link between the new pay systems and the overall business objectives. In fact, a significant number of them are designing pay systems because everybody is doing it.

Companies are beginning to include both financial and operational measures in their compensation systems. In other words, they are beginning to measure performance as a function of profits and returns, as well as quality, safety, and attendance. They are starting to recognize the importance and power of performance measurement. Nolan Norton, a research organization of KPMG Peat Marwick, says, "What we measure conveys to the organization what we think is important. If we measure it, it will happen" (Thornburg, 1992, p. 59). David Engleman, CCP, Director, Compensation for Wang Laboratories, also sees the movement to link organizational objectives with performance-reward plans. "Companies are looking more and more at things like quality, teamwork, responsibility and accountability, and compensation people are looking for ways to support these tenets," said Engleman (*Official Membership of the American Compensation Association*, 1993).

Fairfield Inn has attempted to link salary to performance by implementing a PC-driven check-out game called Scorecard. It encourages guests to provide feedback on the quality of his or her stay and the services he or she received. The system automatically matches each guest's rating for each question to the appropriate service personnel. The data is used as part of a quarterly performance review for every employee. Moreover, half of each quarterly bonus is based on individual performance, and half is based on the performance of the entire staff. This helps promote cooperation and teamwork as well as good individual performance.

Seeking to encourage and motivate employees, many businesses have sought to provide awards and recognition to those individuals and teams who have helped support and promote the organization. "Money is one way to compensate, but it can also include promotions, recognition, advancement, and a better working environment," said A. Daniel McIntosh, national director for planning, compensation, and personal consulting services for benefits consulting firm Alexander & Alexander (Stouffer, 1988). Federal Express team members are perfectly happy with a gold quality award pin and their picture in the company newsletter. Sometimes a little recognition is enough. Also, there is a certain amount of pride that comes from being associated with a team and public recognition can strengthen it.

In order to integrate the principles of TQM with pervasive compensation practices, many HRM professionals and organizations are turning to skill-based pay, broad banding, maturity curves, and peer-review appraisals. The Powertrain division of General Motors' Buick-Oldsmobile-Cadillac group, as well as Zytec Corporation, winner of the Malcolm Baldridge Award in 1992, have done away with supervisor-subordinate appraisals in favor of the team peer review method. They are also employing the use of maturity curves based on work experience, seniority, or skill competencies (Kennedy, 1993). In effect, they are trying to break away from the notion of individual performance and trying to embrace and support collective performance.

Working to develop employees to achieve organizational objectives and goals, a great many companies have turned to self-directed work teams, information sharing, gain-sharing, and skill-based pay. A. David McIntosh notes the movement toward pay-for-performance in steel through gainsharing, where employees share in company profits if certain goals are realized (Lawler & Cohen, 1992). Gainsharing is an excellent compensation tool to promote cooperation and trust among teams and groups. A problem with gainsharing, however, is that the line of sight between a team idea and the size of the bonus is rather weak. Moreover, a team can make a breakthrough idea and only receive a moderate portion of the organizational bonus because the savings or profits are spread among every employee in the company. Still, gainsharing can combat the problem of individual groups or teams within an organization becoming too self-focused and neglecting to take the broad needs of the organization into account. Gainsharing can temper the potentially strong and harmful cohesiveness that can develop within teams and groups (Lawler & Cohen, 1992).

In general, HRM professionals must recognize that the more interdependencies among groups and teams within an organization, the more important it is to design reward systems to function at the organizational level. On the other hand, if teams can stand alone much like project teams, the rewards should be focused at the team level.

There is also a significant movement toward pay-for-performance in the health care industry. This has been triggered by the growing costs of employee compensation, diminishing revenues, and the approval of the Internal Revenue Service. The big advantage of pay for performance is the ability to link compensation to productivity. This is significant because it allows companies to fluctuate compensation costs with company performance. If the company does poorly, then the company can lower compensation.

There is also a recent trend toward broadbanding that undoes job sets and job grades and focuses on individual worker evaluation. Companies are realizing that by continuing to use job-based pay systems, the emphasis will remain on job descriptions rather than individual growth and initiative (Lawler & Cohen, 1992). This is why a number of companies are turning to skill-based pay systems in an attempt to abandon the bureaucracy and focus on the individual. Some examples of skill-based pay are the stair-step models, the job-point accrual model, and the cross-department model. Companies are also turning to skill-based pay to motivate project teams, within an organization. Project teams are normally composed of a diverse group of workers with disparate specialties. In organizations with project teams having the correct mix of skills within the teams is crucial. Skill-based pay can facilitate the right mix of skills within the organization and among the teams (Lawler & Cohen, 1992).

A GLIMPSE OF THE FUTURE

Many organizations are a decade or two behind in compensation designing and compensation structure. One reason for this may be because, for some companies, changes in compensation are like that of a slow moving dinosaur. Some companies are reluctant to make changes in the compensation plan without a great deal of thought and research because it is the single most costly element of the HRM department. In those companies where there is a resistance to making changes in a compensation system, it will be very difficult, if not impossible, for HRM professionals to design and implement state-of-the-art compensation systems for their organizations.

Many companies are responding to the intensely globally competitive environment with changes in compensation design. Unfortunately, many companies are instituting these changes in an effort to catch up to the most successful and proactive companies. These same companies will have to make adjustments to their compensation structure in the coming decade in yet another attempt to catch the competition. This will be an inevitable and costly cycle. In the years to come, HRM professionals must ensure that their companies think in the long-term and anticipate environmental changes, employee concerns, and competitive reactions. In effect, HRM professionals must get their companies to learn to think proactively instead of reactively.

HRM professionals committed to helping their organization develop, implement, and maintain comprehensive compensation systems would do well to learn from well-known and progressive firms such as Saturn Corporation and General Mills. Such programs are aimed at fostering employee commitment and include value-based hiring, career-oriented appraisals, and extensive employee involvement programs. Their compensation plans, therefore, tend to reflect the trust with which these companies treat their employees, and the fact that employees are and should be treated as partners in the business.

The trend in organizations' compensation policies and programs like Saturn Corporation and General Mills is to:

Offer packages of above average pay combined with incentives and extensive benefits.

Build a compensation package that puts a significant portion of pay at risk.

Emphasize self-reporting of hours worked, rather than devices like time clocks.

Build a pay plan that encourages employees to think of themselves as partners, meaning that they should have a healthy share of the profits in good years and share in the downturn during bad times.

Provide a package of benefits that makes it clear that they view their employees as long-term investments. (Dessler, 1993)

The evolving practices in organizations like Saturn provide us with a better understanding of what HRM professionals can expect in the compensation arena. In addition, HRM professionals should be sensitive to some of the changes that will affect compensation.

First, with an increasing emphasis on flexibility and on empowering employees, "In the U.S. companies in the year 2000, most traditional job descriptions and hourly employee job classifications will be fed unceremoniously into the paper shredder" (Rich, 1992, p. 27). Replacing them will be greater latitude for employees to evolve their responsibilities and activities in a job description. Measurement systems and rewards will continue to focus on paying for improved results.

One aspect of this — skill-based pay — will actually be a return to the compensation methods of the far distant past. Under the apprentice systems that started with the guilds of the Middle Ages, apprentices had to demonstrate competence at their trade before being promoted to journeymen, and then to masters. So when firms like General Mills, Saturn, or Motorola condense dozens or hundreds of job classifications into a few broad bands and then base pay differentials on skill levels, we are really returning, to some extent, to the past. In summary, competency or skill-based pay will become increasingly prevalent (Rich, 1992; Dessler, 1994).

One expert also suggests that as firms like IBM break themselves into small, decentralized pieces, the whole concept of centrally determined compensation plans may become obsolete (Smith, 1992). He says that at some point managers of decentralized companies should simply get salary budgets and then set pay levels for new hires, determine pay increases, decide when to give raises, and make all other decisions concerning cash compensation for the employees reporting to them (Smith, 1992, p. 23).

There will also be a growing emphasis on pay for improved results and on nontraditional pay (also called alternative rewards). Traditional pay plans based on job descriptions, job evaluations, and salary structures tend to focus on creating order, reinforcing the hierarchy, and directing behavior (Cumming, 1992). In the future (and for many firms the future is now), the emphasis will shift from paying for the job to paying for the employee's contribution. Thus, the focus will shift from creating order and directing behavior to encouraging involvement and commitment, and to rewarding positive results. Nontraditional or alternative pay plans for doing this include competency or skill-based pay, spot rewards, team incentives, and gainsharing (Dessler, 1994).

HRM professionals will also need to find answers to several questions related to changes in the way work is done and how it is rewarded. For example, if a company tries to discourage the lone-ranger mentality among its employees in favor of group dynamics and group cohesiveness (or increased teamwork), a few problems can arise. For example, where are all those good ideas that the old management-by-objective system models encouraged going to come from? (Thornburg, 1992).

Another question that must be answered is: How can U.S. companies and HRM professionals motivate all employees to address the changes and challenges of the future? For example, it will be difficult to motivate a worker who has been receiving steady increases in pay each year to adopt and accept a pay-for-performance plan.

In the movement away from job evaluations and job analysis toward broadbanding, organizations will have to determine how they will manage individuals and not jobs in the compensation equation. Answers to how organizations will deal with these changes and new responsibilities are unknown.

There is a growing trend toward diversity in the workforce and a market demand for highly educated and skilled workers. As a consequence, HRM professionals and organizations must determine how to attract and retain these scarce resources. Moreover, they must somehow design flexible compensation packages tailored to individual needs, yet continue to work toward promoting a cooperative and team-oriented environment. Unfortunately, providing different rewards to individuals within teams can undermine cooperation and collective effort. The extent to which HRM professionals help their organizations determine how to deal with these teams will have a major impact on the potential success of their compensation efforts.

To ensure the compensation system tracks with the company's overall business plan in the future, HRM professionals must work with their organizations to identify business objectives, assess the current compensation system, and identify new or existing pay systems that can close the gaps. The first step by the organization should be to identify strategic objectives. How can the company gain or maintain a competitive advantage? Will it introduce new products? Will the focus of the organization be customer-service, quality, and/or low-cost?

The next step is to rigorously assess the existing compensation system to determine if it supports the company's objectives and motivates personnel to achieve those objectives. Companies must assess their merit pay system, executive compensation, and employee benefits to determine if they are industry competitive. Companies must analyze each element of their pay plan and ask, Does this element effectively attract, retain, and/or motivate employees? What most employers are finding is that their current pay plan ranks high in the attract and retain function and low in the motivation function. Interestingly, many companies are realizing that their management-productivity incentives, while increasing productivity, are negatively affecting quality and customer service.

The next step is for HRM professionals to ensure that their companies devise a pay plan that will support and reward customer service, quality, and cost reduction. In effect, they need to devise a plan that will fill the holes in the existing plan or devise a plan that will replace it (McNally, 1992).

Companies should seriously consider making a move toward group incentives, gainsharing, or skill-based pay. Which pay plan to choose should be a function of the objectives of the business, and the type of work processes and programs already in place in the organization.

HRM professionals can devise more worker-sensitive compensation systems when they work to see that their companies pay more attention to Vroom's expectancy theory when designing or refining their compensation system. According to expectancy theory, employees perceive rewards in terms of expectancy, instrumentality, and valance. That is, the reward should be performance contingent, desirable, and attainable. Therefore, it is the contention of this book that companies should list all the rewards that it offers employees as well as the purpose of each reward. The company should then conduct and examine a survey of employee perceptions of each reward to see if they align with company objectives. It has been proven and it is logical that rewards that are important to individuals will impact their motivation to perform. Experience shows us that people in organizations behave in whatever ways that will lead to the rewards they value. This is why it is so important for HRM professionals to study their organization's present compensation and incentive system to determine if valued rewards are tied to crucial business objectives.

Compensation plans must be installed as proactive measures, not reactive measures. They must also involve the employees and capture their attention. Compensation plans are most effective when employees are involved in the design and implementation of the plan, and when the organization provides feedback to the employees about the plan. Therefore, in order to promote teamwork and business objectives, companies should regularly communicate their performance to employees and facilitate employee involvement in meeting business objectives. Obviously, if employees are rewarded based on achievement of business objectives, their motivation will increase commensurate with the control they have in attaining these objectives.

When designing compensation systems, HRM professionals should use a task force to design the system. The task force should also have considerable influence in setting base lines, goals, or targets of the plan. The CARS research has demonstrated that organizational performance-pay plans are more effective in promoting business objectives and are rated more favorably when task forces are utilized in their design and installation (McAdams & Hawk, 1992). The task force should be composed of at least one high level manager to demonstrate executive support and commitment. The team should also be composed of a few employees who are broad thinkers, a few employees who are technical specialists in reengineering, and all the members should be from various areas in the organization.

HRM professionals should also make every effort to include all employees in the organization when designing a compensation system, not just selected participants — to do otherwise would promote segregation and discrimination that is detrimental to an organization's culture. For example, a company that is using the compensation system to drive organizational change or the reengineering effort would want to think twice about having an award and recognition program for one group and not the other. An incentive system set up for one selected group could promote an unhealthy and unproductive we or they environment (Kanin-Lovers & Keilty, 1993).

As organizations strive to become more competitive, they will need to find ways to begin to control their compensation costs. Thus, HRM professionals must be prepared to look at staffing needs as determined by technology, quality, competition, and costs. This will require that HRM professionals check out and apply one or more of the various approaches to job evaluation. In addition, they must identify the sources of information they need to price jobs realistically and competitively: benchmarks, wage surveys, market analysis, and the like.

Most people have grown up with the notion that they are entitled to annual raises, regardless of business conditions or their own productivity. That entitlement mentality must be eliminated by HRM professionals. Instead of automatic salary increases, HRM professionals should introduce lump-sum payments and incentive programs to tie salary increases to competitive performance.

Some other things HRM professionals can work on with their organizations to reduce compensation costs are:

Hold across-the-board pay increases to the minimum needed to meet inflation.

Recognize contributions to the organization through development opportunities and job security, in addition to reasonable merit pay raises and salary increases.

Use lump-sum merit increases instead of salary adjustments.

Instead of merit raises use overtime pay for employees who are normally exempt.

Make job-title "promotions"; they are sometimes more rewarding than pay increases.

Increase the number and value of one-time (that is, not built into base salary) incentive rewards.

Review your compensation program regularly, continually monitor market trends and changes in your organization, and adjust compensation to shifts in supply and demand and changing technologies.

Patton (1977) suggests that in compensation policy there are seven criteria for effectiveness. Compensation should be:

Adequate. Minimum governmental, union, and managerial levels should be met.

Equitable. Each person should be paid fairly, in line with his or her effort, abilities, and training.

Balanced. Pay, benefits, and other rewards should provide a reasonable total reward package.

Cost-effective. Pay should not be excessive, considering what the organization can afford to pay.

Secure. Pay should be enough to help an employee feel secure and aid him or her in satisfying basic needs.

Incentive-providing. Pay should motivate effective and productive work.

Acceptable to the employee. The employee should understand the pay system and feel it is a reasonable system for the enterprise and himself or herself.

To the seven criteria for effectiveness can be added:

competitiveness of the wages and salaries with those paid by other organizations in the same industry or locality;

the organization's ability to pay;

whether to give pay increases on the basis of performance, length of service, or both;

what kind of wage and salary differentials there should be between satisfactory and outstanding performers, and between supervisors and their subordinates;

rules of administration — for example, how frequently the pay structure and the pay of individuals should be reviewed, and how fast someone can move through a rate range (a range of possible pay amounts); and what time perspective to have in mind — for example, whether pay decisions should be based strictly on performance over the last year, or whether performance and the organization's ability to pay over the past several years should be taken into account.

A successful compensation system needs to incorporate the equity concerns of all participants in the employment relationship. This is achieved by establishing a system that includes both external and internal comparisons in setting pay levels. In addition, it is more important to focus on the specific employees who are dissatisfied with compensation than on the overall level of satisfaction. If poor performers are dissatisfied, that may be as desired.

CONCLUSION

Traditionally, using pay to recognize an individual employee's contributions has been thought of as a way to influence the behaviors and attitudes of current employees, whereas pay level and benefits have been seen as a way to influence so-called membership behaviors: decisions about whether to join or remain with the organization. However, there is increasing recognition that individual pay programs may also have an effect on the nature and composition of an organization's workforce (Milkovich & Wigdor, 1991). For example, it is possible that an organization that links pay to performance may attract more high performers than an organization that does not link the two. There may be a similar effect with respect to job retention (Noe, Hollenbeck, Gerhart & Wright, 1994).

Continuing the analysis, perhaps organizations that link pay to individual performance are more likely to attract individualistic employees, while organizations relying more heavily on team rewards are more likely to attract team-oriented employees. Although there is no concrete evidence of this yet, it has been found that different pay systems attract people with different personality traits and values (Bretz, Ash & Dreher, 1989; Judge & Bretz, 1992). The implication is that the design of compensation programs needs to be carefully coordinated with the organization and HRM strategy (Noe, Hollenbeck, Gerhart, & Wright, 1994).

Compensation plays an important role in attracting new employees to join an organization and rewarding them for their contributions. However, more recently, the focus of compensation system design is shifting from an emphasis on attracting and retaining employees to an emphasis on motivating employees (McNally, 1992). Moreover, HRM professionals and their organizations are realizing that compensation can be used effectively as a strategic tool. This involves rewarding skilled workers for achieving goals that drive the company objectives. The primary objective of an organizational compensation system has been, and will continue to be, to improve organizational performance. Yet, there have been, and will continue to be, changes made in compensation systems by HRM professionals and their organizations if organizations are going to be successful in the future.

In the coming years, there will be more widespread use of work teams, and a greater emphasis on team rewards, and less emphasis on linking rewards to individual achievements. And with this trend, HRM professionals and their organizations will need to relinquish control and rely more heavily on employees to develop, administer, and communicate new pay programs. The CARS study has already statistically proven that compensation plans have better results when employees are more involved in design and implementation. It is time that U.S. companies and HRM practitioners embrace these results, begin to communicate program results, and broaden employee involvement. Moreover, there will unlikely be an increase in pay-for-performance initiatives filtering down to lower levels in the organization. Therefore, organizations must be willing to move away from pay-for-performance efforts that are strictly reserved for sales representatives or top-level executives.

In the coming years, HRM professionals must take the time to ensure that greater thought and emphasis are given in developing compensation systems to accommodate the changing workforce demographics. The workforce in the future is expected to be more female, more educationally disadvantaged, and older. In fact, according to Hudson Institute study Workforce 2000, three-fifths of all women over 16 will be working by the turn of the century (Stelluto & Klein, 1990).

REFERENCES

Bretz, R. D., Ash, R. A., & Dreher, G. F. 1989. Do people make the place? An examination of the attraction-selection-attrition hypothesis. *Personnel Psychology 42*: 561–81.

Cooper, R. 1986, June 9. Employee incentives pay off. *Business First-Louisville*. 2(44): 26.

Cumming, C. 1992, November/December. Will traditional salary administration survive the stampede to alternative rewards? *Compensation and Benefits Review*: 42-47.

Dessler, G. 1993. *Winning commitment*. New York: McGraw-Hill.

Dessler, G. 1994. *Human resource management*. (6th ed.). Englewood Cliffs: Allyn & Bacon.

Dickens, W. T. & Lang, K. 1986, April. Labor market segmentation and the union wage premium. NBER Working Paper 1883. Cambridge, MA.

Dowling, P. J. & Schuler, R. S. 1990. *International dimensions of human resource management*. Boston, MA: PWS-Kent.

Firth, S. 1981. *The expatriate dilemma*. Chicago: Nelson Hall.

Judge, T. A. & Bretz, R. D. 1992. Effect of values on job choice decisions. *Journal of Applied Psychology 77*: 261–71.

Kanin-Lovers, J. & Keilty, J. 1993, March/April. Designing incentives to support business reengineering. *Journal of Compensation and Benefits*: 55.

Kennedy, P. W. 1993, March/April. Quality management challenges compensation professionals. *Journal of Compensation and Benefits*: 29–35.

Lawler, E. E., III & Cohen, S. G., 1992, Autumn. Designing pay systems for teams. *ACA Journal*: 6–16.

McAdams, J. L. & Hawk, E. H. 1992, Autumn. Capitalizing on human assets through performance-based rewards. *ACA Journal*: 66.

McNally, K. A. 1992, July. Compensation as a strategic tool. *HRMagazine*: 59–62.

Milkovich, G. T. & Wigdor, A. K. 1991. *Pay for performance*. Washington, DC: National Academy Press.

Noe, R. A., Hollenbeck, J. R., Gerhart, B., & Wright, P. M. 1994. *Human resource management: Gaining a competitive advantage*. Burr Ridge, IL: Austin Press/Irwin.

Official Membership of American Compensation Association. What to expect in 1993. *36*(2): 14.

Patton, T. 1977. *Pay*. New York: Free Press.

Reynolds, C. 1986. Compensation of overseas personnel. In J. J. Famularo (ed). *Handbook of human resource administration* (2nd ed.). New York: McGraw-Hill.

Rich, J. 1992, July/August. Meeting the global challenge: A measurement and reward program for the future. *Compensation and Benefits Review*: 26–29.

Selz, M. 1992, February 27. Hiring the right manager overseas. *Wall Street Journal*: B2.

Smith, A. W., Jr. 1992, July/August. Structuralist salary management: A modest proposal. *Compensation and Benefits Review*: 22–25.

Stelluto, G. L. & Klein, D. P. 1990, February. Compensation trends into the 21st century. *Monthly Labor Review*: 38–45.

Stouffer, R. 1988, August 29. More companies turning to pay for performance. *Pittsburgh Business Times & Journal 8*(2): 2.

Teague, B. W. 1972. *Compensating key personnel overseas*. New York: Conference Board.

Thornburg, L. 1992, June. Pay for performance. *HRMagazine*: 58-61.

5

Benefits and Human Resources Management

Stephen C. Caulfield, managing director of William M. Mercer, outlined the key issues facing human resources management (HRM) professionals at a recent Corporate Benefits Management Conference:

Employers in the 1990s must focus on human resource issues — especially employee benefit issues because people will be the assets that differentiate companies in the next few decades. Human resource management will be at the center of efficiency, quality and competitiveness in the 1990s. And, employee benefits are at the heart of management of human resources. Employers must particularly focus their human resource efforts on health cost management and benefit communications. I believe that those two areas are prerequisites for successful management of the human resource agenda for the 1990s. (Kertesz, 1991, p. 12)

Employee benefit programs have become an integral part of most compensation systems. Group life and health insurance programs, retirement programs, paid vacations and holidays, prepaid legal plans, and dental and optical insurance coverage are among the type of employee benefits commonly found in private and public sector organizations.

Administering benefits today represents an increasingly specialized and expensive task. It demands specialized expertise because employees are becoming more sophisticated in financial matters and are, therefore, demanding new types of benefits and because of federal legislation — concerning pregnancy benefits, for instance — requires that benefit plans comply with new laws. Furthermore, benefit plans have become increasingly expensive.

Employers and employees are vitally concerned with indirect compensation (benefits). Aside from its high value, it is a form of compensation on which employees generally do not have to pay income taxes. As the cost of indirect benefits grows in proportion to the total pay cost, organizations are becoming more concerned about the number and type of benefits they provide, the management of benefits, and cost containment. As a result, benefits management by the HRM department has moved off the back burner and into the fireline of strategic management.

This chapter will discuss benefits and the challenges they present to HRM professionals and their organizations. First, we will discuss some of the more common types of benefits. Next, we will identify a number of challenges benefits pose for HRM professionals and some organizational responses to those challenges to date. The chapter concludes with a look at how benefits issues will play a role in the coming years.

TYPES OF BENEFITS

Mandatory benefits are those that are mandated by legislation — either state or federal. For example, in the benefits area, federal legislation supports the Old Age, Survivors, Disability, and Health Insurance Program and a number of legally required benefits associated with that program — social security and unemployment insurance. Another major piece of federal legislation is the Employment Retirement Act of 1978. The Economic Recovery Act of 1981, and other tax laws define, as part of the Internal Revenue Code, the taxable or nontaxable status of benefits. Before 1984, employers were required to give few benefits other than Social Security, workers' compensation, and unemployment. However, beginning with the Consolidated Omnibus Budget Resolution Act of 1984, federal regulations requiring employers to provide additional benefits began to proliferate. More recently, the passage of the Family and Medical Leave Act of 1993 (HR770) provides an additional legally sanctioned benefit that HRM professionals must take into consideration in the benefits equation.

Workers' compensation provides for continuation of salary in the event that you are unable to work due to a work-related injury. Employer paid payroll taxes also provide important benefits in the form of unemployment compensation programs and a retirement system. Unemployment programs are funded through payments of Federal Unemployment Tax Act taxes. The Federal Insurance Contribution Act taxes support the vast Social Security system.

Organizations offer many different benefits to their employees. They are grouped into several types: security; health care; retirement; financial and other insurance; social, recreational; time off, and others.

Security Benefits

Several benefits offer protection and/or security to employees. As noted earlier, some are required by federal and state laws. Others are given voluntarily by the organization or made available through provisions in labor/management contracts. Workers' compensation, unemployment compensation, and Social Security are the most important of the security benefits.

Health Care Benefits

Organizations provide a variety of health care and medical benefits. The most common ones cover medical, dental, prescription-drug, and vision-care expenses for employees and their dependents. Basic health care insurance to cover both normal and major medical expenses is highly desired by employees. Likewise, dental insurance is important to many employees. Many dental plans have orthodontic coverage, which is usually more costly. Some employer medical insurance plans also cover psychiatric counseling. The rapidly escalating costs of health care benefits are a major concern for employers.

Retirement-Related Benefits

A widespread package of benefits offered by most employers attempts to provide income for employees when they retire. Few people have independent reserves to use when they retire. However, financial resources represent only one facet of the broader issue of retirement policies.

Financial and Related Benefits

Organizations may offer workers a wide range of special benefits — financial (for example, credit unions, purchase discounts, employee thrift, savings or stock investment plans, and financial planning and counseling), insurance (for example, life, disability, and legal), educational (that is, educational assistance), and social and recreational (for example, bowling leagues, picnics, parties, employer-sponsored athletic teams, organizationally owned recreational lodges, and other sponsored activities and interest groups). From the point of view of the organization, such benefits can be useful in attracting and retaining employees. Workers like receiving special benefits because they are not taxed as income.

Unusual Benefits

Many organizations offer their employees a wide range of benefits other than those normally provided. Food services, counseling services, paid professional memberships, uniforms, and employee discounts are common ones. Often, the benefits given are tied to the goods and services provided by the organizations. But other organizations offer more unusual benefits as the following examples illustrate (Lawlor, 1993; *Omaha World-Herald*, 1993b):

Free breakfast every day is given to employees at Computer Associates International, based in Islandia, N.Y.

The manufacturer of Budweiser and Michelob beer, Anheuser-Busch, allows employees to take home two cases of beer per month at no cost.

On his or her birthday, each employee at Mary Kay Cosmetics in Dallas, Texas, receives a birthday card and a coupon for a free lunch or movie tickets for two, and after five years with the company, employees receive a U.S. Savings Bond.

A Livermore, California, employer, Lawrence Livermore National Laboratory sponsors over 100 clubs for employees. Employees join based upon their interests and the clubs meet after work hours. Karate, chess, and computers are just three clubs that exist.

Time Off Benefits

Employers give employees paid time off for a variety of circumstances. Paid lunch breaks and rest periods, holidays, and vacations are the most well known. But leaves are given for a number of other purposes as well. A study of time off benefits for organizations with fewer than 100 employees found that those benefits represent a cost of 5 percent of total compensation for an average of 68 cents per hour for each employee (Miller, 1992). Some of the more common time off benefits include holiday pay, vacation pay, and leaves of absence.

CHALLENGES OF BENEFITS TO HUMAN RESOURCES MANAGEMENT

The Aging Workforce

There are many implications that demographic shifts during the next ten years will form a U.S. working society very different from the society of today. Organizations will require that HRM professionals proactively maintain a benefits plan that will keep pace with the changing society and minimize chances for being unprepared. With regard to the workforce structure, "both the population and workforce are likely to grow at their lowest levels since the 1930s. And, the pool of older workers — the aging baby boom generation — will continue to increase" (Geisel, 1990, p. 3).

Furthermore, there is a direct correlation between the age of an employee and the number of physician visits he or she will make.

"Using distribution of physician visits by age as a reasonable surrogate for total health costs by age, it is clear that as people move into their fifties, the number of physician visits, and therefore the total health costs, begin to rise significantly" (Caulfield, 1990, p. 20). Therefore, even if the costs and prices of health care related products and services were frozen from now until well into the next decade, and not affected by inflation, for example, a substantial increase in the utilization of health care would still take place as today's Baby Boomers move from their mid-30s and 40s to their mid-50s. This rapid increase in the utilization of health care, and its vast consumption of corporate profits, poses a major challenge for HRM professionals to review constantly available alternate means for the provision of medical and medically related products and services.

Family Related Challenges

As a result of workforce and social changes, family related issues have received increasing attention. Family related challenges for HRM professionals include leave to care for family members, child-care assistance, and elder care.

An Increasing Presence of Women in the Workforce

In 1940, only 8.6 percent of all working women had children. In 1960, women comprised 33.4 percent of the workforce and 28 percent were married with children. As of 1990, women comprised 58 percent of the workforce (this is up from 46 percent in 1975), over 61 percent of whom have children (O'Neill & Tocco, 1990; Geisel, 1990). The U.S. Labor Department's Bureau of Labor Statistics points out that 67 percent of working women have at least one dependent child under the age of 18, and 58 percent have children under 6 (Shalowitz, 1992). By the year 2000, women will comprise 65 percent of the U.S. workforce, and 80 percent of them will become pregnant sometime in their working lives. Men, too, have a considerable stake in the issue. By the end of the decade, three-quarters of all families will include a two-career couple, up from roughly 56 percent in 1990 (Weisendanger, 1990).

The major difference today, compared to 1940, is that working women are faced with increased financial burdens (that is, an increasing amount are childless, unmarried, and self-sufficient; many others support themselves as well as children). Today's HRM professional, therefore, must make the most suitable and acceptable health care provisions for the single working woman in order to afford her independent financial security even in the event of a sick child. The challenge for HRM professionals is to discover and maintain such provisions so that family-related needs do not interfere with worker productivity.

Dependent Care

Dependent care includes child care, elder care, and care for the ill and infirm who are dependents of those people participating in the workforce. Because of the large numbers of mothers who are in the workforce and who have young children, as well as the significant number of working men with sole responsibility for young children, child-care services are increasingly important. Child-care programs are of several kinds, and sometimes have a combination of features. Information and referrals are the most frequently found services, followed by counseling assistance, help with child-care expenses, and employer-sponsored day-care centers. Other programs that support child care are job sharing, voluntary part-time work, flextime, and flexible leave programs.

Many families that purchase child care commit as much as 20 to 30 percent of their pretax earnings to pay for the services; 45 percent of the families with children six and younger have total incomes between $15,000 and $40,000. Three thousand dollars per year per child is the average cost of full-time child-care services (Caulfield, 1990). A recent Federal Express survey of 30,000 employees from 30 different corporations, within several different industries, showed that 71 percent experience stress from family and work conflicts, especially regarding child care. Almost half of the survey respondents felt the stress affected their work, and 35 percent admitted being absent from work because of child-care problems (Weisendanger, 1990). HRM professionals must recognize that, whether single parents or dual-career couples, these employees often experience difficulty in obtaining quality, affordable child care. Therefore, the major challenge related to child care for HRM professionals today and into the next decade is to create provisions that support parents to be productive at work without experiencing undue stress from child-care concerns.

To date, organizations are addressing the child-care issue in several ways. Some organizations have established on-site day-care facilities. Costs and concerns about liability have been established. At least one study found that on-site child care had a positive impact on employees who used the service. The study found that the greater the use of the care service, the more favorable employees' attitudes toward management (Konesh & Nichol, 1992).

Other options offered by employers include:

providing referral services to aid parents in locating child-care providers;

establishing discounts at day-care centers, which may be subsidized by the employer;

arranging with hospitals to offer sick-child programs that are partially paid for by employers;

developing after-school programs for older school-age children, often in conjunction with local public and private school systems.

The challenges related to elder care and care for the sick and infirm dependents also require HRM attention. Elder care is an area of employee benefits that is gaining more attention. One reason is that demographics are changing dramatically. For example, the U.S. Senate Special Committee on Aging predicts that, by the year 2010, there will be 22 elderly persons per 100 working-age persons — in contrast with 19 per 100 in 1988 — and that by the year 2050, the ratio will be 38 per 100 (French, 1990).

Different organizations have surveyed their employees and found that as many as 30 percent have had to miss work to care for an aging relative (Lefkovich, 1992). The responsibilities associated with caring for elderly family members have resulted in reduced work performance, increased absenteeism, and more personal stress for the affected employees. Many more employees will have to respond to this issue as the U.S. population continues to age.

According to Urban Institute estimates, the need for long-term care nursing homes will rise precipitously over the next two decades. Social scientists observe that the disintegration of the nuclear family is compounded by the geographic dispersion associated with both job mobility and migration changes that are influenced by economics and lifestyle changes (Caulfield, 1990). Besides the economic implications, concern about elderly relatives can have a major impact on employees' peace of mind, attendance, and productivity.

With the increase in the demand for long-term institutional care, HRM professionals will need to ensure that their organization's benefits programs help employees support relatives in need of elder care. As in the case of child care, HRM practices such as flextime, job sharing, and voluntary part-time work can be of assistance to employees with elder care responsibilities.

Family and Medical Leave Act of 1993

In 1993, President Clinton signed into law the Family and Medical Leave Act (FMLA), which covers all employers with 50 or more employees within 75 miles of a workplace, and includes federal, state, and private employers. Only employees who have worked at least 12 months, or 1,250 hours, in the previous year are eligible for leaves under FMLA. The law requires that employers allow eligible employees to take a total of 12 weeks' leave during any 12-month period for one or more of the following situations:

birth, adoption, or foster-care placement of a child;
caring for a spouse, child, or parent with a serious health condition; and
serious health condition of the employee.

A serious health condition is one requiring inpatient, hospital, hospice, or residential medical care or continuing physician care. Employers may require employees to provide certificates by a doctor verifying such illnesses.

Regarding taking leaves, FMLA provides the following:

Employers taking family and medical leave must be able to return to the same job or a job of equivalent status or pay.

Health benefits must be continued during the leave at the same level and conditions. If the employee does not return to work for a reason other than serious health problems, the employer may collect the employer-paid portion of the premiums from the nonreturning employee.

The leave taken may be intermittent rather than in one block, subject to employee and employer agreements, when birth, adoption, or foster-child care is the cause. For serious health conditions, employer approval is not necessary.

Employees can be required to use all paid-up vacation and personal leave before taking unpaid leave.

Employees are required to give 30-days notice, where practical.

All of these provisions will have significant effects on employers and employees alike. Numerous HRM policies have had to be revised as a result of this act. It has also required HRM managers and other managers to do better staffing, planning, and scheduling.

Decreasing Talent Pool

Another demographic factor impacting this area of HRM is the fact that the talent pool for high-tech, high-skill jobs is not keeping pace with the demand. This is a result of two unrelated factors: a crisis in our education system and a decline in our birth rate. It is estimated that the number of Americans in the 16–24-year-old age bracket is 25 percent less than the previous generation. This trend should continue through the year 2000 (Zarowin, 1991).

The education crisis has contributed to a shortage of qualified employees able to begin to contribute to a firm's bottom line. A Colorado manufacturer has reported that of the 2,100 job applicants each year, 70 percent are rejected due to an inability to perform elementary writing skills (Merdinger & Botkin, 1992). The issue, then, facing the HRM professional is to design a relevant, meaningful benefits package aimed at a diverse and continually changing workforce at a price that will help promote competitiveness.

New and Different Workplace Health Risks

Along with the stress factors employees experience related to child care and elder care, HRM professionals must develop benefits that help employees deal with programs directed toward stress management and stress reduction. Although the aforementioned programs contribute to minimizing stress, an on-the-job exercise program — sometimes called a wellness program — can encourage employees to take preventative measures in personal health matters. The challenge for HRM professionals is to adopt a variety of wellness designs that help a firm's workforce lead healthier lives. Prevention of illnesses is a major solution to medical and medically related products and services cost containment.

Benefits in Multinational Companies

A major challenge that confronts multinational organizations is deciding how to provide equitable compensation systems for employees given overseas assignments. This challenge is compounded because employee benefits often vary drastically from country to country or from industry to industry. In Europe, for instance, it is common for employees to receive added compensation in proportion to the number of family members or the degree of their unpleasant working conditions. In Japan, a supervisor whose weekly salary is only $500 may also receive benefits that include family income allowances, housing or housing loans, subsidized vacations, year-end bonuses that can equal three months' pay, and profit sharing (Cascio & Serapio, 1991).

Successful management of employee benefits in a multinational corporation depends on various features. Perhaps the most important one is a corporate policy statement that outlines specific instructions for the development, approval, and administration of all benefit plans. This policy statement should include any payment of company funds to employees other than base salary, such as pensions, medical and life insurance, vacations, and severance pay (Krupp, 1986).

Cost Containment of Benefits

Prior to the New Deal, instituted by Franklin D. Roosevelt in response to economic problems brought about by the Depression, the concept of benefits was foreign to most U.S. working people. The term "wage earner" was appropriate because it encompassed completely the total compensation that a worker could expect to receive — wages. The idea of a day's pay for a day's work in many cases meant just that — you were paid in cash daily.

While other benefits were not unheard of, their status was so minor that the term "fringe benefits" was coined to describe their overall importance to compensation. Very often, the only fringe benefits available might be a short holiday (when the factory closed once a year for inventory) or a small Christmas bonus. This may have amounted to 1 percent of an employee's wages (Zarowin, 1991).

Although the first recorded profit-sharing plan in the United States occurred at a Pennsylvania glass works in 1794, the big push for increasing benefits occurred during World War II (Cohen, 1976). Wartime needs created serious shortages of workers. Since increases in wages were controlled by the federal government, employers and unions came up with new ways to attract and retain employees. Managers offered inducements that were not subject to government controls. If the government would not permit managers to offer greater wages, then the managers offered to pay medical bills, provide life insurance, and subsidize cafeterias instead (Milkovich & Boudreau, 1994).

Tax policies encouraged the continued growth in benefits. Most benefits are nontaxable income to employees and are deductible expenses to employers (McCaffery, 1983). Today, benefits constitute a major portion of labor costs. In 1929, they amounted to only 3 percent of total payroll; by 1969, they were 31 percent; by 1990, benefits had risen to be more than 38.4 percent of wages and salaries; and in 1993, they topped 39 percent (U.S. Chamber of Commerce, 1993). The average employer pays more than $8,000 a year per employee for benefits. In terms of the costs of specific benefits, payments for time not worked (vacations, sick days, and so on) represent just over 10 percent of the average employer's payroll. Medical and related benefits account for about 10 percent of payroll; legally required benefits (Social Security, for instance) represent almost 9 percent; and other benefits, including retirement and savings plans and life insurance, account for the remaining 8.5 percent of payroll taken up by benefits (Milkovich & Boudreau, 1994).

Employers have felt the impact of increased costs, as the following examples illustrate (Clements, 1993; *Omaha World Herald*, 1993a; Thompson, 1992).

The costs of health care benefits add over $900 to every car manufactured by Chrysler, Ford, and General Motors.

DuPont Corporation had health care costs rise 50 percent from 1989 to 1993, with a cost of $6,000 per worker being paid each year.

Xerox Corporation has seen health care costs rise at a rate quadrupling the national inflation rate, despite aggressive cost-management efforts.

Dayton Hudson, a Minneapolis retailer, calculated that it had to sell 39,000 Ninja Turtle toys to pay for one employee to have an appendectomy, and Goodyear Tire & Rubber had to sell 461 radial passenger car tires to pay for an appendectomy.

A 22-employee firm in Florida spent over $95,000 in health care benefit costs in one year; a study of small business found that health care costs annually averaged $3,600 per worker for the typical small business.

As we have seen in the preceding chapter on compensation, the cash wages and salaries paid to employees are just one factor of the compensation equation. In considering the compensation package needed to recruit and retain good workers, it is necessary to recognize that the entire compensation be examined, including the fringe benefits. A careful review of the benefits package by the HRM department is necessary to ensure that there is a proper match between the workforce and the benefits offered. While an HRM professional's organization may be offering a generous package, if the employees do not find it valuable, then the benefits will not have the desired effect of keeping people on board, especially if a competitor firm is offering comparable wages with more attractive benefits.

HRM professionals must recognize that they must not only look at the costs of paying benefits but also pay particular attention to the implications or cost of not paying them or of paying reduced benefits. If HRM professionals fail to ensure that their organization's benefits are competitive within their industry as part of the total compensation package, then there will be little likelihood that the organization will be able to recruit the kind of talent that will make the organization profitable. In a down economy, the organization may be able to attract a competent workforce on a temporary basis, with modest benefits. This is currently occurring in some segments of the economy. However, as positions open up, the organization often will lose its most capable workers to organizations willing to offer better compensation. In a robust economy in which skilled workers are at a premium, all firms will be forced to offer the attractive packages or face losses due to the inability to attract skilled personnel.

In the short and long run, it is usually in the organization's best interest to continue to seek ways to compensate their employees equitably. While some firms have said they cannot afford to pay benefits, the truth of the matter is that they cannot afford not to pay them. The reason for this is that benefits, especially those that are highly valued, will more than likely make for a contented and productive workforce. An employee who feels that his or her organization recognizes his or her worth is more likely to be a good worker, and this sense of value will show up as a plus on the bottom line.

Perhaps the most concrete statistic of the effect that benefits can produce is the reduction in the turnover in the workforce. A recent study done by the U.S. Small Business Administration revealed that the recruiting and training costs to firms with under 100 employees is $1,001 for nonmanagerial employees and $1,738 for managers. Claudia Wyatt, a benefit consultant, states that the consequences of turnover are "lost productivity, recruiting costs, the time it takes to train a new employee, the loss in the company's knowledge base, possibly the cost of a temporary employee and the intangible cost of the impact on other workers" (Shalowitz, 1992).

HRM professionals should take a proactive approach with respect to determining the mix of benefits that will provide the highest value to the workforce. Toward this end, they must be aware of both internal and external factors that affect the firm. Consider, for example, companies that, traditionally, have employed high proportions of women, such as banking and health care firms. We know that close to 60 percent of working women have children under six years old. Clearly, working women with young children will value time off, flexible hours, the ability to work part-time, day care, or work at home. It is in the organization's own interests to accommodate such worker needs. In the case of allowing for family leave, employers will spend three to five times more to replace a worker than it does for the employer to cover the cost of family leave (Shalowitz, 1992).

Communication of Benefits Information

Central to the issues presented above is the challenge of effectively communicating information on employee benefits to current and prospective employees. The HRM department plays a major role in determining how effectively information about benefit programs is provided to employees. Studies over the years have shown that many employees are unaware of some of the benefits that are provided, and many tend to underestimate substantially the costs of those benefits of which they are aware. Lack of awareness, of course, reduces the motivational value employee benefits may have and leads to lack of uniformity in employee use. Lack of awareness can also contribute to inadequate planning by the employee. For example, if an employee does not understand the savings and tax advantages of a salary reduction plan, the employee may not take advantage of it, and may lose eventual retirement income.

The HRM department, therefore, has a major challenge to provide information and counseling about employee benefits. The HRM department also has some information obligations under the law. Under the Employee Retirement Income Security Act, an employee participating in a retirement plan must be furnished with information such as an understandable summary of the plan and an annual report on its financial status. Employees are entitled to certain information upon request, including their total accrued benefits (Ledvinka, 1982).

ORGANIZATIONAL RESPONSES TO COST CONTAINMENT

In attempting to cope with the issue of benefits, most organizations have tended to focus on the most obvious symptoms that also would appear, at first glance, to be the easiest to address — rising costs. A variety of approaches has been tried either alone or in combination. This section will look at the more common ones.

Some firms will take the course of least resistance and view rising cost as a natural inevitability or normal function of time. Their response is actually a nonresponse. They merely accept the price increases and go on with business as usual, either raising prices or accepting a lower return. Some organizations view their commitment to cover employee's health as a solemn trust and have paid the increasing premiums. A practical option to this strategy, while continuing to pay the entire cost, is to shop around to see if other companies can offer a cheaper alternative to the current plan.

A second approach is to attempt to reduce administrative costs. An example of this might be to join a coalition of like organizations to get a reduced rate through a group plan. For example, in Virginia, independent public accounting firms that are members of the Virginia Society of Certified Public Accountants are eligible to join the society's group plan with Blue Cross/Blue Shield, rather than seek a more expensive individual firm plan. There are, likewise, group plans for term life and disability insurance.

As costs increase on any form of insurance, a common way to lower premiums is to increase the deductible, that is, employees must pay more out of pocket before the policy begins to pick up the tab. Traditionally, most policies have had a $100 deductible — the employee paid for the first $100 of medical costs after which the provisions of the policy took effect. Employers are now asking workers to pay the first $250, $500, and in some cases $1,000 of costs before the policy will start paying. The result is that employees do not use the health insurance as much and do not qualify for payments as often. If the insurance carrier is paying out less money for policy users, costs tend to drop.

Where employees are required to share in the cost of a benefit, as costs rise, the cost borne by the employee rises proportionately. This has the tendency of mitigating the effects of price increases on the employer. If the employer is covering two-thirds of the cost of insurance, or some benefit, any price increase will be split two-thirds to the employer and one-third to the employee.

When one plan becomes too expensive, the organization may decide that they just cannot afford that plan any longer. Rather than force employees to pay for the cost, it may be decided to opt for a plan that offers reduced benefits. For example, a company may opt out of the dental or psychological counseling services offered by the premium plan and go with a basic medical plan rather than ask employees to pay.

One of the more innovative and effective means of controlling costs in the area of health care has been the managed care concept. Under this plan, a Health Maintenance Organization (HMO) is set up to administer to the health needs of the employees. Rather than giving workers a blank check as to who to see and what treatments are used, a primary care physician must first be consulted to determine the appropriate treatment. The HMO is a large organization with many specialists and facilities that are for the use of members. The key to the lower costs of an HMO is the efficiency of having all medical services and facilities under one umbrella organization.

Perhaps the most promising development in the containment of fringe benefit costs is one that also addresses the question of giving workers those benefits that they desire most — a flexible benefit program. Under this arrangement, a firm provides for basic medical and pension coverage plus a certain level (measured in cash) of benefit credits to be used on those benefits that he or she finds most useful. An employee can buy additional medical coverage if the basic plan does not provide for adequate services due to a special condition or if an employee has a family and wishes to opt for family coverage. A young, single employee may decide that he or she does not need additional medical coverage and does not wish to contribute to a deferred compensation plan such as a 401-K type plan, but would rather be paid cash to pay down debt. Under a flexible benefit arrangement, unused credits can be converted to cash.

Under current tax laws (Section 125 of the Tax Code administered by the Internal Revenue Service) employees who could divert some income before taxes into accounts found certain benefits. A flexible spending account allows employees to contribute pretax dollars to buy additional benefits. An example helps to illustrate the advantage of these accounts to employees. Assume an employee earns $3,000 per month. He has $100 per month deducted to put into flexible spending accounts. That $100 does not count as gross income for tax purposes, thus reducing his amount of taxable income. Then, the employee uses the money in his account to purchase additional benefits.

These plans have grown in popularity as flexible benefit plans have been adopted by more employers. The strengths of such a plan are that it: empowers employees to choose what is best for them; allows benefit packages to be tailored to meet the different desires and needs of its employees; aids in benefit cost-control efforts; heightens employee awareness of cost and the value of benefits; and helps the organization recruit, hire, or retain employees more easily because of the attractiveness of flexible plans. It also is a way of dealing with the central idea to group insurance — subsidy, that is, the healthy help pay premiums for the unhealthy on medical insurance. Of course, such plans and their tax advantages can be changed as Congress passes future health care and tax-related legislation.

Such flexible plans are not without their drawbacks. The major problems are: the complexity of keeping track of what each individual chooses, especially if there are a large number of employees; increase in benefit communications costs — inappropriate benefit packages may be chosen by employees; and advance selection, which means that only higher-risk employees select and use certain benefits (that is, because many insurance plans are based on a group rate, the employer may face higher rates if insufficient numbers of employees select an insurance option.

Due to the rate at which the cost of employee benefits have increased recently, especially health care, and also due to changes in the makeup of the workforce, the first five organizational responses to cutting benefit costs have just about outlived their usefulness. The benefit question is multifaceted and these responses are reactive in nature to just one of the drivers of this issue — cost.

Managed care is proactive in its approach to health care cost containment but does not go beyond this one issue. The flexible benefit spending plan, or some derivative, appears to hold the most promise for providing individual employees with the benefits that are most desired as well as helping management contain costs. The ability to match benefits to differing employee needs, while also controlling some costs, is so attractive that employers will try to find ways to overcome the disadvantages while attuning their benefit plans to the coming years.

Other Benefit Concerns That Must Be Addressed

While communication of the importance of benefits to employees can be addressed, escalating benefit costs that are driven in particular by double-digit increases in health care costs are less controllable by HRM professionals.

In dealing with the problem of spiraling costs associated with employee benefits — most notably health care — the natural question we ask is how expensive can this become? Using current data regarding the increase in prices and projecting current trends 20 years, it appears that medical costs alone will be 100 percent of salary costs. Add to this the other benefits that are increasing, and the compensation equation may be one-third salary and two-thirds benefits. This is not necessarily a bad situation, but it does point out that doing business in the United States in the twenty first century will be an expensive proposition.

Key questions remain concerning how to address cost increases. Should they be passed along to employees, swallowed by employers, or shared? What is the most advantageous way? What is the role of the government in providing affordable health care for Americans and the globalization of the economy? One actuary opined that the situation of spiraling health care costs "might ultimately require some kind of government intervention, but it will not happen for several years" (Haslinger & Shannon, 1992). This statement was made in January 1992. When one considers that a central focal point of the past presidential election was this very issue, one has to think what a difference a year makes. The extent to which government becomes involved in health care will have a profound effect on the whole question. We would hazard to guess that costs will not be reduced but rather shifted. Government mandated health plans will be to health care what social security benefits are to a retirement plan — basic, but one would not want to depend on it as one's sole means of health care.

The continuing globalization of economic activity is the other major question facing business that will have a bearing on the benefits received by U.S. workers. Like it or not, we have come to the realization that the era of Pax Americana, which followed World War II, is now over, at least economically. We are no longer the sole player in the world economy, and all industries are subject to this competitive pressure. The implication to the U.S. worker is that he will have to be competitive both in productivity and in cost reduction. As we have seen, a major component of employee cost is benefits.

Because U.S. businesses are truly international, they are not restricted in production of goods to the shores of the United States. As a consequence, they also are not restricted to the U.S. labor market. What this means is that U.S. companies will continue to manufacture products and expect to earn a good return for stockholders but will only employ U.S. workers if it makes economic sense.

The North American Free Trade Agreement provides an illustration of this thinking. This agreement does away with all trade barriers among the three North American countries of Canada, Mexico, and the United States, creating one unified market. As a result of the North American Free Trade Agreement, corporations will go to those areas where they can earn the highest return. Recently, there has been a major move among U.S. companies to shift operations to Mexico, where wages are about one-eighth of the U. S. rate. This type of pressure will have the effect of decreasing the levels of total compensation in this country. It has already occurred in some industries, where labor has had to make wage concessions.

Another recent trend among U.S. businesses that may affect the level of benefits in labor markets is reengineering. We noted earlier that U.S. businesses have experienced a shortage of skilled workers due to lower birth rates and problems with U.S. education. Reengineering is a process whereby business redesigns the workplace to make the process more streamline. It can entail rearranging workstations so work flows more quickly, using computers to automate departments, or using state of the art manufacturing technology, such as robotics.

The end result is that fewer workers are required to obtain the same output. This is precisely the effect that has taken place. In a recent story in the *Wall Street Journal* on reengineering, it was estimated that over the next two decades as many as 25 million of the 90 million jobs provided by the private sector could be eliminated through reengineering processes (Ehrbar, 1993). The combined result of shipping jobs to offshore manufacturing plants and reengineering could have the effect of producing a buyer's labor market that would drive compensation (benefits) down.

A GLIMPSE OF THE FUTURE

In the future, with a diminishing supply of new workers, the HRM department will take on an increasingly important role, with the focus on attracting and retaining key talent. Benefits will unlikely play an even more important role in this process and will impact companies' ability to compete for these key resources. The availability of flexible benefits will prove to be instrumental in attracting and retaining employees. A recent Gallup poll indicated that 90 percent of employees would prefer a job that includes flexible benefits (Thompson, 1991).

In the future, growth in the penetration of flexible benefits will continue, as small and large businesses alike will realize the advantages associated with flexible plans and, accordingly, will jump on the bandwagon. In the 1990s, more companies will have philosophies similar to Coca-Cola Company. C. Ron Chelley, director of corporate employee benefits, said, "Our primary motive in adopting flexible benefits was to insure that we would continue to be able to attract a high caliber workforce" (Baker, 1991). The cost savings of its Select plan was a positive side benefit.

In the future, a key challenge within the area of benefit plan administration will be the critical need to change or update current benefit plans to meet the diverse needs of a demographically disparate population. The U.S. labor force and population has changed considerably in the last 20 years. An increasing number of women in the labor force, higher divorce rates, and an increase in births outside of marriage have led to an increase in less traditional families. The realization of the changing workforce and the future implications was the primary driving force behind the introduction of flexible benefits. Clearly, characteristics and corresponding by-products of the introduction of flexible benefits have served to address the key issues that HRM professionals will need to tackle within the benefits arena.

Not only will there be a limited supply of highly educated/highly skilled workers but also the workforce will be even more diverse. Estimates say that by the year 2000, some 65 percent of new entrants to the workforce will be women, only 15 percent of the available new workers will be white males, and over 75 percent of all families will be dual career families (Guinn, 1989). These changing demographics, including a greater proportion of women and particularly mothers with young children, will require companies to offer benefits that meet these employees' diverse needs. In particular, a life-cycle benefit orientation will be necessary. Accordingly, cafeteria plans will need to constantly evolve to meet their changing needs.

Benefits that appear to be state of the art in 1993, such as child care, elderly care, legal services, adoption assistance, hearing care, financial counseling, and discounted heart and liver transplants (currently offered by PepsiCo) will become standard over the next decade or so. In fact, benefits may become just as important or more important to employees as salary.

The aging of the population, as Baby Boomers and yuppies get older, will make elder care benefits particularly necessary as a flexible benefit offering. Long-term care insurance plans as well as gray area benefits, such as job sharing and flextime, will be important for individuals who need to take care of aging parents. Other benefits that will be expanded include employee assistance programs, educational saving, and saving for first mortgages. Multi-purpose flexible spending accounts may also emerge, whereby employees could use the funds for different purposes at different stages of their lives. Reimbursement funds may also be funded by employers in lieu of wage increases. As with salary, benefits may also become performance based rather than based on seniority, age, and life situation.

The never ending quest for cost containment must continue in the years ahead. The key challenge is how to deliver desired benefits without continuing to dump extra costs on employees. As employers limit their benefit liabilities, employees will have to pick up increasingly larger shares of benefit costs. Even Blue Cross/Blue Shield no longer pays all total health insurance costs for employees. Increasing pressure on employees will cause more consumerism as greater cost consciousness by workers encourages them to shop for reduced prices, particularly for economic health care providers. Companies will reward employees' efforts for cost containment. Current cost containment measures will continue and will likely accelerate. Concurrent reviews, mandatory second surgical opinions, pre-admission testing, and other procedures will become standard practice. Additionally, managed flex, that is flexible benefits that encourage managed care, will be the norm.

Other efforts to reduce or stabilize health care costs will include having a medical team on site for preventive health care maintenance; the pursuit of alternate delivery systems such as surgical centers, preferred provider organizations (PPOs), hospices, home health care and birthing centers; and implementing wellness programs.

Wellness programs, in particular, seem to have high potential to help reduce spiraling medical costs. Paying for employees' health club memberships may become an important wellness benefit. Baker Hughes Inc., a company that provides products and services to the petroleum industry, introduced a wellness program in 1990 after a task force discovered that the majority of health care charges were a result of employees' lifestyles. They implemented a $10 surcharge on tobacco users and initiated wellness check-ups. A non-smoking employee who passes his or her wellness physical receives a $100 pre-tax credit annually. Over three to five years, BHI estimates it will save $2.4 million annually due to the wellness program (Baker, 1991). Findings from a five-year study of over 11,000 Johnson & Johnson employees showed that the wellness program that they have in place saves about

$1 million annually through improved productivity, reduced absentee-ism, and lower health care costs (Shadovitz, 1988).

Unless benefit costs and health care costs stabilize or are reduced over time, there may be a shift toward more contingent or part-time workers in order for companies to reduce their benefit spending in the future. The hiring of part time workers has already begun in a number of organizations and will likely increase in the coming years.

In the future, it will also be necessary to continue an ongoing communication effort to ensure that employees have a greater understanding of benefits and thus are more conscientious toward usage. More conscientious employees are less likely to take benefits for granted and over utilize them. The real challenge for corporations is to dispel the mindset of diminishing entitlement of benefits and encourage employees to regard such compensation as part of a partnership in controlling health care costs (Duggan, 1992). Because companies can no longer afford to offer the widespread coverage U.S. workers have come to expect, employees need to expect less from their companies and learn to budget for health care in the same way as they budget for clothes, food, or any other living expense (Baker, 1991).

Another area that will become increasingly important in the benefits administration area is the subject of retirement benefits. With the over 65 population expected to increase from the current level of 32 million individuals to nearly 40 million by 2010 (Thompson, 1991), retirement benefits need to be reassessed. A number of companies are initiating flexible benefits for retirees in an effort to cap their exposure. While most companies are reluctant to tackle current retirees, future retirees will likely see changes in their benefits packages. Moving retirees to flexible benefits may balance the unwelcome news of cutbacks while allowing more effective monitoring of costs. In many cases, flexible options may be chosen immediately upon retirement and may not be able to be changed after that point in time. Only a few companies (TRW, Pillsbury, Quaker Oats, Vons) have moved to flexible benefits for existing retirees with defined contributions. Retirement benefits are also getting increased attention because of new Financial Accounting Standards Board (FASB) rulings that require that companies put aside monies for current and future medical costs, thus impacting pre-tax earnings. Companies must also record future retirement expenses as current liabilities on the balance sheet.

A great deal of uncertainty exists and a lot of questions remain unanswered concerning the future of flexible benefit plans and employee benefits in general. In the near future, specific types and levels of health benefits will likely be mandated by the government for all Americans (as evidenced by President Clinton's efforts to develop a national health plan). This nationalized health care system could cause significant changes in flexible benefit programs, specifically flexible spending accounts (FSAs). Government regulations will also likely change benefits like FSAs with a potential loss of their tax benefits. FSAs are considered unfair subsidies that benefit individuals with higher incomes disproportionately. Medicare funding may also have an impact as recent estimates predict that Medicare will go broke in two years.

Organizations will continue to face increasing pressure to provide benefits. Several reasons why employers will continue to face increasing pressure to provide benefits follow.

A major reason is that federal and state governments want to shift many of the social costs for health care and other expenditures to employers. This shift would relieve some of the budgetary pressures facing legislators to raise taxes and cut government spending.

Also, demographic changes in the United States mean that more workers will need child care and older citizens will require more health care. Mandated benefit coverage will continue to force employers to fund more of these benefit costs.

To date, employer reactions to efforts to mandate benefits have been swift and vehement. Employers emphasize that small businesses are more heavily burdened because they have smaller staffs to handle the increased work of benefit administration. Fears about the costs of providing the mandated benefits also trigger the reaction. One study estimated that labor costs for businesses would increase at least $40 billion per year if all of the mandated benefits proposed were enacted (*Nation's Business*, 1988). As the U.S. workforce ages and becomes more diverse, other benefit issues will arise in which mandatory benefit coverage may be attempted or may occur. Undoubtedly, employers also will continue to resist and lobby against efforts to mandate benefits.

In the future, benefit administration will take a total compensation approach as there is a further blurring of what defines pay versus benefits. When hiring individuals, salary and benefit estimates will likely be combined to give a total compensation dollar amount. With the competitive nature of the workplace, it will be increasingly important to regularly assess and update the current benefit program via obtaining ongoing employee feedback. HRM professionals must take a proactive approach and always be looking toward next generation benefits. It will also be important to assess how each company compares relative to key competitors in its industry and market. With the anticipated changes in benefits, HRM professionals will need greater expertise in a number of areas, such as tax accountant, attorney, and effective forecaster. These challenges will necessitate better planning and objective setting by HRM professionals with a greater long-term strategic focus.

Probably the most important challenge for HRM professionals and other organizational managers in the future is the effective management of benefit programs. When top managers make benefit and services decisions, they must consider the following facts: mandated programs *must* be funded; there is little evidence that benefits and services really motivate performance — nor do they necessarily increase satisfaction; most employees view benefits and services as entitlements; unions, competitors, and industry trends continue to pressure managers to provide or increase voluntary benefits; and costs of benefits and services continue to escalate dramatically.

To manage the benefit program effectively, HRM professionals should ensure that their organizations follow these steps:

Develop objectives and a benefit strategy (pacesetter, comparable benefits, or minimum benefits).

Involve employees and unions in benefit decisions (find out what those involved desire in benefits and involve union leadership when the organization is unionized).

Communicate the benefits effectively (various communications media can be used: employee handbooks, company newspapers, magazines or newsletters, booklets, bulletin boards, annual reports, payroll stubbs, employee reports, filmstrips, cassettes, open houses, and meetings with supervisors and employees).

Monitor the costs closely (in addition to considering costs in choice of benefits, it is vital that managers make sure the programs are administered correctly — like reviewing insurance claims and using computerized administration procedures).

Together, HRM professionals will find that these four steps will improve the effectiveness of any benefit program.

Finally, HRM professionals will need to be increasingly sensitive to issues of equity. As benefit programs are developed and proposed in response to changes in demographics and a more global marketplace, it is particularly important that differences in benefits among groups of employees be justifiable and readily explained. In the end, because it will be increasingly difficult to anticipate every circumstance that might arise in the administration of a given benefit program, HRM professionals should keep good records of decisions made in order to treat people consistently and to clarify policies when necessary. Such record keeping can help the HRM department identify practices that need to be curtailed.

CONCLUSION

A review of where the organization has been is generally a good place to start in order to determine where it is headed. Sixty years ago, benefits were equal to about 1 percent of salary; today they are more than 40 percent. Additionally, the variety of benefits offered has increased just as dramatically. From a short vacation to an offering so varied that they are referred to as cafeteria plans, the package of the future must reflect the needs of the diverse workforce.

The continuing trend of increasing numbers of women in the U.S. workforce will, likewise, continue the trend of benefits targeted at their needs and accommodations for their situations. Programs that, 20 years ago, were considered revolutionary, such as child care, split shifts, and flexible hours, are now considered standard fare. Consider a workforce that by 2005 will be 64 percent female, and two-thirds of whom will be responsible for the care of a child. Such numbers will eventually generate political power that will produce major workplace reform legislation. The number of female legislators is beginning to increase, reflecting the growing political strength of this group. This, along with the numbers of females in the workforce, will create a critical mass, sufficient to change, radically and forever, corporate America.

The changes will be gradual but dramatic with more emphasis placed on child care issues. Workers may be willing to accept lower wages for payment-in-kind such as an on-site nursery.

One of the most important fringe benefits provided by employers is the payment of health insurance premiums and other health expenses. Health costs have, by far, outstripped all other costs and have greatly contributed to overall employee costs. Over the past four years, the cost of health insurance for single coverage has increased at a compound rate of over 17 percent in one city. This statistic is in line with the national average, which was reported at greater than 17 percent for a three-year period. The result of this ever increasing cost is that, within 20 years, health costs will account for 100 percent of payroll costs (Merdinger & Botkin, 1992). Perhaps a more telling statistic, in terms of what the consumer pays for health costs, is that it has been estimated that each automobile built in the United States carries as part of its price tag $1,000 in health care costs paid for the employees of the automobile industry. The implications, with respect to the competitiveness of U.S. products, are obvious.

In helping to draft the benefit policy statement, HRM professionals see that two general objectives must be kept in mind. First, the organization's overall welfare must be given primary consideration. Second, employee benefits must be competitive on the international level if a multinational corporation is to attract and retain the dynamic, aggressive kind of leadership that is required to be successful (Krupp, 1986).

In the final analysis, businesses will do what is necessary to survive. If this requires them to provide the benefits, it is the mission of the HRM professional to provide the means to satisfy employees. To summarize, examining the role of the HRM professional with respect to this issue raises two central concepts: survey people to find out what they need and have a package that is flexible enough to accommodate the needs of a diverse workforce. This should serve HRM well even as the environment changes.

REFERENCES

Baker, E. L. 1991, December. Cafeteria compensation. *Across the Board*: 48–54.

Cascio, W. F. & Serapio, M. M., Jr. 1991, Winter. Human resources system in an international alliance: The undoing of a done deal? *Organizational Dynamics 19*: 63–74.

Caulfield, S. C. 1990, December. Benefits in a changing workforce. *Employee Benefits Journal*, pp. 19–20.

Clements, M. 1993, March 12. DuPont shifts burden onto employees. *USA Today*, p. 2B.

Cohen, J. 1976. The evolution and growth of social security. In J. P. Goldberg, W. Haber, & R. S. Oswald (eds.). *Federal policies and worker status since the thirties*. Madison, WI: Industrial Relations Research Association.

Duggan, P. 1992, March. A new age for flexible benefits. *Risk Management*, pp. 95–99.

Ehrbar, A. 1993, March 16. The price of progress. *The Wall Street Journal*, p. A1

French, W. 1990. *Human resource management* (2nd ed.). Boston, MA: Houghton Mifflin.

Geisel, J. 1990, May 7. Workforce changes beget 'family' benefits. *Business Insurance*, p. 3.

Guinn, S. L. 1989, December. The changing workforce. *Training & Development Journal*, pp. 36–39.

Haslinger, J. A. & Shannon, E. S. 1992, June. Designing flexible credits: marketplace forces can help control costs. *Pension World*, pp. 25–27.

Kertesz, L. 1991, August 19. Benefits at forefront of a new age. *Business Insurance*, pp. 12–13.

Konesh, E. E. & Nichol, V. 1992. The effects of on-site child care on employee attitudes and performance. *Personnel Psychology 45*: 485–507.

Krupp, N. B. 1986, September. Managing benefits in multinational organizations. *Personnel 63*: 76.

Lawlor, J. 1993, July 20. Offbeat perks can perk up workers. *USA Today*, p. B2.

Ledvinka, J. 1982. *Federal regulation of personnel and human resource management.* Boston: Kent Publishing Company.

Lefkovich, J. L. 1992, June. Business responds to elder-care needs. *HRMagazine*, pp. 103–8.

McCaffery, R. M. 1983. *Managing the employee benefits program*. New York: American Management Association.

Merdinger, P. & Botkin, P. 1992, January. Times "a changing" as benefits continue to reflect society. *Pension World*, pp. 18–20.

Milkovich, G. T. & Boudreau, J. W. 1994. *Human resource management* (7th ed.). Boston, MA: Irwin.

Miller, M. A. 1992, March. Time-off benefits in small establishments. *Monthly Labor Review*, pp. 3–8.

Nation's Business. 1988, April. How costly are mandated benefits? pp. 12–14.

Omaha World-Herald. 1993a, February 28. Xerox pushed HMOs hard, p. G1.

Omaha World-Herald. 1993b, April 11. Perks can make the difference, p. 1G.

O'Neill, K. J. & Tocco, A. L. 1990, March/April. Are child care assistance programs a critical investment? *Financial Executive*, pp. 19–23.

Shadovitz, D. October, 1988. Six ways to cut employee health costs. *Financial Manager*, pp. 58–62.

Shalowitz, D. 1992, April 27. Benefits administration: More companies discover family-friendly benefits can help them save money. *Business Insurance*, pp. 3–7.

Thompson, R. 1991, July. Switching to flexible benefits. *Nation's Business*, pp. 16–23.

Thompson, R. 1992, February. Benefits update; costs for firms set a record. *Nation's Business*, pp. 42–43.

U.S. Chamber of Commerce. 1993. *Employee benefits 1993*. Washington, DC: Chamber of Commerce.

Weisendanger, B. 1990, July. Child care groups up. *Sales & Marketing Management*, pp. 92, 96.

Zarowin, S. 1991, December. How to find and keep the best employees in the 21st century. *Journal of Accountancy*, pp. 34–38.

6

Human Resources Information Systems and Human Resources Management

The issue to be discussed in this chapter is computers and human resources management (HRM). Why are computers an issue in HRM? To answer this question, we must first understand the underlying reason for the existence of business organizations, which is to maximize profits. To maximize profits, organizations must not only maximize revenues but also minimize costs. The most productive way to minimize costs is to become more efficient. This is why computers are an HRM issue. If used properly, computers, with their speed and accuracy, can increase the efficiency of the HRM department, not to mention the entire company, thereby maximizing revenues while minimizing costs.

In order to understand the impact computers can have on HRM, we must analyze the sub-issues of computers in HRM. Some of the more important issues are the need for computers in the HRM department, what to include in an HRM computer system, implementing the system, maintaining the system, and finally, ensuring that the system is secure.

Are computers needed in HRM? In short, the answer is yes. The driving force for computers in HRM is increasing efficiency. There are many reasons HRM must become more efficient. One of them is caused by organizational growth and/or consolidation. The larger an organization is, the harder it is to maintain, manage, and use employee information. Richard Fremon (Warren, Gorham & Lamont, 1992) states that "the most important characteristic of the computer is that it can be programmed to do repetitive operations rapidly, reliably, cheaply and tirelessly." This is important when dealing with a large number of employee records. Another reason HRM must become more efficient has to do with preparing the various reports periodically required by government agencies, such as the Equal Employment Opportunity

Commission or Office of Federal Contract Compliance Procedures. The computer's ability to store, as well as quickly process and access large amounts of data, make it particularly suited for this task. Finally, in this increasingly competitive world, organizations are beginning to recognize that one of the keys to efficiency and success is the proper management of their human resources. To do this, HRM must minimize the time requirements of its administrative and record keeping duties and maximize its time allocated for strategically planning the usage of human resources for both short-term and long-term projects. An HRM department that is not bogged down with employee record maintenance and report writing can be more proactive in the organization. Not only does the HRM department become more productive but also the human resources of the organization become more productive as well.

HUMAN RESOURCES INFORMATION SYSTEM DEFINED

The information requirements of a human resources planning system are staggering. In addition to basic human resources data, managers need instant information about related corporate financial, planning, business, and operational factors. They also need to update demographic and statistical data, make projections and forecasts, show trends, test models, perform measurements and statistical analysis, and generate reports, including graphics.

To accomplish all this and retain a measure of sanity, organizations and their managers need a computerized system, known generically as a human resources information system (HRIS). HRIS is any organized approach for obtaining relevant and timely information on which to base human resources decisions. HRIS is an automated means of collecting, analyzing, and reporting personnel data quickly, inexpensively, and safely. An effective HRIS is crucial to sound human resources decision making; it typically employs computers and other sophisticated technologies to process data that reflect the day-to-day operations of a company, organized in the form of information to facilitate the decision-making process. Information requirements associated with the HRM function are numerous. For example, assessing the personnel supply involves keeping track of employees throughout the organization. Recruitment, selection, training and development, career management, compensation, and labor relations programs also require timely and accurate information for decision making. Furthermore, personnel reporting requirements of governmental legislation can be time-consuming, expensive, and cumbersome endeavors without an HRIS that provides rapid retrieval and consolidation of pertinent data. A full-function, top-of-the-line personal computer-based HRIS can handle all personnel record keeping and reporting requirements, plus several related functions. It can help HRM professionals identify future needs and immediate requirements.

An HRIS need not be complex or even computerized. HRIS can be as informal as the payroll records and time cards of a small boutique or restaurant, or as extensive and formal as the computerized human resources data banks of major manufacturers, banks, and governments. HRISs can support planning with information for labor supply and demand forecasts; staffing with information on equal employment, separations, and applicant qualifications; and development with information on training program costs and trainee work performance. HRISs can also support compensation with information on pay increases, salary forecasts, and pay budgets; and labor and employee relations with information on contract negotiations and employee assistance needs. In every case, their purpose is to provide information that is either required by human resources stakeholders, or supports human resources decisions.

The main components of a HRIS are the database, the hardware, and the software. The heart of the system is the database, where all the information is stored. The construction of this database controls the ease of data storage and retrieval. The next component is the hardware, or the actual computer system that the HRIS runs on. The hardware consists of a central processor, disk drives, monitors, scanners, printers, and other peripherals. The hardware can consist of any computer ranging from a large mainframe, on which resides many other computer functions to minicomputers that might be tied together into a network of users in various departments that can access data simultaneously. The hardware might be personal computers (PCs), either single, stand-alone units, or a group of PCs tied into a network, with the ability to share data and programs among themselves. The software consists of the packages of program instructions that tell the computer(s) how to process the data. The price of software can vary from several hundred dollars for single-function, single-user PC programs, to $500,000 and up for highly-sophisticated, multi-functional mainframe computer programs requiring management information systems (MIS) departments to maintain and run them. Software is being developed every month, so new applications are being written as this book is being written.

HISTORY OF HUMAN RESOURCES INFORMATION SYSTEMS

The issue of computers in HRM departments is not revolutionary. The many different applications — some currently utilized to their full potential, others still in the planning and testing phases, and still other applications not yet conceived — are what will carry HRM departments into the twenty-first century. It is exactly this uncertainty concerning the precise role of computers in HRM that poses the biggest challenge for the future.

HRM departments have historically been paper driven operations. From the potential employee's resume and signed application form, to the pension fund records and resignation letter of the retiring employee, collecting and filing paper documents has been the norm for HRM departments. Fortunately, manual record keeping is finally beginning to lose favor among HRM professionals. But simply deciding to automate is not enough. Just determining which pieces of the enormous quantities of information usually found in even a small HRM department should be stored in a new computer system can be a formidable and expensive task. Further, there is no single, best HRIS. Companies must assess their own needs and choose a product that meets those needs and is economical as well.

The growth of HRISs has been strongly influenced by the growth of computer technology and by government regulations (Kavanagh, Gueutal, & Tannenbaum, 1990; Ceriello & Freeman, 1991). The emergence of HRISs began slowly in the 1960s and a company's information about hiring, firing, promoting, transferring, and paying its employees resided in paper files. It was difficult to use this information for planning or decision making because one had to go through each file by hand and find the needed information. Applications related to HRM were written primarily for expensive, large, mainframe computers that required the users to be experts in computer technology.

The introduction of a company's information system was not without considerable resistance by the employees involved in the change. Although advantages of automating an HRM department may seem clear to an outsider, convincing the employees involved was not so simple. HRM managers had to decide which areas of their operation would be the most likely candidates for change. In many cases in the 1960s, the payroll function was the first to automate. During the 1970s, mainframe computers became more widely available. They were used to assist with the calculation of cost data, such as accounts receivable or inventory control.

Automating the payroll department first may have actually been the best choice, despite the limited HRM capabilities of such systems. Employees who were reluctant to give up the old manual ways of conducting business might have been more motivated when success involved the proper printing and disbursement of their own paychecks.

By starting with the payroll records, every employee in the entire company was necessarily entered into the computer system. This created a powerful database of information. Although, as stated above, HRM capabilities of these early payroll systems were limited, the fact that all employee records were part of the database meant that some reports, formerly done manually, could then be generated in a matter of minutes. This faster information processing was one of the greatest advantages of installing an HRIS.

Tax reports, mailing labels, and some basic statistical reports concerning salary information were just a few of the possible HRM applications of these early systems. Even the relatively simple task of changing an employee's address was further simplified by this automation.

Unfortunately, these early computer systems ran primarily on expensive mainframes. Professional computer programmers were needed to keep those systems operational. And changes to a system, however slight, might cost thousands of dollars. Most programs were tailored to the individual company who purchased the system, making companies even more dependent on professional programmers.

The explosion of computer technology in the late 1970s and throughout the 1980s lowered the cost of mainframe systems, of PCs with the same storage capabilities and data-manipulation speed as mainframes, and of software applications targeted for HRM. Thus, even smaller companies were able to afford HRISs.

DESIGNING AND CREATING A HUMAN RESOURCES INFORMATION SYSTEM

To date, no single best way to design and implement an HRIS has emerged. For our purposes, an HRIS should be designed to provide information that is:

Timely — A manager must have access to up-to-date information.

Accurate — A manager must be able to rely on the accuracy of the information provided.

Concise — A manager can absorb only so much information at any one time.

Relevant — A manager should receive only the information needed in a particular situation.

Complete — A manager should receive complete, not partial, information.

The absence of even one of these characteristics reduces the effectiveness of an HRIS and complicates the decision-making process. A system possessing all of these characteristics enhances the ease and accuracy of the decision-making process.

It is widely agreed that the first and most important step is specifying the system requirements, especially the target users and the decisions the system is designed to support. These specifications include decisions about the type of data to collect, the amount of data to collect, how to collect the data, and when to collect it.

The next step is business system design. It involves answering questions about who will use the system, how they will access it, how it will be updated, and so on. Technical design includes software system development and programming. Then the system is tested at certain locations and evaluated. Once in operation, the system is evaluated, improvements are planned, and the process begins again (Milkovich & Boudreau, 1994).

A more detailed description of a design process of an HRIS that will conform to the HRIS criteria presented earlier includes the following four steps: study the present system; develop a priority of information that key stakeholders need; develop the new HRIS; and choose a computer.

1. Study the present system. In defining the requirements or assessing the existing information system, three questions need to be answered: What is the present flow of information? How is the information used? How valuable is this information to decision making (Adams, 1990).

2. Develop a priority of information that stakeholders need. Once the current system is thoroughly understood, it should be used to develop information priorities. A manager must have certain information in order to make proper decisions. Other information is nice to have, but is not essential to the manager's decision making. The HRIS design must ensure provision of high-priority information. Data having a lower priority should be generated only if the benefits exceed the costs of producing it.

One approach is to have individual managers develop their own priority lists and then integrate them into a list for the entire organization as a whole. In such cases, the needs of the entire organization may well be the controlling factor.

3. Develop the new HRIS. The organization-wide priority list should govern design for the HRIS. Information judged not worth the cost should not be included. A system of required reports should be developed and diagrammed. The entire organization is treated as a unit to eliminate duplication of information.

4. Choose a computer. In today's organization, it is reasonable to assume that the HRIS of most organizations will be computerized. Since the human resources software for PCs is almost always the responsibility of the HRM department, HRM professionals should be computer literate. Such knowledge increases the likelihood that the right computer will be chosen to help meet the organization's HRIS needs.

These steps are not separate and distinct — in fact, they overlap considerably. Development of an HRIS is not merely a matter of properly designing the system. Creating a smoothly functioning and operational HRIS is virtually impossible without a major commitment from top management. However, following the four steps can result in an HRIS design that could become an effective system if supported strongly by top management. The design of an effective HRIS would also produce several important reports and forecasts related to business operations. For example, routine reports that would go to different levels of managers (that is, weekly and monthly employment status reports may be sent to the general manager, whereas quarterly reports may be forwarded to top management), exception and on-demand reports, and forecasts.

In many of today's organizations, employees, line managers, and a variety of HRM and other staff use the information in the HRIS directly through their PCs, telephones, or in written form. This trend is likely to continue with users demanding a more active role in the design of the HRIS. In any case, the design of an HRIS must meet the HRM needs of the organization. Among the hundreds of computer applications available today, three types have been used in HRM: transaction processing, reporting, and tracking; decision support systems; and expert systems (Broderick & Boudreau, 1992; Lawler, 1992).

Transaction Processing, Reporting, and Tracking

Transaction processing refers to computations and calculations used to review and document human resources decisions and practices. This includes documenting employee relocation, payroll expenses, and training course enrollments. This type of application helps companies comply with regulations, such as federal laws, or track adherence to company policies. For example, the Equal Opportunity Act (1991) requires employers with 50 or more employees to provide the government (in the EEO-1 report) with information regarding employees' race and gender by job category.

Decision Support Systems

Decision support systems are designed to help managers solve problems. They usually include a what-if feature, which allows users to see how outcomes change when the assumptions or the data change. The systems are useful, for example, in helping organizations determine the number of new hires they need based on different turnover rates or the availability of employees with technical skills given a change in customer or product demands.

Expert Systems

Expert systems have three elements:

a knowledge base that contains facts, figures, and rules about a specific subject;

a decision-making capability that, imitating an expert's reasoning ability, draws conclusions from those facts and figures to solve problems and answer questions; and

a user interface that gathers and gives information to the person using the system.

Expert systems are designed to stimulate the decision-making process of human experts. The system recommends actions that the user can take based on the information the user provides. The recommended actions are those that a human expert would take in a situation with similar characteristics.

The use of expert systems in HRM is relatively new. Some companies use them to help employees decide how to allocate monies for benefits or to help managers schedule and determine the labor requirements of projects. In reality, the major use of HRIS is in the area of human resources planning.

Human resources planning involves four distinct phases or stages: situation analysis or environmental scanning, forecasting human resources demands, human resources supply analysis, and action plan development (Page & Van De Voort, 1989). HRISs are typically subdivided into three major categories for inclusion into human resource planning: operational systems, tactical systems, and strategic systems (Schultheis & Sumner, 1989).

Operational Systems

Operational systems supply the manager with data to support the personnel decisions that occur regularly. The payroll subsystem of the financial system collects and reports data pertaining to operational human resource needs. Position information systems identify each position in the organization, the job category in which the position is classified, and the employee currently assigned to the position. Employer information systems consist of a personnel file and a skills inventory that contains information about each employee's work experience, work preference, test scores, interests, and special skills. The employee evaluation information system consists of performance appraisals, and the performance and productivity measures used in employee evaluations. The government reporting information system includes all data and reports required from affirmative action and equal opportunity laws, Occupational Safety and Health Administration data, and immigration and nationality data. The applicant selection and placement systems are used to screen, evaluate, select, and place job applicants. To ensure legal compliance, these procedures must be fully documented and carried out in a structured manner.

Tactical Information Systems

Tactical information systems provide managers with support for decisions that emphasize the allocation of resources. The job analysis and design information systems describe the jobs, specify the skills required, provide Position Analysis Questionnaires and task inventories, and are useful in developing and refining job titles, the salary structure, and promotion paths. Recruiting information systems provide the organization with a bank of qualified applicants from which it may fill vacant positions. This system is necessary to collect and process the many types of information necessary to construct the recruiting plan. Compensation and benefit information systems are used in monitoring work attendance, time worked, overtime, payroll deductions; building wage structures; tying wage structures to results of wage surveys and incentive pay systems; and administering benefit options. Employee training and development systems must administer training programs so that they meet the needs of the jobs that are available, and are directed to those persons interested and capable of benefitting from them. The labor negotiations information system must be able to track disciplinary action and grievances, what-if scenarios on spreadsheet applications during negotiations, and have on-line capabilities to access Bureau of Labor Statistics and labor law information networks.

Strategic Human Resources Information Systems

These systems ensure that the organization has the right kinds and the right number of people in the right places at the right times to achieve its objectives. The first strategic planning function is manpower planning. Manpower planning involves identifying the human resources needed to meet the objective specified in the strategic plan. This means forecasting the supply and demand of the required workforce. The second strategic planning function is to develop the policies, procedures, and activities that will achieve the human resource needs spelled out in the manpower plan. These include job analysis, design, and recruiting.

HUMAN RESOURCES INFORMATION SYSTEM CHALLENGES FOR HUMAN RESOURCES MANAGEMENT

A few challenges organizations and HRM must meet when dealing with the need for an HRIS are finding a system that can make the HRM department more efficient, managing the costs associated with a computer system, convincing upper level managers that a computer system is needed, and addressing the security and privacy concerns.

Will the Human Resources Information System Increase Efficiency?

There are many HRM computer systems that will make the HRM department more efficient and productive. An HRIS can increase efficiency by providing both direct and indirect benefits (Walker, 1993).

Some of the direct benefits are:

total displacement of staff by eliminating task specific staff;

partial displacement of staff caused by the reduced time spent on a specific task or function (increased productivity);

reduction or elimination of costs associated with outside firms performing various human resources functions;

improved data quality and accuracy;

faster response to manager and employee questions (improved service);

reduced overtime, clerical expenses, and contractor payments; and

reduced space requirements.

For these direct benefits, it is easy to see how costs will be reduced, efficiency increased, and the range of services expanded. Now for the less obvious, indirect benefits of automating the human resources department via an HRIS:

faster, more reliable, and accurate information for decision making, promotion and transfer tracking, payroll, and benefit administration;

comprehensive data on the work force throughout the organization;

reduced litigation costs with the availability of more complete and accurate employee data;

faster response times to manager and employee questions;

faster turn around time on medical claims payments; and

reduced employee turnover.

These indirect benefits are often only measurable in terms of employee morale and increased speed and accessibility to information. These benefits are difficult to measure in dollars.

What Are the Costs Associated with a Human Resources Information System?

Although there are many benefits that can be obtained through the usage of an HRIS, there is also a very real and important disadvantage. The largest obstacle an organization must consider when contemplating an HRIS is its associated costs. Some costs affiliated with automation in HRM are hardware, software, installation, training, consulting, and maintenance. Hardware related costs include PCs or mainframes, monitors, printers, and ergonomically designed work station furniture that enables the equipment to be operated by employees over long periods of time without incurring health problems. The budget for software should cover three types of programs: general office packages including word processing, spread sheets, and graphics; utility programs including antivirus, backup, and hard-disk management packages; and HRM applications software (O'Connell, 1992b). Programs are available for practically every human resources function imaginable and will be discussed later. Costs pertaining to installation are the initial loading of employee information, software customization, vendor support for setting up hardware and configuring software, and lastly, developing or redesigning forms to be used in conjunction with the new software. One of the necessary and often overlooked costs of an HRIS is training. Underestimating the need and budget for training will result in underutilization of the HRIS, which leads to the high costs of lost productivity. Another cost to consider is the use of consultants. Consultants are necessary to provide the expertise needed to plan, select, and implement hardware and software. Finally, maintenance costs must be assessed. O'Connell (1992b) says that "maintenance fees for software can cost from 10 to 20 percent of the purchase price" (p. 31). Other maintenance costs include hardware maintenance, future expansion of the system, and periodic training. When added together, the costs associated with an HRM computer system can be quite formidable. This leads to the next challenge — convincing upper management that a computer system is needed.

Is Top Management Convinced of the Need for a Computer System?

Convincing management of the need for automation in HRM is very important because management often holds the purse strings. Few HRM departments are empowered to make such an expensive capital investment without upper management approval. Three hurdles HRM managers must overcome to gain acceptance and funding are the lack of political support, the lack of strong HRM commitment, and finally, the inability to prove some of the cost savings claimed.

The lack of political support for HRM automation stems from the belief that HRM is not essential because it does not generate any revenue. Another reason is that line managers do not fully appreciate the amount of data handled and the paperwork that is generated by the HRM department.

The second hurdle is caused by barriers inside the HRM department itself. Because automation in HRM is relatively new in most organizations, many of the older and senior managers are not as computer literate as their counterparts in accounting and finance. O'Connell (1992b) notes that "many (HR managers) have shied away from learning about computers and their impact on operations, so they are unable to articulate their needs" (p. 32). O'Connell also asserts that thorough business analyses that present a rationale for automation are often not done.

Finally, the benefits of an HRIS given earlier are frequently hard to estimate. This problem is especially evident when attempting to estimate indirect benefits. More importantly, these benefits are likely to be viewed with skepticism by upper managers. Walker (1993) explains: "Managers may doubt the credibility of the entire document if it appears to be 'padded' with superfluous, unsubstantiated benefits" (p. 241).

How Are Security and Privacy Issues Related to Human Resources Information Systems Addressed?

While the benefits of ready access to computerized HRM information are often compelling, this technology creates new obligations and responsibilities for the HRM professional. What does security mean when talking about computer systems? Computer security has two aspects: protecting against unauthorized access to sensitive personnel data and protecting against data tampering from both people and virus programs. Security is an issue because privacy is an area of growing concern among employees, managers, and government. Some states have even enacted privacy laws to enforce the issue. It is also an issue because the computer system's database represents a large investment in both time and money and should be protected from tampering.

Ensuring security is a challenge to the HRM department in two ways. First, with the increasing reliance on computerized information systems, sensitive information is becoming more centralized. We can see that, when combined with the user friendly microcomputers and their expanding networking capabilities, the information is continually becoming more accessible by more people. The second challenge is to protect data from tampering in the form of computer viruses. A computer virus is a program that attacks and damages both programs and data files. They are introduced into the system through computerized bulletin boards or floppy disks.

HRM managers are answering the challenge of securing their data by employing several methods. Access to data files is being limited to personnel through the use of multilevel passwords. With multilevel password protection, one person will be able to access a certain level of information where another person, with a need for greater access, will be able to access a wider range of information. Other techniques to limit access are limiting access to terminals with key card access to the computer room or by simply installing locks on computer terminals.

The data stored on computerized systems is often confidential and private and should be accessible only to approved individuals under controlled conditions. Every data field included in the human resources database should be there for a clear business reason. For example, managers should question the reason for including information regarding employees' religious beliefs or political affiliations. HRM professionals should periodically audit employee databases and remove outdated, irrelevant, or inaccurate information.

One of the major advantages of HRIS is also a potential liability. Employees have access to information that can be useful for decision making. However, most of that information (for example, salary information, financial account information, personal information) needs to remain private. Various laws regulate the extent to which employees, company representatives, and parties outside the company can have access to the information in employee records. Therefore, HRM professionals must be aware of all relevant privacy legislation.

HRM professionals must also ensure that their organizations develop policies regarding the disclosure of information to government agencies, credit companies, and marketing organizations. The most difficult questions relating to information disclosure involve information provided to other companies about former employees. HRM professionals must ensure that neither they nor the organization's managers provide information that could be judged slanderous by the courts.

Protecting the information system against unauthorized access is important because employees can often use PCs to link up with mainframe computers where confidential information is stored. Most software packages provide features, such as passwords, that limit employees' ability to view and change specific types of data.

Another challenge for HRM professionals related to the HRIS is computer viruses. A virus is a destructive, unauthorized computer code that someone has intentionally built into a piece of hardware or software. Viruses erase data stored in memory or cause pictures or diagrams to appear on computer monitors, thereby keeping the computer's operating system from functioning. Viruses usually enter computer systems either on purpose (for example, a disgruntled employee) or because naive users have entered a data set or application from a separate storage medium (such as a contaminated floppy disk). To protect against viruses, a virus-detection program should be installed on all computers. These programs identify and destroy viruses before they can cause damage. Viruses are being dealt with by the use of antiviral software and implementing antiviral policies. Antiviral software scans disks and files for viruses and eliminates them when found or alerts the user to their presence. All software applications and disks should be examined by the virus-protection program, particularly if they are from sources outside the organization. Some antiviral policies being implemented are: banning the use of all unauthorized disks and software, limiting employees from taking disks home to use on their own computers, and enforcing the use of backup procedures. The problem with these procedures is that not all people take them seriously, not even HRM managers. However, as time goes on, and more organizations are affected by their lack of a secure computer system, this will change.

Specific steps that HRM professionals should take to secure HRIS are (Adams, 1992):

Train all users how to securely use and handle the equipment, data, and software.

Train employees to sign off PCs after they are through using them.

Do not allow passwords to be shared. Change them frequently.

Run software through a virus-detection program before using it on the system.

Ensure that backup copies, data files, software, and printouts are used only by authorized users.

Make backup copies of data files and programs.

Ensure that all software and mainframe applications include an audit trail (a record of the changes and transactions that occur in a system, including when and who performed the changes).

Use edit controls (such as passwords) to limit employees' access to data files and data fields.

The growing use of computers in HRM is proof that HRM departments are meeting the challenges of automating HRM. HRM managers are conducting thorough needs analysis in the early planning stages. Some are including the end users and other departments in this analysis. Including these people ensures that the company will get computer systems that will be used, and thereby increase its efficiency, while providing employees and departments with any new services that may be needed both now and in the future. This also minimizes the costly rework and schedule overruns that occur when the system does not perform as desired or expected in the testing phase of implementation. Including end users in such a large undertaking makes sense and will definitely become commonplace in the future. The attitudes of HRM managers are also changing. Automation is not seen as a convenience or a threat but as a necessity to just keep up with the increasing demands on the HRM department by both the government and the organization. By performing studies on the benefits computers can have on HRM, such as the time savings for various HRM tasks, HRM professionals can provide the proof top managers need. The attitudes of top management are also changing. Top management is realizing the impact proper management of their human resources can have on the bottom line. In addition, they realize that automating HRM will give their managers the ability to manipulate and analyze information for more informed decision making. These attitude trends, as well as the need to respond quickly to the business environment, will continue in the future, further ingraining computers into HRM.

What Should Be Included in a Human Resources Information System?

This question poses a challenge to HRM because there is so much out there. There are so many different types of software and hardware to choose from that HRM professionals must really do their homework both in-house with needs analysis, and out of house, finding a system to meet their needs.

The area of HRM automation with the most selection by far is software. The selection of software will be directly determined by the needs of the HRM department and the organization. The following are some different types of software HRM should consider for its computer system. The first type is relational databases. A relational database will reduce the need to enter and maintain duplicate information. Data is entered into the database only once and the computer knows how to find and can combine it to produce reports and analysis. HRM personnel should also consider query programs. One of the most important abilities of the computer system is to provide management with information needed in decision making. A query program will allow managers and employees to do what-if analysis using the information stored in the computer system and to produce unique reports. Finally, HRM professionals must consider what types of applications software are needed. As discussed earlier, the HRIS is a very broad database-like program. Here, applications software would be very specific. O'Connell (1992a) describes the difference between the two as follows:

> While the HRIS focuses on employee records, applications software is designed to support the work of specific human resource functions such as compensation, benefits, training or affirmative action. It is different in many ways from the HRIS. . . . Applications systems are often transaction-driven rather than providing a record of information . . . and are generally much easier to use than an HRIS. (p. 31)

Although there is not as much selection when dealing with hardware, the decision on what to use is no less challenging. The key concern is choosing the right technical platform, that is, mainframe or microcomputer. Both platforms provide advantages and disadvantages. The differentiating factors are the amount of data to be stored, how long it will take to do typical processing for an application, how easy access should be, how many people must have simultaneous access to the information, and cost. Typically, mainframes offer more memory storage, can process large amounts of data faster, are more secure, and allow greater simultaneous access to information. On the other hand, microcomputers are much less expensive and their software is much more user friendly. This user friendliness is the driving force behind the use of microcomputers. Microcomputers, with their spread sheets and databases, allow managers and HRM users to process information, do analysis, and do special report writing without the assistance of computer programmers.

HRM professionals are meeting the challenge of selecting the right software for their organization by performing thorough needs analysis.

The key steps in performing a software needs analysis are as follows: reviewing the current system and procedures, interviewing key users, analyzing the findings, and preparing the document (Adams, 1990).

A very important aspect of this process is considering future needs. What will the system be required to do in the future? Defining these needs and ensuring that they are within the system's capabilities, or that the system is flexible enough that it can be easily updated, can save the organization large modification costs down the road. In the future, there will be orders of magnitudes and more programs and systems to choose from, each with its own subtle differences. This will put more pressure on HRM professionals to do a thorough needs analysis in order to find the software that most closely matches their needs.

HRM professionals have answered the hardware question by combining microcomputers and mainframes to obtain the advantages both platforms have to offer. Silverman (1991) states that "For many organizations, it makes sense to maintain a corporate database on the mainframe and decide how to maximize system functionality through the use of communication technology and PC applications software" (p. 30). This allows time consuming jobs, such as payroll processing, to be done much faster on the mainframe via batch processing while correspondence intensive jobs, such as what-if analysis, can be done in the user friendly environment of the microcomputer. This is the approach that Silverman's company, PHH Corporation, employs. When discussing her company's mainframe software, she states, "They are extremely appropriate for the complex reporting typically done by corporate staff. . . . However, for the many 'search and sort' type reports run on a daily basis, a menu-driven report writer on the PC would be ideal, saving mainframe processing time and facilitating training" (p. 30). The trend today is toward more use of the microcomputers. In the future, with advances in networking and computing technology, the microcomputer will be able to take over more of the current mainframe responsibilities.

How Should a Human Resources Management Computer System Be Implemented?

Implementation of a computer system is the phase that involves installing the hardware and software, converting or entering the initial data, preparing and documenting procedures, and finally, training users. This issue poses a challenge for HRM because, without full implementation, the system may perform but often leaves gaps that are not apparent until reports contain invalid data or inaccurate totals or the systems specialist departs for another position (O'Connell, 1992c).

Implementation is the area where improvement is most needed. However, a number of HRM professionals have learned that a phased implementation of a computer system over a period of time is more advantageous than implementing the system at one time. The phased implementation process allows users to learn and more thoroughly test the subsections of the system. Any problems or shortcomings of the system found in these stages can be dealt with much faster and cheaper than if the problems were discovered during the actual use of the system after installation.

Some areas of implementation that HRM professionals must improve in are testing, procedure documentation, and training. Testing is important because it ensures that there are no glitches in the system and that it performs the desired functions. HRM departments must include many dimensions in the testing phase. A few are: testing to ensure that erroneous data is detected when entered, ensuring files and procedures that have been interrupted can be recovered, checking that data remains accurate once entered and is not corrupted, and determining that the system meets the requirements of the end users. Documenting procedures is also an important implementation requirement needing improvement. These procedures control how data is entered, processed, and distributed. This provides consistency in the way the database is used, which increases the accuracy of the information. Lastly, the HRM department must improve the training of its staff and other users. This training must go beyond which buttons to push and provide users with an understanding of all aspects of the system.

Why Is Maintaining a Computer System an Issue?

Maintenance is important because it protects an organization's sizable investment in an HRIS. Maintenance is a challenge to HRM in several ways. First, maintenance is expensive. Second, HRM professionals must decide on what aspects to include in a maintenance program in order to keep the system up and running in the present and ensure that the system will not be out of date in the future.

A rule of thumb for a system's maintenance costs is 10 to 20 percent of the retail price of the system. HRM professionals and organization mangers generally realize the need for adequate maintenance of large capital investments and, therefore, factor funding into the HRM budget. Typically, maintenance contracts are purchased from the vendor at the same time as the system. This gives the HRM department access to a consultant that is knowledgeable about the system and also provides updates to the software to keep the system current. Software updates are a necessary aspect when we consider, for example, how much changing legislation affects various HRM functions. Other ways mangers are maintaining their computer systems are by providing operating and maintenance procedures. Operating and maintenance procedures ensure that both the hardware and software are not damaged through misuse or neglect. Maintenance procedures also include procedures to periodically create backup disks for the information currently in the system's memory. Backing up memory can save the organization time and money if an accident occurs and information in the system's memory is damaged or lost. The HRM department also provides for training new users. This training, however, is often inadequate and not done periodically to ensure users are maximizing the system's capabilities. HRM managers and staff must also become more creative in maximizing their system's capabilities in the future. With the rapidly changing demands in the business world, the computer system can easily become outdated if users do not devise ways to meet current needs with existing equipment.

How Will Mergers and Acquisitions Affect Human Resources Information Systems?

Mergers and acquisitions (M&As) present certain facets to HRIS that are unique. Flexibility and security are two key issues in M&A control. Client/server data relationships are being established to provide controlled distribution of data while still allowing top management quick access to vital decision-making data (Leckonby, 1992). HRIS can simplify acquisitions in the following areas:

Compensation

Salary codes can be used for both companies to segregate salaries by company. Environmental features of each company may not allow salary mixing.

Employee Benefits

Different companies have different packages that have different characteristics. HRIS can track each company separately if needed.

Pension Plans

Pension plans usually follow an employee to a new company. HRIS can easily track both companies' plans.

Government Compliance Reports

After an acquisition, the makeup of the workforce must meet equal employment opportunity guidelines. HRIS can allow easy data export from the new company to the parent company for reporting purposes.

Divestiture

The challenge here is to be able to segregate data, not integrate it. Keeping individual HRM records makes good business Other issues to consider in M&A activity include staffing levels and restructuring to meet new business demands (Spoor, 1992).

CONCERNS RELATED TO HUMAN RESOURCES INFORMATION SYSTEMS THAT MUST BE ADDRESSED BY HUMAN RESOURCES MANAGEMENT PROFESSIONALS

One concern with the general use of computers that HRM is just beginning to become aware of is health concerns. Bettendorf (1990) says "computer-terminal operators have always complained about the effects of the Video Display Terminals (VDTs) on their vision. . . . However, more serious problems such as Cumulative Trauma Disorders (CTDs) are beginning to appear in the office work force" (p. 35). CTD is caused by repetitive motions over long periods of time and have usually been associated with forms of manual labor but are now emerging in the office environment. Managers often do not take complaints by employees seriously and, thereby, compound the problem. If left unaddressed, these complaints could materialize into large medical and workers' compensation expenses and, if the problems grow, a result may be costly government legislation.

The solution to the problem is ergonomics, which is the science of fitting the job to the worker. HRM professionals should ensure that an ergonomic policy is put into place. This policy should consist of training managers to take employee's complaints seriously. Managers should also be trained to recognize potential problem situations, and how to remedy them before employees complain. In addition, ergonomically designed work stations should be purchased. This can mean anything from purchasing very expensive work stations to a simple desk light or foot rest. Employees also need to be trained in ways to make their work station more comfortable in order to reduce the risk of developing a CTD.

Another concern that was briefly discussed earlier has to do with the myth of an integrated HRM computer system. An integrated system is one that is deeply rooted into each HRM function to allow the HRM department to maximize its efficiency. This is promised by every software vendor but seldom realized. In reality, most software is only used to about 20 percent of its capacity. The culprit? A woeful lack of training (O'Connell, 1990). The blame should be divided between the vendor and the HRM department. The vendor is to blame for not making all the features obvious that will make the HRM department's functions more efficient. They are sometimes out of touch with what HRM professionals do, and the real life situations they face in their jobs. During the implementation stage, vendors often do not offer services that allow users to make full use of all the software's features (Leonard, 1991b). Furthermore, the vendor manual is usually written in language that is too technical for the layperson to fully understand. However, the blame ultimately lies with the HRM department for not demanding these things from the vendor.

The HRM department must also arrange for comprehensive initial and periodic training for employees. This training should teach the employee both how to do his or her specific job and demonstrate the other features of the system so that he or she can make full use of the resource.

Another concern with the introduction and the use of computers in HRM is the human relations problem that arises between the HRM department and the MIS department. Some of the reasons for this conflict are the competition for limited resources, the mainframe verses microcomputer mentality, and the use of commercial software (Johnsen, 1990). HRM and MIS must often compete for funds allocated for computer services, and with HRM becoming more computerized, they are also competing for computer programmers and operating personnel. The last two reasons for conflict are due to fundamental differences in the ideology of what characteristics are most important in a computer system and how software should be developed. MIS has historically used mainframe computers and is used to working in that environment. They have the technical expertise needed to create the software in-house to meet the needs of the organization, whereas, HRM is more user oriented. They do not possess the technical skills of MIS and, therefore, prefer more user friendly systems like microcomputers with off the shelf software.

A related question is, HRIS: Is it human resources or information systems? Or is it a separate entity? In recent years, human resources is evolving into a more strategic function, and HRIS is strategically important to HRM. The increasing need to manage HRM on line more efficiently and the growing sophistication of available technology contribute to a company's competitive advantage. The HRM department of the future will have developed an HRIS that provides management with timely and accurate information to plan and make decisions. With this in mind, the function critical to achieving the HRM department's most important mission should be under the control of the department. Or should it? Computer science requires technical knowledge and expertise institutionalized in MIS. Also, the HRIS operation, especially mainframe computer related expenses, may be the responsibility of MIS, finance, or some other non-HRM department. The trend today is toward HRIS being either internal or adjunct to the HRM departments. They are helping themselves by also hiring their own computer professionals. The question remains as to whether HRIS will continue to become an HRM function, whether it will begin migrating back to MIS, or whether it will become an autonomous department only related to HRM functionally.

HRIS advancements, wondrous as they have been, have moved so far so quickly that the user community has been left in the technological dust. Users are not convinced that they need the latest and greatest in technology. They are now demanding to see how products contribute to productivity gains before spending corporate dollars to purchase them. The number of users that have bought much more than they require, both in capabilities and technology, are beginning to get smarter about their purchases. A question that remains is when will vendors start concentrating on integrated, usable systems, rather than techno-gizmos. Why are some HRIS implementations failing? The software is not being integrated with existing departmental structure in a way that matches the mission of the departmental objectives. The question is how many of these failures will take place before organizations and software/hardware vendors alike can match their needs with the proper HRIS. The vendors that offer the services capable of combining functional and technical aspects of HRIS will be the biggest winners in the HRIS marketplace (Leonard, 1991a).

Another question to be answered, if one already has an HRIS, is when to, or whether to, modify the software. Extensive code modification in HRM software could result in:

the inability to add vendor enhancement because the code has been so drastically modified;

software maintenance, because of unique modifications, becomes increasingly difficult and expensive in the long run;

documentation of program changes will fail to keep pace with actual code changes; and

user training falls short because modified software outlasts the people who made changes, documentation is inadequate, and HRIS turnover creates a growing gap between resident skills and company-specific systems.

The keys seem to be understanding the system and questioning procedural needs. Technical system modifications can be minimized or avoided by possibly changing existing company policies and procedures. Verify that the new system is already giving valid information, just in a different but usable format. The goal of packaged system modifications is to make the system work for the organization and departmental users. The history of failed HRIS implementations has been marked by undue emphasis on technical sophistication or data systems gimmickry, with little or no input from the HRM specialists who will use the system, and for whom the system is supposedly being designed and installed.

Different government reporting entities have put pressure on organizations to change from sleepy personnel departments to proactive human resource divisions whose mission is to recruit, monitor, and evaluate the firm's labor force while complying with federal and state legislation. HRM professionals must ask themselves whether or not they will be able to continue to respond to the never ending laws that require them to produce more and more data. Answering this question is especially important when one recognizes that each new law creates demands for charts, logs, data, and reports to assure compliance. As examples of recent legislation, the Employment Retirement Income Security Act of 1980 prohibits discrimination in private pension plans and requires detailed analysis of payrolls; the Occupational Safety and Health Act requires business to keep records on employee accidents; the Age Discrimination and Employment Act requires pay and promotion tracking records; the Equal Pay Act requires tracking job characterizations and correlating these with payroll data to ensure male-female pay equality. The Toxic-Substances Control Act requires employers to keep daily records on contact with toxic substances. Section 89 of the 1986 Tax Reform Act required firms to embark on a new barrage of data gathering and reporting regarding employee benefit and pension plans. These firms had to prove that their plans did not discriminate in favor of owners or highly compensated employees (Laudon & Laudon, 1991).

The new Americans with Disabilities Act of 1990 ruling says employers must be able to demonstrate that hiring and promoting decisions are based solely on the employee's skills and abilities. Job descriptions must be specifically designed and documented well before applications are taken or promotions are given. An applicant tracking system would make it easier to prove that the company has complied with the new law. Resume scanning systems can speed up the process of selecting potential job candidates. Electronic record-keeping systems can facilitate all legislative compliance issues (Harriger, 1992).

A GLIMPSE OF THE FUTURE

With the emergence of a more global marketplace, HRM professionals must wait to see what new, unforeseen problems will arise for their departments as this trend continues. But one thing is certain. When new problems arise, new and better software products will be developed to handle them. Just as the ancient payroll systems of the 1960s would be unable to cope with the payroll problems of the 1990s, so will the HRISs of today be unable to handle all of the problems that might occur in the future.

Unlike those earlier programs, the programs of the 1990s are for the most part user friendly. Changes of the type alluded to here are now usually quite simple to make and are often done by the end user, not a professional programmer. If it is possible to use the past to predict the future, it is reasonable to assume that massive technological advances will be made in HRISs that will render obsolete the systems being used today. It is in this way that the resources of the past will be less than adequate to solve the problems of the future. Because of this, HRM professionals must consider the future when choosing a new system. Specifically, they must consider the compatibility of any new system with any existing system.

The amount of training time needed for employees on a new system should also be a factor in any decision of this type. Too often, employees are handed a new system with little or no real training on that system. This can lead to inefficient and inconsistent operations. Employees in this undesirable situation often know little about the potential uses of the HRIS. This lack of training in and underutilization of HRISs should be a major concern for HRM professionals. Very careful consideration must also be given to the manner by which the information will be put into the new system, because data that cannot be accessed properly, serves no useful purpose. These are all critical issues that cannot be overlooked. Finding answers to these problems should be the top priority of HRM professionals in the future.

Mandell (1992) offers the following observation:

Despite the potential payoffs, users, consultants and even vendors say HRISs are not without some drawbacks. For starters, many companies may find large systems difficult to install. In fact, one vendor estimates that 30% of companies abandon their attempts to install HRISs . . . (and . . . some of the blame must go to buyers themselves). Many customers underestimate the complexity of full-blown HRISs, and simply don't assign enough resources to get these complex modular systems running. (p. 128)

It might be safe to infer from this statement that one of the critical questions HRM professionals must answer is how they plan to get the company-wide cooperation needed to make any HRIS work. Without this cooperation, even the best computer system will be under-utilized. HRM managers are going to have to act as public relations representatives for their system of choice. Because of the broad range of services these systems can provide as depicted, this should not be as difficult an undertaking as it has been in the past.

The future will bring vast changes in the way the HRM departments function. Three trends that will most likely continue into the future are: the widespread adoption of computers into HRM, accompanied by more powerful and useful equipment and software; the growing use of expert systems in the individual functions of HRM; and the increasing independence and liberation of non-HRM personnel.

In the future, the mystique of computers will have dissipated. People will have been exposed to computers from the early stages of their lives. Computers will have become a fundamental tool in all education institutions. Our society will become much more computer literate. The fear and threat the computer brings to today's managers, due to the lack of understanding, will not exist. In addition, hardware and software technology advancements will play a major role in computer usage. As technology increases, so will the capabilities of the systems. Increased capabilities will, with the proper training, be transformed into increased efficiency in the entire organization, not just in the HRM department. The competition in the business world will drive computers into all aspects of organizations due to the potential increase in efficiency. In the future, organizations that maximize the potential of their computer systems will be so efficient that they will have totally displaced businesses that do not use computers.

One such technical advancement in the arena of software is the expert system. Expert systems provide consistent information in a timely fashion. Although they are very expensive and the bugs have not been totally worked out at present, this will not be the case in the future. Expert systems will greatly improve training in the future. In a sense, each employee will have his or her own private tutor who can provide interactive customized training. It is, however, unlikely that expert systems will totally displace human experts. For example, there are certain types of training, like hands on training, that humans can do more efficiently and effectively than computers.

Another change coming is the challenge to integrate computer imaging technology into the HRIS. Potential imaging applications fall into three categories:

Archiving Applications — This use will take advantage of the compact nature of images stored on optical disks. A disk the size of a music compact disk can store the equivalent of 12,000 letter-size pages. Optical images, compared with microfilm, are easier to retrieve, storage conditions are less critical, and reproduced images offer better quality.

Librarian Applications — These applications require online storage of large quantities of documents to facilitate information reference. Typical applications include storage of union agreements, arbitration case documentation, and industry statistics.

Document Processing Applications — These applications should be converted from paper to image at the earliest possible time. Typical human resources applications include resume processing, benefits and workers' compensation claims, accident reports, and reimbursement claims, just to name a few (Tolson, 1992).

Key issues confronting HRIS in the next decades include several areas. In international tones, emerging nations will be closing the earnings and cost gap with the United States, putting more pressure on U.S. human resource planning and production. More HRM issues will be concerned with elder care, an older workforce, child care, and job-sharing. We will see new combinations of video, data, text, and sound in computer systems, as well as more price-performance and storage capabilities. This adds up to quicker and cheaper movement of data. Trends of today, including downsizing and decentralization, will continue to push firms to sustain the competitive advantage. This source claims that the company of the future will rely more on technology than it does today, and human resources will become more technically oriented because most management information and administrative processes will be automated (Walker, 1987).

In the future, computers and HRIS will be more closely aligned with the corporate mission. The human resources planning function will support the corporate mission by focusing on its people inventory system. Staff development will become even more of an issue than it is today. Also, new issues concerning privacy and security will be researched. Among the key programs that will be addressed are: human resources planning, career planning and development, skills inventory information, succession planning, and employee cost information (Pasgualetto, 1988). These programs are currently on today's agenda for HRIS development, but their importance will be magnified greatly as more and more firms realize the strategic importance of a technically superior HRIS to address current and forthcoming human resources needs.

HRM systems of the 1990s are not just used for payroll purposes. Prepackaged commercial systems are expensive, but most offer a multitude of practical applications and are user friendly. This is in sharp contrast to the type of HRM packages that were available just 20 years ago. Most systems on the market today offer a wide range of services. They "track compensation, payroll, benefits, insurance policies, career paths and employee history" (Mandell, 1992, p. 128).

Individual companies have different needs when they shop for an HRM system. What companies usually find is a wide range of choices of HRM systems that perform tasks their HRM department had perhaps never even considered. Purchasing an HRIS is an expensive proposition. To receive maximum benefit, companies must look to the future and anticipate what problems might occur and what information might be useful to store on the computer system. This type of internal brainstorming, often done with the help of an outside consultant, should lead to a more informed decision in purchasing an HRIS. Many companies have had to make a decision concerning what HRIS to buy in the last decade. It is important that they continue to make well informed decisions in the future.

The popularity of new client/servers, many of which can be run using Microsoft Windows, another relatively new and popular computer product, is proof of a statement made earlier. It is the uncertainty concerning the precise role of computers in HRM that presents the biggest challenge for the future.

It is difficult to predict what additional information might need to be accessed or how that information might be used in the coming years. However, HRM professionals have a unique responsibility to remain informed about not only advances in technology but also ways that technology might be used to streamline operations in their departments.

Finally, in the future, the increasingly user friendly computer systems and increasingly computer literate managers will further integrate computers in HRM and allow managers to operate more independently. It will be easier for managers to perform their own HRM analysis and prepare their own reports to use for decision making and planning. This independence will give managers the access to higher quality and customized information, thus, increasing the quality of their decisions and their own efficiency.

CONCLUSION

As the world's population continues to grow at an accelerated rate, so by necessity will the world's businesses expand to keep pace. Clearly, it is true that whatever products or services the people of the world demand, businesses will exist to meet those demands. The increased population will almost certainly lead to increased demand for goods and services of all types, a trend that is always welcomed by the business community. And as new businesses open their doors and existing businesses expand, HRM departments will be expected to keep up, and their choice and utilization of HRISs will be their key to success.

Also, as the idea of a global marketplace gains favor throughout the business community, HRM departments will find themselves challenged in ways that were unimagined just a decade ago. Organizations that want to compete in the global marketplace in the 1990s must be more efficient, focused, and responsive to customer and employee needs. Companies that want to remain competitive will find that computers will be the most important single organizational tool that their HRM departments will use in the coming decades.

Finally, business climates forecast an increasing role for the HRM professional as a result of HRIS. Mergers and acquisitions are becoming commonplace, with HRIS trying to combine numerous, usually non-compatible, systems and the immediate inclusion of hundreds of new employees into new systems on short notice. System complexities deepen when various software products are combined. HRIS now has evolved from a one- or two-person function to a multilayer echelon comprising numerous specialties. HRM professionals are now being included in divisional as well as corporate environments, doing consulting, planning, and support, as well as day-to-day functions. The bottom line is that properly used HRM computer programs will help the organization to save not only time but also significant amounts of money as they continue to improve their competitive advantage.

REFERENCES

Adams, L. E. 1992, February. Securing your HRIS in a microcomputer environment. *HRMagazine*: 56–61.

Adams, T. R. 1990, January. Buying software without the glitches. *HRMagazine 35*: 40–42.

Bettendorf, R. F. 1990, March. Curing the new ills of technology. *HRMagazine 35*(3): 35–36, 80.

Broderick, R. & Boudreau, J. W. 1992. Human resource management, information technology, and the competitive edge. *Academy of Management Executive 6*: 7–17.

Ceriello, V. R. & Freeman, C. 1991. *Human resource management systems*. Lexington, MA: Lexington Books.

Harriger, D. 1992, July. Software systems aid compliance with regulations. *HR Focus*: 8.

Johnsen, J. L. 1990, January. Getting Along with Your System Staff. *HRMagazine 35*(1): 20.

Kavanagh, M. J., Gueutal, H. G., & Tannenbaum, S. I. 1990. *Human resource information systems: Development and application*. Boston: PWS-Kent.

Laudon, K. C. & Laudon, J. P. 1991. *Management information systems*: New York: Macmillan Publishing.

Lawler, J. J. 1992. Computer-mediated information processing and decision making in human resource management. In G. Ferris & K. Rowland (eds.). *Research in personnel and human resource management*. Greenwich, Conn.: JAI Press, pp. 301–44.

Leckonby, B. 1992, September. HRIS criteria: Protect corporate assets during times of change. *HR Focus*: 12.

Leonard, B. 1991a, July. Open and shut HRIS. *Personnel Journal*: 59–62.

Leonard, B. 1991b, September. The myth of the integrated HRIS. *Personnel Journal*: 113–15.

Mandell, M. 1992, April 6. Managing the human assets. *Computerworld 26*(14): 128.

Milkovich, G. T. & Boudreau, J. W. 1994. *Human resource management* (7th ed.). Burr Ridge, IL: Irwin.

O'Connell, S. E. 1990, April. Making the case to management. *HRMagazine 35*: 30–32.

O'Connell, S. E. 1992a, April. Information management issues and the ADA. *HRMagazine 37*(4): 31–32.

O'Connell, S. E. 1992b, July. The HR automation budget. *HRMagazine 37*(7): 31–32.

O'Connell, S. E. 1992c, December. Implementation is the key to automation. *HRMagazine 37*(12): 25.

Page, R. C. & Van De Voort, D. M. 1989. Job analysis and HR planning. In W. F. Cascio (ed.). *Human resource planning, employment, and placement*. Washington, DC: Bureau of National Affairs. pp. 34–72.

Pasgualetto, J. 1988, August. Evaluating the future of HRIS. *Personnel Journal*: 82–86.

Schultheis, R. & Sumner, M. 1989. *Management information systems, The manager's view*. Homewood, IL: Richard D. Irwin.

Silverman, F. 1991, December. Stepping onto the right platform. *HRMagazine 36*(12): 30–31.

Spoor, J. 1992, January. HRIS and acquisitions: A smooth transition. *HRFocus*: 17.

Tolson, R. 1992, November. Imaging technology: Imagine the possibilities. *HRFocus*: 18.

Walker, A. J. 1987, November. Human resources: Preparing for the next century. *Personnel Journal*: 107–12.

Walker, A. J. 1993. *Handbook of human resource information systems*. New York.: McGraw Hill Inc.

Warren, Gorham, Lamont. 1992. *Compensation strategy and management*. Research Institute of America Inc.

7

Human Resources Management and Employee Training and Development

One-tenth of U.S. workers receive formal training before starting work or on the job. Out of 3.8 million businesses in the United States, approximately 0.5 percent, about 15,000, provide training experiences for their employees. That is, they spend approximately $30 billion, or 1 or 2 percent of their payroll, on formal training. Compared to Japanese and German employees, who spend 8 to 10 percent of their work time in training, U.S. employees of Fortune 500 companies spend only 2.5 percent of work time in training (Baber, 1991). Competitive pressures in a global arena will require U.S. businesses to improve the productivity of the workforce through employee training and development.

Training can be used by companies to gain a competitive advantage. As noted above, typically, U.S. companies have not used training for this purpose. Lack of investment in training is an often-cited reason for why U.S. companies are losing market share to foreign competition. For example, on average U.S. firms spend about $2,600 per worker per year on training, while Japanese firms spend about $6,500 per worker per year (*Chicago Tribune*, 1992). However, companies like Federal Express, Solectron, Anderson Consulting, and other U.S. companies believe that training plays an important role in increasing productivity and competitiveness. As a result, they invest from 3 to 5 percent of their payroll in training (Henkoff, 1993). For example, to achieve its quality objectives, Xerox spent $125 million on training, in addition to the 2.5 percent of revenue it spends on training each year. The investment in quality training has paid off handsomely, since the company has regained market share from the Japanese in the copier market. Motorola provides each employee with about three and one-half days of training per year (Carnevale, Gainer & Villet, 1990).

This chapter is concerned with the human resources management (HRM) department's role in employee training, or human resources development (HRD), and the accompanying challenges and issues that HRM professionals will need to address in the coming years. The chapter will also discuss organizational responses to date to address a number of training challenges and will conclude with a discussion of future challenges that HRM professionals must deal with in the coming years.

HUMAN RESOURCES DEVELOPMENT CHALLENGES FOR HUMAN RESOURCES MANAGEMENT

Today's business environment is rapidly changing, and, because of the rate at which change is increasing, even the old adage, "the only thing constant around here is the rate of change," no longer holds true. In order to survive, businesses and individuals must either adapt their behavior to fit this new environment, or effect changes in the new environment for their survival. The HRM challenge is to ensure that businesses, through their employees, acquire the necessary skills and knowledge to adapt to or change this new environment.

It has been estimated that, in response to these environmental changes, workers born after 1958 will likely change occupations four times, and that two of the four occupations do not even exist as yet (Johnston & Packer, 1987). The major driving forces behind the rapid rate of change in the business environment are: global competition, technological advancement, and demographic changes in the labor force. Careful analysis of the many different concerns and issues in current HRD literature will usually identify one of these three key forces as the primary causal factor.

Global competition appears frequently in business literature because of its profound effect on many different aspects of the business environment. Competition in today's global environment means rapidly responding to customer needs with high quality products, supported by world class customer service, and at internationally competitive prices. Of particular concern to HRM professionals is understanding what knowledge, skills, and abilities (KSAs) will be required by employees, thus enabling businesses to meet the challenge of global competition, and determining the most cost effective way of imparting these KSAs.

The need for rapid response to both domestic and global customer needs is resulting in a major restructuring of U.S. businesses from moribund centralized bureaucracies to agile decentralized strategic business units (SBUs). The flattened management structure and increased autonomy of the SBUs pushes decision making to lower levels in the organization, thereby empowering employees, while at the same time creating the need for all employees to have a more generalized and less specialized knowledge level. Necessarily included here is the need for employees to understand the international markets in which SBUs operate. Maintaining an available pool of knowledgeable and highly skilled employees provides a strategic advantage to organizations through increased flexibility and the capability of responding rapidly to changes in the market environment.

Global consumer demand for high quality products has required U.S. companies to implement various quality improvement programs and total quality management concepts. Implementation of these programs typically requires employees to make cultural changes as well as to learn the skills necessary to perform effectively in the quality measurement arena. Similarly, the demand for world class customer service is also requiring cultural changes and new skills.

Developing employees to provide world class customer service is particularly important for HRM professionals. World class customer service means providing customized solutions to specific customer problems. Thus, employees directly interfacing with the customer must be able to accurately analyze the customer's problem and have sufficient knowledge of potential solutions for the problem to recommend specific products or a course of action that will correct it. Training must provide the initial level of knowledge as well as assist in implementing the cultural shift from a product focus to customer focus. Once these initial hurdles are cleared, the employees' level of knowledge must be maintained in a constantly changing environment.

Developing and maintaining cost competitive products at internationally competitive prices requires companies to make the most effective use of all resources involved in the production process and requires the cost of these resources, including labor, to be measured against a global standard. Because the cost of labor is significantly higher in the United States than in the countries of a number of competitors, U.S. businesses are working to reduce the use of the labor resource through improvements in labor productivity. While organizational streamlining has been, and will continue to be, an important part of the solution, working smarter is also required. Here again, only improved employee knowledge and skills can provide the means.

Technological advancement has historically served as the engine for productivity improvements and has been responsible for the high level of productivity achieved in U.S. agricultural and manufacturing sectors (Johnston & Packer, 1987). In today's organizational environment, technology continues to serve in this role, although at an accelerating pace. This shift provides many unique challenges for HRM professionals, and, at the same time, exacerbates the challenges posed by other factors.

Technological advancement is the driving force in the ongoing shift from a manufacturing-based economy to a service-based economy in the United States. Successful application of technological advancements continues to improve manufacturing sector productivity, thus permitting increased production without requiring additional manufacturing sector employment. Currently, more than 75 percent of the private sector labor force is employed by the service sector and virtually all net job creation in the 1980s occurred in this sector (Ehrbar, 1993).

The service sector, traditionally the most labor intensive segment of the U.S. economy, is being forced to undergo significant productivity improvements to remain globally competitive, especially given the United States' relatively high labor costs. As with other sectors of the economy, this renewal effort is primarily focusing on improving products and human resources productivity through the use of technology. Contrary to popular belief, however, the majority of new jobs created in the service sector require more highly trained, not less skilled, employees. In fact, it is projected that the majority of service sector jobs created in the 1990s and beyond will require post secondary education (Johnston & Packer, 1987).

Globally competitive organizations understand the benefits of technology, realize that it must be applied to their businesses if they are to remain globally competitive, are incorporating it in their products, and are embracing it in their workplaces. HRM professionals are being called upon to ensure that employees have both general and specific knowledge of technological advancements. A general knowledge is necessary for employees to understand how the latest technological advances might be incorporated into new and existing products or applied to existing programs and processes to improve workplace productivity. Specific and detailed technological knowledge is required for those technologies used in employees' current positions as well as for those that will be used in future positions.

While technological advances create their own unique HRD requirements, telecommunication and computer technology developments, in particular, have increased the rate at which the marketplace in general is changing. The increasing use of technology and the rapid pace at which technology is changing has created the need for ongoing training programs. These programs are required by all organizations hoping to function effectively in this rapidly changing environment.

The final factor responsible for a number of the current challenges in HRD is the changing demographics of the labor force. The days of a homogeneous workforce are long gone. Economic growth, coupled with a decrease in the growth in the labor force, is changing the composition of the workforce. The net result is that these changes in the workforce are forcing employers to change how they have traditionally viewed and valued the human resource.

Because the labor force is growing more slowly than in the past, competition for workers in the labor market is increasing. This trend effectively forces companies to be less selective in hiring entry level workers at the same time global competition is demanding a more highly skilled and knowledgeable workforce. Compounding this trend, not only is the average knowledge level and skill of the entry level worker decreasing, but the mismatch between required and available skills and knowledge is increasing. Consequently, increased demands are being placed on HRM professionals to provide basic job skills training in addition to all the other training required to transform an entry level worker into a productive member of a world class workforce.

The slower growth in the labor force, resulting from lower birthrates, also has the effect of increasing workforce diversity. As total employment grows with increasing economic activity, jobs are necessarily being disproportionately filled by women and immigrants entering the workforce. Thus, women and minorities now comprise a greater percentage of the total workforce. As a result of this change in demographics, HRM professionals are increasingly being called upon to provide diversity training, particularly in larger corporations. The theory behind providing this type of training is to create a workplace environment that is "conducive to retraining and promoting a diverse workforce" (Johnston & Packer, 1987).

The slower growth in the labor force also increases the average age of the workforce, creating many human resources challenges for organizations as highlighted throughout this book. The specific HRD challenge posed by increasing workforce age, however, centers around the need for retraining due to the changing business environment and technological advances. While older workers tend to be more stable, more highly educated, and more reliable than young workers, they also tend to be less adaptable to change. Thus, retraining an older workforce that is more set in its ways and was not raised in today's lifelong learning environment requires the application of more non-traditional training methods.

The U.S. government also is increasingly becoming a vital influence on training. This has been happening in two ways. One is the pressure for equal employment opportunities and human rights. Equal employment legislation makes it illegal to discriminate unfairly against applicants or current employees on the basis of the person's age, race, sex, religion, or national origin. Several aspects of an organization's training program must, therefore, be assessed with an eye toward the program's impact on women and minorities. For example, when adverse impact exists and relatively few women or minorities are selected for the training program, you may have to show that the admissions procedures are valid — that they predict performance on the job for which the person is being trained.

The second way government influences training is that it provides many training programs. These programs frequently have public policy purposes, such as reducing unemployment, upgrading the incomes of minority groups, or increasing the competitiveness of underdeveloped regions of the country. In the United States, the federal government, through the Comprehensive Employment and Training Act (1974) and other workforce legislation has allocated large sums of money for the training of potential workers for jobs. The government reimburses training organizations (schools, business, unions) or trains the workers itself. In addition, in an effort to expand the pool of entry-level job applicants, Congress has revised the Job Training Partnership Act (JTPA) to focus more attention on youth. The JTPA is the federal government's prime job training program to help the economically disadvantaged and long-term unemployed. Under the JTPA, the government pays up to half the costs associated with supervising and training full- or part-time employees (*Personnel*, 1990). More recently, legislation like the Americans with Disabilities Act is placing new expectations on HRM professionals to ensure that their training efforts are responsive to disabled employees. Finally, the Clinton Administration sees education and worker training as key to raising U.S. productivity, economic growth, and living standards through increasing cooperation between government, business, and labor.

In summary, global competition, technological advancement, changing demographics, and the U.S. government are driving forces in today's rapidly changing business environment. Each of these factors separately and combined poses its own unique demands on the HRM function in general and HRD efforts in particular. For example, HRM professionals are challenged to ensure that training programs are effectively aligned with the organization's business strategy. The HRM manager must be a strategic planning partner, working alongside other top executives, in order to create a training function that translates organizational objectives into the knowledge and skills needed to implement the organization's strategic plans. Starting from the top will ensure managerial support for training programs. The cumulative effect of these trends is very clear, however, HRD will command a steadily increasing share of the resources of HRM and their organizations in the future, and will be critical to future success.

ORGANIZATIONAL RESPONSES TO HUMAN RESOURCES DEVELOPMENT

The purposes served by training today are much broader than they have been in the past. Training used to be a fairly narrow and routine affair in most organizations. The aim was usually to impart the technical skills needed to do one's job. This might involve training assemblers to solder wires, salespeople to close a deal, or teachers to devise lesson plans.

Training is used by more and more organizations today to achieve two additional aims. First, other broader skills are being taught to the organization's employees. These skills include problem-solving, communication, and team-building. Second, organizations are taking advantage of the fact that training can enhance employee commitment. Few things illustrate an organization's commitment to its people more than providing continuing opportunities to better themselves. Therefore, training opportunities can help mold employee commitment. This is one of the reasons why some organizations (for example, Toyota and Saturn) provide about two weeks of training per year for all employees.

The expansion of training's role reflects the fact that "the game of economic competition has new rules," as one expert says (Carnevale, 1990). In particular, it is no longer enough just to be very efficient. Surviving and thriving today and tomorrow requires speed and flexibility on the part of the organization. And they require responding to customer needs with respect to quality, variety, customization, convenience, and timeliness. Meeting these new standards requires a workforce that is more than just technically trained. It requires people who are capable of analyzing and solving job-related problems, working productively on teams, and shifting from job to job.

Unfortunately, a training gap exists and may even be widening. While some organizations — Motorola, Texas Instruments, and Xerox, for example — devote 5 to 10 percent of their payroll dollars to training activities, the average training investment by U.S. firms (while large in dollar terms) is less than 2 percent of payroll (Carnevale, 1990). Experts estimate that between 42 and 90 percent of U.S. workers need further training to get them up to speed (Carnevale, 1991).

Further evidence of the training gap is evident by the fact that organizations increasingly find they need employees with analytical skills, independent judgment, and the ability to work closely with others in complex operations. An example can be seen in manufacturing, where the practice of having workers perform simple, repetitive, assembly-line tasks is giving way to the concept of teams with interchangeable skills, and the broad operational responsibilities. These teams need members proficient not only in math and reading but also in the application of computers to manufacturing and service operations. In the construction industry, for instance, workers now use new-generation, power-driven machines, lasers, and robots that require levels of training far ahead of those needed less than a generation ago (Szabo, 1993).

What is happening in construction is but one example of the widening gap between job requirements and the skill levels of many job seekers. This chasm is impeding growth for organizations and the economy as a whole and posing new challenges for HRM professionals as they attempt to ensure that employees are effectively trained to do their jobs.

Projections by the American Society for Training and Development (ASTD) of job needs through this decade alone spotlight the trend. The ASTD association of employer-based training professionals, forecasts that by 2000 (Szabo, 1993): more than 65 percent of all jobs will require some education beyond high school and 23 million people will be employed in professional and technical jobs — the largest single occupational category — that require ongoing training. In addition, ASTD says, almost 50 million workers need additional training just to perform their current jobs effectively. In a related trend, the distinction between management and labor is narrowing, intensifying the need for greater KSAs across a broader cross section of the workforce. Since it is likely that the task demands of jobs will continue to be unstable because of volatile technology and market conditions, requiring more training so that employees can meet current effectiveness standards, HRM professionals will be challenged to find ways to eliminate the widening gap. In any case, training is moving to center stage as a means of improving organizations' competitiveness.

For training to move closer to center stage, HRM professionals must help their organizations realize that training can (Goldstein & Gilliam, 1990):

increase employees' knowledge of foreign competitors and cultures, which is critical for success in foreign markets;

help ensure that employees have the basic skills to work with new technology, such as robots and computer-assisted manufacturing processes;

help employees understand how to work effectively in teams to contribute to product and service quality;

ensure that the company's culture emphasizes innovation, creativity, and learning;

ensure employment security by providing new ways for employees to contribute to the company when their jobs change, their interests change, or their skills become obsolete; and

prepare employees to accept and work more effectively with each other, particularly with minorities and women.

Most businesses now recognize the need to significantly increase their investment in employee training and development. Their experience to date with demographic trends alone has caused them to realize that the long standing strategy of going to the labor market to hire required skill levels as they are needed in the workplace is becoming increasingly difficult, if not impossible, to implement. Thus, organizations are increasing their training expenditures as a percentage of total payroll costs in an attempt to guarantee themselves access to the skills required to maintain a globally competitive workforce.

Organizations next face the question of how to allocate total available training resources. Organizations are confronted with essentially infinite training needs yet constrained by finite resources. All too frequently, businesses focus only on perceived needs, and opt to apply training dollars to correct existing knowledge deficiencies in the workplace, not prepare for future change. While this approach may correct an existing performance problem, it may not prepare an organization for future market situations.

Faced with rising training costs into the foreseeable future, some organizations are stepping back from training to meet current business needs, and are adopting a more proactive approach to training. As organizations such as Rohm & Haas and IBM reformulate their strategic plans, they are determining what new skills will be required and formulating training programs accordingly. Rohm & Haas developed a major training program for supporting the implementation of work teams following an organizational restructuring. IBM developed and implemented a company-wide voluntary job enrichment training program to upgrade the skills of production employees that resulted in the net savings of one production support employee for each eight workers trained (Reid, 1992).

Today's ever changing environment frequently forces organizations to undergo major cultural changes. Here again, progressive organizations are using training programs to provide the knowledge required by employees to implement the desired corporate culture. Parisian, an Alabama-based department store chain, utilizes HRD resources to instill in their sales force the company culture of providing "extraordinary customer service in an industry in which it is difficult to distinguish one store's merchandise from another's" (Thornburg, 1992).

Implementation of quality improvement programs to achieve world class products also imposes large demands on the training efforts of HRM professionals, both for company and supplier employees. The Welch Allyn Company, a world class producer of medical diagnostic instruments, discovered this in 1986 when it made the decision to implement Total Quality Management (TQM). In addition to initial program familiarization and statistical methods training required for all employees, Welch Allyn employees now spend an average of 60 to 80 hours each year in training. Even large demands such as those imposed by the implementation of TQM can pay off. In fact, in 1987, Motorola reported that it saved $30 for every $1 invested in statistical process and control and problem solving methods (Carnevale, 1992). More recently, Motorola opened Motorola University, where it spends $24 million a year to teach TQM to its own employees. It also teachs TQM to faculty from business and engineering schools (Wiggenhorn, 1990).

Customer service is becoming increasingly important as the shift toward a service sector economy continues. Many organizations are beginning to use training and development programs in their quest to provide world class customer service. The basic aim here is to train all employees to treat the company's customers in a courteous and hospitable manner. The saying the customer is always right may be an old one, but it is one that has been rediscovered and is being emphasized by countless organizations today.

Xerox designed and implemented a program to ensure that both their sales and support employees understand the total document solution process in order to completely satisfy a customer's information processing needs. This program departed from some previous attempts to improve customer service by focusing on improving the employees' knowledge of the integrated Xerox product line, rather than the development of better interpersonal skills (Thornburg, 1992).

Siemens — one of the world's leading manufacturers of high-technology equipment — conducts a variety of training programs for many of its 27,000 employees, as well as for its customers, all across the United States (Schuler & Huber, 1993). Siemens USA courses are designed to meet the special needs of customers and their markets. For example, on-the-job training for customers ensures that all the capabilities of the company's technologically advanced systems are fully utilized and all their benefits are fully realized. Similarly, the special classes for Siemens engineering, manufacturing, service, and administrative personnel are designed to sharpen skills, enhance professional knowledge, and improve personnel expertise and effectiveness. Constant, specialized training is one of the ways in which Siemens is fulfilling its commitment to keep customers and employees ahead of the competition in a fierce, changing, tough, complex, high-technology marketplace.

Revco, D. S., a large Ohio-based drugstore chain, identified three behaviors that were critical for creating a good customer-service environment. The behaviors included: greeting customers when they entered the store, asking customers if they needed assistance when they observed them looking for a product, and making eye contact with customers when they spoke to them. Their approach to customer-service training, although simple, emphasized how managers' involvement and support for training can ensure its success. Each store manager was given a training guide that described the three customer-service behaviors and emphasized that managers were responsible for observing and coaching employees to ensure that they were using the behaviors. A five-minute video, prepared by the chief executive officer explaining his enthusiasm for the program, was distributed to all stores. To evaluate the effectiveness of the program, Revco sent secret shoppers into the stores to check on employees' use of the three customer behaviors. The shoppers reported that employees demonstrated the three behaviors more than 90 percent of the time (Piskurich, 1991).

Technological advancement is having a major impact on organizations in both the manufacturing and service sectors. As organizations increasingly turn toward technology in their search for productivity improvement, the need for training increases significantly. Branch Electric Company illustrated this process in preparing for a move into a new computer automated distribution center. A two-week training course was developed with the software supplier and structured so that some or all segments of the training could be taken, depending on an individuals involvement with the system. Training was given to the managers who were then responsible for training their subordinates. This highly successful training program allowed the new system to be brought on line, division by division in a phased department-by-department approach, as had traditionally been used (Reid, 1992).

Due to the rapid rate of change in technology, organizations are increasingly finding it necessary to implement retraining programs. Clorox and Quad Graphics are two such companies. Clorox worked with an outside consultant and established two ten-week voluntary programs for its employees to increase their understanding of technology. During the first ten weeks, classes that incorporated job related technology were offered to employees before and after their shifts. The initial program was supplemented with a second ten-week follow-up program. Quad Graphics adopted a more holistic approach to retraining and its continuing training program includes "human resource and processing skills" as well as technical skills (Overman, 1992, p. 41).

Graphic Controls Corporation, a manufacturing firm in Buffalo, New York, has turned to cross-training some of its skilled employees to meet many HRD challenges. Originally, cross-training was implemented to allow the company to continue meeting production needs in the absence (because of illness or emergency) of skilled workers. The Designated Trainee Program goals are "to produce a well-trained and versatile work force qualified and willing to work where the need arises, and at the same time, to provide individuals with cross-training, skills enhancement and job enrichment" (Santora, 1992, p. 162).

The additional training received on the job is enabling employees to master skills necessary for advancing to higher-paying positions. This not only boosts employee morale, but also promotes retention of talented employees. Cross-training at Graphic Controls Corporation has helped to address the status of women and minorities in the workplace. Women and minorities benefit because they receive education and training in higher skill-level positions, thus increasing their chances to move upward in the Graphic Controls Corporation workforce. Cross-training benefits management through reduced downtime and reduced need for hiring outside temporary help, both of which enhance the organization's ability to meet the challenges created by restructuring by providing employees qualified to perform expanded jobs and accept expanded responsibilities.

HRM professionals need to work with organizational managers to identify the prevailing business strategy to ensure that they are allocating enough of their budgets to training activities, that employees are receiving training on relevant topics, and that employees are receiving the right amount of training. A good example of how business strategy influences training practices is Travelers Corporation. Travelers' strategic objective is to become the number one provider of financial services in the United States (Hickey, 1988). To achieve this goal, all employees must be trained to use data-processing technology, and managers need to learn how to manage in a company in which data-processing technology makes more information available at the lower levels of the organization and in which products are more tailored to customers' needs. In the past, managers at Travelers were expected to be product experts; now managers must know how to determine customers' needs and identify financial experts who can meet those needs.

At Travelers, the role of the training function has changed to support the company's strategic objective. The training function supports the corporate strategy of automation not only by developing and administering programs designed to improve employees' computer literacy but also by using computer-based instructional systems, such as interactive video, tailored to the computer demands of each job. A new management development program has been implemented to educate managers about how to share power and serve as a resource for employees.

Some organizations are beginning to improve their competitiveness by attacking literacy problems through training. Methodist Medical Center of Illinois offers courses in reading, English, and math. The program is offered to employees during work time. Employees in housekeeping, food service, linens, and supply processing and delivery are participating in the program. Instructors use items the students are familiar with to improve literacy levels. For example, employees learn how to use a calculator while learning numbers. Supervisors report that the most notable change resulting from the program is employees' improved confidence in themselves and their ability to perform their jobs. Supervisors also report that the quality of employees' written assignments (for example, schedules, documents, and worksheets) has improved (Solovy-Pratt & Vicary, 1992).

The Brenlin Group, an Ohio metalworking manufacturing holding company with 4,200 employees, has learning centers at company work sites. These learning centers include self-paced, computer-aided instruction designed to bring employees to a minimum eighth-grade reading and math level. Three years after the learning centers opened, the company experienced lower turnover, increased sales dollars per employee, and increased employee involvement (Bureau of National Affairs, 1992).

Magnavox Electronic Systems Company, a high-technology manufacturer of satellite communications and navigational equipment located in Torrance, California, found that 52 percent of hourly employees were functionally illiterate in reading and 36 percent were illiterate in basic math. The company developed several classes designed to improve employees' deficiencies. These classes included two English-as-a-second-language classes for foreign-born employees, a language class for English-speaking employees, and a math and communication skills class. The courses used documents, tables, and calculations that employees actually used on the job. The program results were impressive — reading skills for the students who completed the program improved 15 percent, and math skills improved

21 percent. The average monthly efficiency of employees who completed the program increased 45 percent (Ford, 1992).

A number of U.S. organizations are taking advantage of business opportunities around the world. Along with these opportunities comes the need for organizations to train expatriates and foreign nationals (employees from the host country) in a wide variety of topics, including language and computer skills. HRM professionals must ensure that their organizations carefully consider whether the training methods they use in domestic facilities are appropriate for overseas operations. HRM professionals in the United States believe that experiential, hands-on training methods are most effective. However, for employees of other cultures, hand-on methods may be counter to cultural norms. For example, Asian and Arab employees prefer observing trainers demonstrate skills, rather than participating in role playing. The use of interactive video as a training strategy is inappropriate in Japan and other societies where people prefer to learn and work in teams.

Johnson Wax's team-building course has not been delivered at the company's Brazil facilities. Because Brazil's culture strongly emphasizes teamwork, asking employees to take a team-building course would be insulting. To avoid the problems associated with trying to adapt training programs to the cultures of different countries, Agvet, a division of Merck and Company, Inc., which produces livestock and agricultural products, develops most of its training programs in the United States, but they are delivered in different ways. For example, to train salespeople in each subsidiary, Agvet will often train a line manager to deliver the training. Line managers are able to adapt the training course to meet the norms of the local culture (Gerber, 1989; Marquardt & Engel, 1993).

Training employees abroad involves more than translating existing programs into other languages. Cultural differences influence both the applicability of training material and the reactions of trainees to the programs. Some suggestions for conducting training programs abroad are (McCarthy, 1990):

Understand the taboos and turn-ons of the participants' culture. For example, in Japan, risk-taking is by and large taboo. You may, therefore, find that you get no volunteers to participate in a training role-play exercise because doing so requires taking a risk.

Critiquing other people in public is taboo in some Far Eastern cultures. Therefore, even something as simple as getting a volunteer to be an observer in a training discussion or role-play could be difficult with trainees here, because the role of the observer is often to critique the other participants' behavior.

Saving face and not putting people in embarrassing situations are important not just in the Far East. In Middle Eastern countries, in East and West Africa, and in some European cultures, including Spain and Italy, criticizing trainees or making them look foolish is not advisable. In fact, putting them in any activity in which their behavior will be discussed, debriefed, or criticized can create problems.

In some cultures, you will find it difficult to get feedback on your effectiveness as a trainer. Even if you violate a taboo, the trainees may be reluctant to tell you so, because to do so would be to criticize you and cause you to lose face.

Make sure to understand how the job you are training your trainees to do is viewed in their native culture. In the United States for instance, it is appropriate to tell salespeople to write introductory letters to high-level executives to gain entry to their organizations. In Japan, doing so would be highly unusual. Instead, repeated personal visits to drop off business cards are often required to gain entry.

Consider the effect of jet lag and diet changes. For example, while it may be 4:00 P.M. in Boston where you are doing your training, your French participants' body clocks may be set to a more tired 9:00 P.M. Similarly, Japanese participants may expect a rice meal, and all participants fresh from overseas would probably do better with mineral water than soda.

With a workforce that is becoming increasingly diverse, many organizations find they have to implement diversity training programs. As an HRM manager for one organization put it: "We're trying to create a better sensitivity among our supervisors about the issues and challenges women and minorities face in pursuing their careers" (Santora, 1992, p. 74). Diversity training often involves creating greater sensitivity among non-supervisors as well, with the aim of creating more harmonious working relationships among an organization's employees.

Aetna provides company-wide training on managing diversity. The thought process was "if you can't [shed old prejudices about gender, race, and ethnicity], you won't be effective in anticipating your customer's needs, and this will have major business consequences" (Thornburg, 1992, p. 47). Aetna's training program focuses on core competencies, including such skills as planning and development, managing resources, teamwork, and adaptability.

A supervisory training program at Kinney Shoe Corp. provides an example (Santora, 1992). The organization conducts eight-hour seminars for Kinney Shoe executives and store managers. The program is called Valuing Diversity. In part, the seminars are aimed at showing participants how their own upbringing affects the assumptions they make and their behaviors. For example, the organization's studies indicated that managers responsible for hiring might make an assumption about an applicant's intelligence based on the person's accent and poor English-speaking skills. The manager might assume that the person lacks the skills to sell shoes, although he or she actually could sell effectively.

The Kinney Shoe Valuing Diversity program also shows how people from different cultures react differently to situations in the workplace. It does this by presenting a number of situations. For example, one situation illustrates that a Native American worker might be embarrassed by public praise from his or her supervisor.

While the current training thrust for progressive organizations is toward the proactive, there will always be a place for reactive training. The competitive marketplace is very unforgiving and employee knowledge deficiencies must be corrected expeditiously if product sales and quality reputation are to be maintained. The caution here is to perform sufficient evaluation of the problem to ensure that the performance problem is truly caused by lack of knowledge and not some other problem such as inefficient work procedures or processes.

Regardless of the specific reason for conducting training, as HRD demands increase, HRM professionals must decide as to the most pressing needs, and training resources must be allocated accordingly. Companies such as Florida Power are demanding that a training needs analysis be performed to support all requests for HRD resources (Gordon, 1991). The purpose of the needs analysis is to ensure that a knowledge deficiency exists and that formal training is the most effective means for correcting the deficiency. Additionally, these assessments include a cost benefit analysis to determine whether the projected return to the business from correcting the deficiency is greater than the cost of providing the training.

A continuously challenging aspect of HRD is selecting the most effective method of delivery. HRM professionals are being forced to be innovative in this area as training requirements increase. Various methods are being used including: working with community colleges and vocational schools to provide required basic or advanced skills training; adopting apprenticeship programs; using consultants to assist in the design and/or delivery of training classes; using on-the-job training programs, team or individual; providing formal training classes delivered by company training specialists; providing self-study programs; and utilizing computer assisted training programs. HRM professionals can provide valuable assistance to companies in obtaining maximum value for every training dollar spent.

Finally, and perhaps most frequently neglected, organizations are beginning to measure training effectiveness through the return on investment (ROI) realized from HRD programs. Federal Express conducted its first ROI pilot program for skills training in 1989 and has been active in this area since (Gordon, 1991). In 1991, Federal Express used the evaluation model developed during the pilot program to perform ROI studies on six major training programs affecting 50,000 employees. The result was that Federal Express was able to quantify the cost savings from the various training programs and was able to use this information to determine what training should be provided and to whom.

U.S. organizations have serious concerns about both applicants and employees. These concerns have less to do with quantity of applicants available than with their quality. A large and growing segment of the population does not have the basic educational skills to do today's jobs. The abilities to read, write, and do arithmetic are bona fide occupational qualifications in a job market dominated by technology. Yet, 20–30 million adults in the workforce have serious problems with these basic skills. More than half of the Fortune 500 companies report they have to conduct remedial training to bring employees to a minimal level. It costs those firms over $300 million each year. A survey of small and medium companies found that one-third of their employees are deficient in basic educational skills as well (Mathis & Jackson, 1994).

Over the next decade, the mismatch between job skill requirements and the available pool of workers will get worse. HRM professionals must understand and help their organizations respond to trends unfavorable for employers that will further affect the mismatch, such as a decline in population growth, scarcity of educated immigrants, changing employee values, and the need for more job flexibility.

Faced with these challenges, HRM professionals and their organizations have begun to explore a number of avenues:

forging partnerships with public school districts and community colleges,

establishing advocacy groups to promote better schools and funding,

testing prospective employees' basic skills, and

establishing in-house basic skills training.

Major unions, the National Alliance of Business, the Department of Labor, and other organizations are increasingly calling on businesses to achieve an educational partnership with public and private schools (Ropp, 1989; Milkovich & Boudreau, 1994).

Beginning with the 1994 seniors, the Los Angeles Unified School District (the nation's second largest) offers a warranty on the basic skills of reading, math, communication, problem-solving, reasoning, integrity, self-management, initiative, and responsibility. Perhaps such efforts eventually will pay dividends, but they are clearly a long-term solution, not an immediate one.

Organizations are testing prospective employees' basic skills. For instance, of 1,005 companies that responded to an American Management Association survey on workplace testing, 345 companies (34.3 percent) indicated that they conduct basic skills testing (Sherman, 1989). In 89 percent of the responding companies, job applicants who are deficient in basic skills are refused employment. At about 3 percent of the other companies, current employees and candidates for promotion are tested (and often rejected) based on their literacy scores.

One simple approach to remedial training used by organizations is to have supervisors focus on basic skills by giving employees writing and speaking exercises. After an exercise is completed, the supervisor can provide personal feedback (Sherman, 1989). One way to do this is to convert materials used in the employees' jobs into instructional tools. For example, if an employee needs to use a manual to find out how to replace a certain machine part, he or she should be taught how to use an index to locate the relevant section (Bureau of National Affairs, 1987).

Another approach is to bring in outside professionals, such as teachers from local high schools or community colleges to institute a remedial reading or writing program. In-house programs designed by HRM professionals and other organizational members are growing, such as the agreement between General Motors and the United Auto Workers Union that commits funds and manpower to a formal literacy program. Ford and Chrysler established similar programs in 1983 and 1987, respectively. So far, General Motors operates classrooms in 30 of its facilities and plans to put classrooms in all of them soon. Kansas City Power and Light has collaborated with Penn Valley Community College to hire and train lineworkers through a 45-week Lineworkers Training Program (Baber, 1991).

Smaller companies are getting into the act as well. The Hach Company in Loveland, Colorado, offers its 820 employees basic math and writing — 42 courses in all.

Another approach is to use an interactive video disk. This technique combines the drama of video with the power of microcomputers (Bernardon, 1989). An example is Principles of Alphabet Literacy. This program uses animated video and a computer-stored voice to enable nonreaders to associate sounds with letters and letters with words, and to use words to create sentences. A second interactive video disk program is called SKILLPAC. This program, subtitled English for Industry, was designed for nonnative English speakers. It combines video, audio, and computer technologies to teach language skills in the context of the specific workplace situation in which those skills will be used (Bernardon, 1989).

While organizations have increased their use of in-house programs, HRM professionals have recognized that, unfortunately, in-house programs are not a guarantee, and many programs fail. However, basic training will have to be done somewhere by someone. Today's and tomorrow's organizations cannot have high-technology complex jobs if their employees cannot read and write.

As this discussion indicates, remedial training is a major issue confronting HRM professionals and their organizations in the coming years. HRM professionals must also be aware that the training and retraining of individuals for the jobs of the future may determine the success of many U.S. organizations.

A large number of U.S. organizations are attempting to address the current HRD challenges, some by choice, most by necessity. The methods described above are but a few of what some progressive and innovative employers are doing in the HRD arena. Unfortunately, not all U.S. businesses are as progressive and innovative when it comes to resolving HRD challenges. Although some companies are doing a number of things right, it still remains difficult to identify HRM professionals and their companies that are doing all the right things.

TRAINING FOR TEAMWORK

In the past two decades, there has been a tremendous increase in the use of teams in the workplace. An increasing number of organizations today use empowerment and work teams to improve their effectiveness. These organizations organize the work to be done around close-knit teams and establish some form of teamwork as part of their organizational culture. In addition, the organizations empower these teams to get their jobs done, which means giving them the authorization and the ability to do their jobs. An emphasis on teamwork and empowerment are both components of what many organizations call employee involvement programs.

Employee involvement programs aim to boost organizational effectiveness by getting employees to participate in the planning, organizing, and general management of their jobs. The team approach has been linked conclusively to higher productivity and product quality, as well as to increased quality of worklife. Change strategies are usually dependent upon the ability of employees to pull together and refocus on the new common goal.

However, many organizations find that teamwork does not just happen. Instead, HRM professionals (and others) must work to train employees to be good team members. That is why organizations such as General Electric and Saturn spend considerable sums training new employees to be good team members. Such efforts often devote hours to training new employees to listen to each other and to cooperate. Throughout the training process, the organization's dedication to teamwork is stressed. Short exercises are used to illustrate good and bad teamwork and to mold new employees' attitudes regarding what good teamwork is.

Empowering employees (either individually or as teams) almost always requires a lot of training. It is rarely enough to just tell the members of a group that they are empowered to do all the buying and selling and planning involved in producing, for example, the auto component they are responsible for. Instead, HRM professionals must recognize that extensive training is required to ensure they have the skills to do the job.

Xerox and Texas Instruments' Defense Systems and Electronics Group are both Malcolm Baldridge National Quality Award winners that credit training for part of their success. Xerox spent $100 million and five years training employees in the tools of quality by throwing out the pie charts and providing simple step-by-step methods emphasizing interactive skills and teamwork. Texas Instruments' Defense Systems and Electronics Group empowered 700 levels, with training that included changes in work roles, decision making, holding meetings, communication, and cross-functional skills (Caudron, 1991; Drake, 1992).

Research showing how to create and train teams effectively suggests the following guidelines that HRM professionals can use for team training (Goldstein, 1992; Swezy & Salas, 1991):

Encourage team communication that supports the desire to work as well as encourage and support team members' input.

Emphasize interaction and the need for members to depend on each other.

Emphasize the team and member goals and responsibilities, and allow learning of all team members' responsibilities.

Challenge the team to react to changes and unexpected events.

Emphasize teamwork skills and provide examples of both acceptable and unacceptable teamwork.

A GLIMPSE OF THE FUTURE

As we have seen, both economic and demographic trends suggest radical changes in the composition of the workforce of the 1990s and organizations in general. Other factors that affect the number, types, and requirements of available jobs include automation, the need for continued worker education and retraining, and the call for increased accountability of organizations.

These issues suggest that training in organizations will be pivotal in helping organizations meet their strategic requirements. As a result, HRM professionals must ensure that training is an outgrowth of any organization's strategy. When training is driven by organizational strategy, the support of top management is assured. And when the organization as a whole understands the thrust of the strategy and accepts its validity, training moves from the periphery to near the center of organizational activity.

To ensure that training is aligned with organizational strategy in the future, HRM professionals must recognize that certain communications and relationships are required. The organization strategy must be transmitted to those who plan and provide and to those who receive training, and strategy must be formulated in the light of reliable information about the capacity of the organization to train and be trained. When HRM professionals representing training are not represented in strategy formulation, the organizational strategists miss two important pieces of advice. They may set their sights too high because they cannot be sure that the organization has, or will have at the right time, the KSAs required to carry out their plans; they may set their sights too low because they do not know what new KSAs the organization might acquire through training within the strategic period.

The coming radical changes suggest four reasons why training will become more important and the time and money budgeted for training will increase during the next decade (Goldstein & Gilliam, 1990):

1. the number of unskilled and undereducated youth who will be needed for entry-level jobs;
2. increasingly sophisticated technological systems that will impose training and retraining requirements on the existing workforce;
3. the need to train currently underutilized groups of minorities, women, and older workers; and
4. training needs stimulated by the internationally competitive environments of many organizations.

These changes suggest a dual responsibility for HRM professionals and their organizations in the future: HRM professionals must be responsible for providing an atmosphere that will support and encourage change, and ensuring that individual employees derive maximum benefit from the learning opportunities provided. As a result, HRM professionals must ensure that their training efforts provide a payoff and are indeed worthwhile.

Training Management

To enhance the success of training in the future, HRM professionals must also understand that training must be effectively managed. Applying the basics of good management to training departments, HRM professionals must promote cooperation between employee's supervisors (managers) and the training staff. As with many staff functions, responsibility for training is shared between line and staff management. In the future, effective training will require that HRM professionals and other organizational supervisors and managers are able to work closely together on all phases of the training process, and that all parties recognize and understand their shared responsibility. When HRM professionals, staff, and line managers are unwilling to approach the training process cooperatively, they will find that training does not help their organization.

In the future, HRM professionals will also have to be prepared to take responsibility for implementing effective cost reduction programs that have these characteristics:

establishes specific quantitative objectives for each cost reduction area;

includes provisions for quarterly reports of dollar savings;

encourages training personnel by assigning high priority to implementing cost reduction ideas and gives appropriate recognition for the idea; and

utilizes analytical tools and methods to identify opportunities for savings.

Some of the specific areas of emphasis in such cost reduction programs will include the following: training and training-support programs; major items of training equipment (for example, audiovisual); and training property and facilities.

The resource implications of all training objectives and programs will also need to be analyzed systematically. For example, short- (six months to two years) and long-range financial plans (three- to five-year) to support the goals of the training department must also be formulated. The long-range financial plan should be reviewed and updated annually and is based on full consideration of training needs, enrollment forecasts, projected training product and process changes, probable standards, expected new programs, new training strategies, desired auxiliary and support services, anticipated equipment procurement and replacement, organizational changes, and prospective staffing policies (Sims, 1990; Sims, 1993).

The basics of good management will continue to require that HRM professionals responsible for training also receive top management support for the HRM department's training efforts, ensure that personnel who conduct on-the-job training know how to train and are rewarded for their training efforts, build flexibility into the scheduling process, recognize the performance problems that can — and cannot — be solved through training, design an objective training evaluation system, and periodically audit the overall training initiative (possibly with the help of an outside consultant).

HRM professionals will also need to ensure that the department markets its training programs both inside and outside the organization. For example, the marketing potential of in-house training programs and training packages should be systematically surveyed and, when possible, plans should be made to sell the programs and packages to outside customers. In marketing training programs, emphasis should be placed on the development of efficient, attractive, and validated training packages that produce the desired job performance at reasonable cost.

Training individuals to be productive employees and contributing members of their organizations and communities begins with the ability to read, write, solve problems, do math, and communicate with others. In an age when jobs are getting more complex and technology is changing daily, organizations must provide a great deal of training and retraining for their employees. Training will continue to be critical to developing the basic skills of the U.S. population and enabling organizations to be productive. As organizations change and implement new technologies, employees need to be retrained. For example, those organizations that are replacing typewriters with computers must teach the workers affected by those changes how best to capitalize on the new technologies. In addition to providing skills, programs for retraining enable an organization to offer employment security and, thus, create greater loyalty and commitment.

Training and retraining are critical to future organizational success because they provide the skills needed both now and in the future. Together, training and retraining ensure the skills and employee commitment needed for high-quality goods and services and, thus, organizational effectiveness. Because training is important, organizations will have to want to do it as effectively as possible.

Design of Training

In the future, the realization of training benefits in an organization will continue to be contingent on the degree of training planning and effort expended designing and evaluating training programs. Haphazard training programs will result in wasted resources, poorly motivated employees, and few measurable increases in employee performance or organizational productivity. On the other hand, programs that are designed, conducted, and evaluated properly will have innumerable benefits to both the employee and the organization.

With inevitable budgetary constraints for training in the future, HRM professionals will need to consider the following when designing training programs:

Training should have the intent of ensuring that trainees are capable of solving problems and attaining training-related goals.

Training should provide employees opportunities for professional growth and development.

Training programs should seek to overcome deficiencies that result from stringent hiring policies or other inabilities to hire employees who possess appropriate skill and knowledge levels.

Training goals must be expressed in terms of both monetary expenditures and employee time.

Training should be designed after a thorough analysis of employee, task/job, and organization needs. Such assessments facilitate the design of improved training programs.

Training programs need to be user friendly. The information must provide a framework that the participant can digest and remember without extensive memory training. Only then can we expect trainees, at any level, to make the lessons learned part of their daily life.

Individual and group training plans need to be reviewed for consistency. If materials are not reviewed, participants may be inundated with masses of conflicting, and in turn, unusable information.

Training programs have to be presented with adequate application and practice, and, too often, this is not the case. For example, if participants do not get to try different styles of communication in a training session, when do we expect they are going to test this new behavior?

Contradictions between models used in training programs and the actual workings of the organization must be eliminated. These contradictions, which can occur at any level of the organization, can deal a deadly blow to even the most effectively designed program. For instance, a group of entry-level trainees have just been taught to answer the phone in three rings, yet the department to which they are assigned is so understaffed that it is quantitatively impossible to respond to all the incoming calls.

In judging how effective a particular training program design is likely to be, HRM professionals will need to answer the following questions:

Is the content of the program sufficient to achieve the program objectives?

Is the content only what is needed to achieve the program objectives?

Does the program make correct assumptions about the current knowledge and skills of learners?

Does the program make use of the best available delivery systems?

Does the design of the program make the best use of the delivery system?

Do program design and delivery take account of the latest knowledge about adult learners?

Is documentation of the program sufficient to ensure its maintenance and quality control?

Does the design of the program provide for measurement, evaluation, and validation from the beginning?

In the future, appropriately designed training programs have the potential for being the most powerful tool in helping HRM departments use training to achieve organizational quality and productivity. An important component of an appropriately designed training program will be the extent to which the program attempts to train for competence, clarify the psychological contract, and identify training needs (Sims & Sims, 1991).

Training for Competence

Competence includes not only job-related skills but also well-rounded training that prepares employees to apply integrated knowledge in a practical and job-related manner. Thus, the challenge for HRM professionals and their organizations will continue to be one of selecting appropriate competencies, specifying evaluation indicators, and developing a functional training system.

Failure to design training programs that train for competence will result in inadequate design or implementation of a training program. This means the program, even if implemented effectively, will not meet an organization's needs because it will provide no improvement in employee performance. Training based on desired competencies can be evaluated to measure the extent to which the competencies have been achieved. This means that HRM professionals should ensure that training programs focus on outcomes rather than development of knowledge alone.

Transfer of Training

Like yesterday and today, the future will require that HRM professionals continue to find ways to increase the transfer from the training environment to the job as a means of increasing the payoff for training. After all the design and implementation are finished, training still will only be effective if in-class results translate to job behaviors. Transfer will only be enhanced when HRM professionals ensure that the training activities, environment, and responses closely resemble the work situation, as when secretaries use the same computers and work materials in training as they use on the job. Although this may seem obvious, continuous changes in technology will continue to make it tricky.

Perhaps the most important element of training transfer that HRM professionals must be sensitive to in the future concerns the training program itself. A measure of transfer climate is the degree to which the work situation provides opportunities and rewards for using what is learned in training. This will require creating situational clues to show when to use the training and consequences that reward trainees appropriately for using it (Roullier & Goldstein, 1990). In the future, it will be increasingly important that HRM professionals understand that transfer of training is a responsibility shared by employees, management, and the training department.

CONCLUSION

As with most challenges, the responses of U.S. businesses to the emerging trend for highly skilled employees have varied. Some companies are well along the learning curve and are actively attacking the training challenges HRM professionals are facing. Other businesses, particularly those with fewer resources, are not nearly as far along. In either case, HRM professionals will continue to be challenged to find ways to help their organizations train and develop their employees.

In the future, HRM professionals can increase the likelihood that their training efforts will be worthwhile and more successful by incorporating the following ten critical ingredients of successful training adapted from Peters (1987):

1. Focus extensive training on knowledge, skills, and abilities that go beyond the mechanics of performing a job. Organizations should be willing to train employees in a variety of areas, for example, improving their skills in communication and interpersonal relations.

2. Treat all employees as potential career employees. All employees should be trained in the context of career development.

3. Require regular retraining. All company employees should be required to receive some type of training regularly; constant broadening of knowledge, skills, and abilities should be a goal of all employees.

4. Spend time and money generously on training. Organizations should be willing to give employees time off for training regularly and provide tuition contributions where possible. Companies must also ensure that high-quality, effective training is offered; and recognize that throwing money at a problem is unfailingly stupid.

5. On-the-job training is important. HRM professionals must work to make sure all supervisors and managers are good coaches and evaluate them on their effectiveness as trainers.

6. There is no limit to the skills that can be taught. If the courses are well conceived, almost any employee can learn relatively complex subjects.

7. Consider training an important part of the company's strategic thrust. Training must be recognized as a vehicle for strategic change and should be an accepted part of any organization's strategic planning process.

8. Emphasize training during a time of crisis. Organizations should resist the normal temptation to cut the training budget during times of fiscal stress or crisis; rather, increase it!

9. Training should be line-driven. Supervisors and managers should be fully involved with HRM professionals in planning training and teaching. Without this input, they will feel little stake in the programs. HRM professionals responsible for training should be considered experts in organizing training, but supervisors and managers should be viewed as the content leaders.

10. Use training to teach organizational vision and values. Training should be seen as a prime way to teach employees at all levels company values. HRM training staff must make sure top management is involved in training when transmitting the organization's vision.

REFERENCES

Baber, A. 1991, September. Corporate report: Can training save America? *Ingram's*: 58–59.

Bernardon, N. L. 1989, January. Let's erase illiteracy from the workplace. *Personnel*: 29–32.

Bureau of National Affairs. 1987, December 17. *Bulletin to Management*: 408.

Bureau of National Affairs. 1992. Department of Labor's LIFT awards recognize successful training programs. *Employee Relations Weekly*: 1116.

Carnevale, A. P. 1990, November. America and the new economy. *Training and Development Journal 44*: 31ff.

Carnevale, A. P. 1991, March. The training gap. *Training and Development Journal 44*: 9–12.

Carnevale, A. P., Gainer, L. J., & Villet, J. 1990. *Training in America: The organizations and strategic role of training*. San Francisco: Jossey-Bass.

Carnevale, E. E. 1992, July. Eyeing the future, intensifying training. *Technical & Skills Training*: 24–27.

Caudron, S. 1991, April. Xerox won the Baldridge. *Personnel Journal*: 98–102.

Chicago Tribune. 1992, June 14. Sec. 1, p. 18.

Drake, S. 1992, December. Empowering the people. *Human Resource Executive*: 32–35.

Ehrbar, A. 1993, March 16. Price of progress. *Wall Street Journal*: A1.

Ford, D. J. 1992, November. The Magnavox experience. *Training and Development*: 60–61.

Gerber. B. 1989, September. A global approach to training. *Training*: 42–47.

Goldstein, I. L. 1992. *Training in organizations* (3rd ed.). Pacific Grove, CA: Brooks-Cole.

Goldstein, I. L. & Gilliam, P. 1990. Training systems issues in the year 2000. *American Psychologist 45*: 134–43.

Gordon, J. 1991, August. Measuring the goodness of training. *Training*: 19–25.

Henkoff, R. 1993, March 22. Companies that train best. *Fortune*: 62–64, 68, 73–75.

Hickey, J. V. 1988. The Travelers Corporation: Expanding computer literacy in the organization. In J. Casner-Lotto and Associates (ed.) *Successful training strategies*. San Francisco: Jossey-Bass, pp. 19–34.

Johnston, W. B. & Packer, A. H. 1987. *Workforce 2000: Work and workers for the twenty-first century*. Indianapolis, IN: Hudson Institute.

McCarthy, P. 1990, November. The art of training abroad. *Training and Development Journal*: 13–18.

Marquardt, M. J. & Engel, D. W. 1993. *Global human resources*. Englewood Cliffs, NJ: Prentice-Hall.

Mathis, R. L. & Jackson, J. H. 1994. *Human resource management* (7th ed.). St. Paul, MN.: West.

Milkovich, G. T. & Boudreau, J. W. 1994. *Human resource management* (7th ed.). Boston, MA: Irwin.

Overman, S. 1992, August. Retraining puts workers back on track. *HRMagazine*: 40–43.

Personnel. 1990, December. Congress revises job training program: 6.

Peters, T. 1987. *Thriving on chaos*. New York: Harper & Row.

Piskurich, G. M. 1991. Service training made simple. *Training and Development Journal*: 37–38.

Reid, R. L. 1992, April. On target: Retraining to retain workers. *Technical & Skills Training*: 22–26.

Ropp, K. 1989, August. Reform movement for education. *Personnel Administrator*: 39–41.

Roullier, J. Z. & Goldstein, I. L. 1990. Determinants of the climate for transfer of training. Paper presented at the Society for Industrial and Organizational Psychology. St. Louis.

Santora, J. 1992, September. Kinney Shoes steps into diversity. *Personnel Journal*: 74–76.

Schuler, R. S. & Huber, V. L. 1993. *Personnel and human resource management*. St. Paul, MN: West Publishing Co.

Sherman, E. 1989, July. Back to basics to improve skills. *Personnel*: 22–26.

Sims, R. R. 1990. *An experiential learning approach to employee training systems*. Westport, CT: Quorum Books.

——. 1993. *Training enhancement in government organizations*. Westport, CT: Quorum Books.

Sims, R. R. & Sims, S. J. 1991. Improving training in the public sector. *Public Personnel Management 20*(1): 71–82.

Solovy-Pratt, L. & Vicary, R. M. 1992, November. A hospital's perspective for illiteracy. *Training and Development*: 60–61.

Swezy, R. W. & Salas, E. (eds.). 1991. *Teams: Their training and performance*. Norwood, NJ: Ablex.

Szabo, J. C. 1993, March. Training workers for tomorrow. *Nation's Business*: 22–25, 28, 32.

Thornburg, L. 1992, August. Training in a changing world. *HRMagazine*: 44–47.

Warren, Gorham Lamont. 1993. The training function. *Human resources: Policy and practices*. Research Institute of America.

Wiggenhorn, W. 1990, July/August. Motorola U: When training becomes an education. *Harvard Business Review*: 71–83.

8

Downsizing and Human Resources Management

Beginning in the 1980s, and continuing into the 1990s and beyond, companies are finding themselves in a new global marketplace, where business is intensely competitive. New markets, products, and distribution channels have emerged, forcing firms to be more dynamic, forward-thinking, and flexible in their strategies to achieve profitability. At the same time, since 1990, the world has plunged into a recession that has increased the pace of corporate restructuring. Large-scale, cost-cutting measures have become vital to remaining competitive and retaining market share.

Many organizations have yet to finish reshaping themselves in the face of increasing global and domestic competition. Other companies are still attempting to eliminate unnecessary management layers. The movement toward slower growth is a long-term trend driven by several factors. Among these are the use of information technology in lieu of human resources, increased automation, flatter organizational structures and redesigned, flexible workforces. Therefore, downsizing is expected to be a continual process for U.S. organizations. Furthermore, downsizing and delayering are not only occurring in the United States but also in many European and Japanese companies.

Since a human resources management (HRM) department handles personnel issues, a major concern in downsizing needs to be the extent to which the HRM team is involved with and prepared for the management of the downsizing task. Questions need to be addressed regarding the types of programs and human resources support systems that currently exist within an organization to handle the implementation of a workforce layoff, as well as the size of the HRM staff that will be implementing the downsizing programs. HRM departments must play important roles in workforce layoffs, because of the serious financial consequences of a poorly conceived downsizing plan. This chapter is concerned with the role HRM professionals should play in helping their organizations better address the challenges of downsizing. It will also discuss some organizational responses to downsizing to date. The chapter concludes with a look at some potential issues that HRM professionals must confront in the coming years.

DOWNSIZING CHALLENGES FOR
HUMAN RESOURCES MANAGEMENT

Slower economic growth and corporate restructuring pose many challenges for HRM. During periods of slower growth in organizations, the critical issue facing private sector firms is cost reduction; the most difficult challenge is how to accomplish the necessary cuts. One of the common and visible methods of reducing costs involves downsizing an organization, a term that has become a buzzword for the 1990s, frequently referring to large layoffs in the workforce. From the moment a company considers downsizing in this way, many specific problems and challenges arise that will ultimately determine the success of the downsizing effort as well as corporate survival and future profitability of the organization.

A key difference between today's downsizing and other efforts in the past is a wave of corporate restructurings that are permanently eliminating job positions. Even as the economy shows signs of recovering, few jobs are being restored. Thus, it appears that even when the current economic recession ends, staying lean will remain embedded in the corporate consciousness.

An important concern that develops for senior management is balancing the immediate need to lower costs versus the complicated and laborious effort required to accomplish the downsizing endeavor. Management often visualizes the short-term balance sheet benefits of cost reductions without realizing long-term consequences of their actions in terms of the effects on the corporation's workforce. For example, an important hurdle for a firm to overcome is the stock market notion that "demand and sales may be weak, but . . . profits are only a payroll cut away" (Boroughs, 1992, p. 50). This type of short-term financial approach to cost cutting excludes vital human resources concerns and may leave an organization competitively disabled in the long run.

On a more fundamental level, any firm preparing to downsize its workforce is faced with the issue of successfully overcoming human resistance to change. Downsizing implies massive organizational changes, and it is a natural human tendency to resist these changes. As one consultant relates: "Change is exciting when it is done *by us*, threatening when it is done *to us*" (Kanter, 1985, p. 52). The firm, therefore, is challenged not only with designing and implementing the necessary changes, but also with developing ways to overcome resistance to these changes. Frequently, the HRM department will be charged with this arduous task.

Because of the statistics that have already been compiled on the results of corporate downsizing, the organization that reduces its workforce by downsizing is facing a difficult, uphill battle for success. According to a recent consulting firm study, "fewer than half the companies that downsized expressly to cut costs actually met their expense-reduction targets. Only about a third improved profitability to their satisfaction, and a paltry one fifth met their goals for improving return on investment" (McGoldrick, 1992, p. 79). In addition, downsizing is six times more likely to occur in a firm that has already downsized once (Heenan, 1991), creating intense pressure for all involved in the downsizing process.

Careful HRM planning is required in periods of slow growth, and is essential for all steps of the downsizing process. Proper evaluation processes must be in place to ensure that the right people are let go and that essential employees are retained. Voluntary programs, such as early retirement offerings, should be subject to management approval to ensure that essential employees are retained. Communication of corporate plans to all employees is essential, and dismissal of employees must be accomplished in a dignified, professional manner. A fair severance package should be offered to those terminated, and much attention must be given to the grieving process of remaining employees. Retained employees must clearly understand the company's strategy and their place in the redefined company. Poor morale of remaining employees will undermine productivity and is a key factor in the failure of corporate restructuring to improve profitability. If possible, alternatives to layoffs should be sought. These include job redesigns, retraining, reduced working hours, and other measures. With proper HRM planning, restructuring is viewed as rightsizing and not downsizing. This concept involves maintaining the proper core of permanent employees and supplementing this core with temporary or part-time workers.

Effective communication is essential at all levels of the process. If improperly handled, downsizing can demoralize retained workers who fear future loss of their own jobs. These employees must understand the corporate strategy and the role they play in it. Reduction of middle-management layers will require lower tier employees to make decisions previously made at higher levels. Employees must be secure in their job positions after the restructuring in order to respond to this empowerment of new responsibilities. Another aspect of delayering and restructuring is that the proving ground for upper managers (that is, middle-management positions) no longer exists. Alternative ways of training managers must be utilized.

All of the above are challenges presented by downsizings and the corporate restructuring of organizations. As noted earlier, slow growth and downsizing affect virtually every aspect of HRM.

Major challenges and issues posed for HRM in periods of slower growth and restructuring of organizations are as follows:

Determination and management of human resources needs. What core staffing requirements are needed to fit strategic objectives?

What options should be pursued to reduce staff — layoffs versus other options?

Severance issues. What type of severance package will be offered to terminated employees?

Legal issues. Does the restructuring violate employees' legal rights? Do termination and job reclassification of survivors satisfy Equal Employment Opportunity Commission (EEOC) and other legal requirements?

How do we manage periods of renewed increased growth (use of temporary or part-time workers versus permanent rehires)?

Does the evaluation system support HRM objectives to reward and retain essential workers and discourage continued employment of poor workers?

It is important that any downsizing be properly planned and managed to ensure that the proper employees are laid off, that the layoff is handled in a professional, dignified manner, and perhaps most importantly, that morale of the remaining workforce is not adversely affected. Even for organizations that do not actually lay off employees, slower growth will result in many of the same HRM issues (hiring freezes, lack of promotion opportunities, employee motivation problems, etc.). In fact, the issue of downsizing in periods of slower growth impacts virtually all aspects of HRM.

Clearly, there are a number of HRM challenges that need to be addressed in corporate downsizing. The fundamental challenge, however, is the immediate involvement of HRM in cost reductions and strategic thinking that often falls to senior management under the auspices of the chief financial officer (CFO). According to Robert Blakely, CFO of Tenneco, the CFO is the hub of five principal activities in the downsizing process: identifying the problem, quantifying its magnitude, designing a solution, implementing it, and selling the plan in the marketplace (McGoldrick, 1992). While the CFO must consider downsizing and its effects on the balance sheet and earnings outlook, several of the principal activities identified by Blakely overlap the responsibilities and expertise of HRM. Human resources must establish a close link with the chief executive officer, CFO, and others behind the downsizing strategy to ensure that the relevant personnel issues are addressed in any workforce reduction.

Another key challenge for HRM is the design and implementation of a downsizing plan that addresses the concerns of terminated employees as well as the remaining employees. Questions must be answered as to how many employees will be terminated and what criteria will be used to determine which employees will remain. Also, extensive HRM staff are needed to handle the implementation of most downsizing plans that include extensive severance packages and the coordination of outplacement services for terminated employees. Outplacement services may need to provide additional services to address the psychological consequences of layoffs through counseling services for terminated employees. The application of these services and other programs are also crucial for the employees who often harbor guilt feelings for remaining employed with the corporation.

The creation of a survivor plan is a key challenge for all senior management because of the difficulty of overcoming low employee morale. HRM professionals must be especially concerned with the need for developing additional job retraining for the surviving employees. There is a corporate myth behind ignoring the survivors in an organization. The idea is that remaining employees are so happy to have survived with jobs that management can ignore them (Moskal, 1992). The risk in adopting this strategy is trading potential financial gains for additional future losses.

One of the primary challenges is to determine the proper human resources needs to fit the company's strategic objectives. Many companies first get rid of people, then they make decisions about organizing those who remain. Only when they find that their remaining staffs cannot do the work, do the companies start to consider work priorities (Overman, 1991). Eastman Kodak's stock price surged in 1986 when it announced layoffs and cost-cutting measures; however, the stock subsequently declined to a value below 1982 levels. The experiences of Kodak and hundreds of other restructured companies suggest that few companies can slash payrolls without encountering downsizing's unintended consequences: low worker morale, lawsuits, and disappointing financial results (Boroughs, 1992). Many companies eliminate the workers but not the actual work. To be effective, organizations need to redesign their companies from top to bottom. In 1989, Sea-Land Shipping eliminated six layers of bureaucracy, cut approximately 800 people, and reassigned half of its remaining employees. However, Sea-Land is different than most organizations. The company spent eight months planning before it made an actual move, and resulting financial results have been successful (Boroughs, 1992). Unfortunately, fewer than half of the companies that downsized from 1987 to 1992 had planned to do so a year in advance (Wallfesh, 1991; and Fuchsberg & Bennett, 1992). Effective management planning of human resources needs is required. As examples, if too many employees are laid off, or if essential personnel are allowed to retire prematurely, the company may have to hire to refill these positions. It is imperative that HRM knows where the company is headed strategically, and integrates this into their strategy to deal with periods of slow growth. Often, layoffs can be avoided, or the negative effects of the layoffs mitigated, by human resources planning. Sensitivity to human issues can make the difference between success and failure of corporate reorganizations (Wallfesh, 1991).

Successful restructuring demands a working relationship between HRM and line managers. "The line must see things from a human resource perspective to avoid exposing the company to lawsuits. And the human resource staff must understand the business needs of line management in order to cut costs, raise productivity, and improve services" (Wallfesh, 1991). In a study of 30 manufacturing organizations between 1986 and 1990, HRM professionals advocated and helped implement several strategies in the effective firms. These strategies included extensive analyses of strengths and weaknesses and value-added activities. Management of human resources was given priority, information on costs was widely shared, bottom-up participation and implementation of downsizing was encouraged, and downsizing was viewed as a continual process and not a one-time target (Cameron, 1991). HRM must also develop and implement policies dealing with severance packages, training and development of retained employees, and several other issues, and it is important that HRM planning be consistent with corporate strategic objectives. Additional emphasis on HRM strategic planning will be needed in the next decade. As noted earlier, fewer than half of the companies that downsize plan to downsize by at least a year in advance. All corporations will need to have downsizing plans in place. Further emphasis must also be placed on alternatives to layoffs, training, and development of management given the new delayered corporate structure and other factors.

Another HRM challenge is to decide what options to pursue to curtail or reduce manning in periods of slow growth. Is a layoff required or is there a better option that can be pursued? Although economic conditions may necessitate reductions in force, massive layoffs are rarely the best remedy to cut costs. Consequences of layoffs are subtle but potentially lethal. Employee loyalty, morale, and innovativeness generally decrease and layoffs result in lost opportunities for the organization to make real gains (Cameron, 1991).

At a time when U.S. businesses are embracing a total quality management approach, many are undermining their own efforts through improperly planned and chaotic staff reductions. If companies want to increase quality, they must have an efficient, content, and productive workforce (Messmer, 1992). Several alternatives exist to layoffs. Many of these are across-the-board actions, such as early retirement options or attrition. These approaches can quickly reduce the numbers, but it is difficult to predict who will survive and what talents or expertise will be lost. The best downsizing strategies were recommended and designed by employees, not top managers. Although effective downsizing required top management initiative, the task was accomplished most effectively when lower-level employees had input to the process (Wallfesh, 1991). Some companies have pursued innovative alternatives to layoffs. Two of the furniture industry's leading companies, Herman Miller, Inc. and Steelcase, Inc., turned to voluntary programs to cut labor expenses (Heenan, 1991). Two hundred Miller employees at its Zealand, Michigan, headquarters were allowed to take several weeks of voluntary unpaid leave. Steelcase asked its employees to take up to 60 days leave of absence at reduced pay. There are many opportunities for HRM to pursue in this area in the coming decade. Although quick fixes, such as layoffs and restructuring, have been and will continue to be a major trend, evidence shows that layoffs have many unwanted HRM side effects.

HRM professionals will need to develop different strategies to deal with slow growth and rightsizing of organizations. Many organizations have already made the quick fix, either by hiring freezes and attrition, early retirement offers, or layoffs. As pressure continues to reduce costs further in the coming decade, HRM professionals must develop innovative ideas to meet corporate human resources needs without the negative effects of continual layoffs.

Severance issues must also be considered by HRM for companies that downsize. In 1992, Right Associates published the results of a comprehensive survey of severance policy in the United States (Louchheim, 1991/92). The pace of downsizing has made severance policy a key HRM issue. Written severance policies are necessary to set legal limits on severance benefits. Severance plans typically extend medical benefits for a certain period of time, provide job outplacement services, and compensate employees on the basis of some set formula, such as one week's pay for each year of service. It is important to have a legal, written plan. In the Right Associates survey, 24 percent of the companies with such plans were still involved in lawsuits. Costs of laying off workers versus early retirement offers or other payroll reduction plans must be weighed. Studies have shown that it is 23 to 40 percent more costly to retire employees ages 55 and over while retaining workers 40 to 54 years of age (Wallfesh, 1991). Other costs, such as unanticipated retirement of critical personnel, should also be included in the analysis.

It is clear with the continuing trend to downsize companies and layoff workers that severance will continue to be a significant HRM issue in the decade ahead. Further efforts and innovations will be needed to establish written severance policies that reduce the legal risk and costly lawsuits that have occurred in the past. Further analytical work concerning the cost benefits and tradeoffs of severance versus other payroll reductions is also needed.

Legal issues are a key HRM concern in periods of slower growth. These involve several different issues, such as the legality of the severance policy (discussed above), age discrimination issues involved with early retirement programs and EEOC compliance. As management layers are eliminated, job descriptions redefined, and employees laid off, it is essential that HRM be involved to ensure EEOC and other legal HRM issues are complied with. A recent survey by the law firm of Jackson, Lewis, Schnitzler & Krupman, which specializes in employment and benefit issues, found that more than half of the companies that have terminated workers during a downsizing have been sued, which, given the surge in downsizings, could lead to an explosion of litigation by 1994 (Boroughs, 1992, p. 52). It is clear that the legalities of HRM practices during reductions in force will be closely scrutinized, and that clearly, much attention must be given to these issues in the 1990s.

Another HRM issue is how to handle subsequent periods of increased growth. As the company downsizes, or more appropriately rightsizes, for periods of slow growth, it must have a plan for dealing with increased human resources needs during business upswings. Four out of five executives would prefer to have their departments slightly understaffed; this can avert layoffs, but can lead to overworked, unproductive workers. The rightsizing concept can be applied to separate those tasks that can potentially be done by specialized temporary workers versus permanent staff. Rightsizing attacks the one-person, one-job paradigm that assumes a 100 percent permanent staff (Messmer, 1992). The issue is whether to rehire permanent staff to suit business upturns, or to utilize temporary or part-time workers. The correct answer to this depends on several factors, such as future business trends, the availability of skilled temporaries who can handle the new tasks, and other factors. A major advantage of the rightsizing concept is that it protects core employees from repeated rounds of layoffs and downsizings.

Rightsizing involves analyzing a department's personnel needs based on its long-term objectives and finding a combination of permanent and temporary employees with the best skills to meet those needs. The temporary labor pool today encompasses accountants, systems analysts, engineers, lawyers, and other professionals; specialized temporaries now represent 20 percent of the temporary workforce. While the concept of rightsizing and temporaries is useful in many applications, additional work and innovation in this area is needed in the coming decade. Other potential courses of action are flexible workforces with high levels of interdepartmental cross training. This could allow reassigning existing personnel as needed to suit business conditions. This issue will continue to receive HRM visibility in the 1990s as costs of health insurance and other benefits for permanent employees increase.

A major HRM challenge during periods of slower growth is to develop an evaluation system that will lead to rewards and retention of skilled core workers and discourage continued employment of poor workers. The importance of developing and utilizing specific standard criteria in evaluating employees cannot be overemphasized. A recent law firm study showed that more than 50 percent of companies that have fired workers have been sued (Boroughs, 1992). Hoffman-La Roche, a pharmaceutical company, has been entangled in a lawsuit since 1985 related to downsizing charges of age discrimination. Workers are claiming that older employees with higher salaries were singled out for termination, while the company denies any wrongdoing. Meanwhile, the lawsuit remains unsettled, and Hoffman-La Roche has accumulated over $1 million in legal costs (Boroughs, 1992).

Robert M. Tomasko has identified four key HRM actions relating to periods of slow growth and downsizing (Wallfesh, 1991). The first action is to make it hard to get hired. Selection criteria for new recruits must ensure that employees fit the overall company culture as well as the job requirements, and part-time or temporary workers should be utilized. A second key factor is to make it hard for poor performers to stay. This involves putting teeth into the evaluation process. It should be cautioned here that evaluation systems need to be in place prior to downsizing. Most experts advise not to evaluate a person solely to support a reduction in force. Another factor emphasized by Tomasko is to slow down the upward-only fast track and to design career paths that cover more horizontal territory than vertical. The fourth key factor is to keep the pay system from building excess management back into the system. Consideration should be given to applying skill-based pay to staff workers.

While many downsizing efforts are created to lower costs by reducing the workforce, one critical issue that is often inadequately addressed concerns how to handle the work left by terminated employees. If this issue remains unaddressed, as it did for Unisys Corporation, downsizing becomes only one part of a complicated, costly cycle leading to employee burnout, uncompleted work, more new hires, and potentially culminating in further downsizing. For instance, between 1986 and 1990, Unisys hired at least 6,000 people a year at a hiring cost of $6,000 per employee, while eliminating thousands of positions at $100,000 per worker (Boroughs, 1992).

Following periods of downsizing, surviving employees have poor morale and fear loss of their own jobs. Retained employees must understand that they are valued by the organization, but that performance is key to personal and corporate success. These employees will have to assume more autonomy with elimination of management layers. Also, there will be fewer promotional opportunities for the star performers. Money helps, but star performers want to be told that the company has a bright future and that eventually their professional opportunities will soar. This is not always possible with the elimination of management positions. Therefore, companies need to give some control and authority to employees through increased team work, autonomous work units, or other measures (Weinstein & Leibman, 1991).

Additional training may also be needed as employees have to assume tasks previously performed by others. This is often difficult, as training budgets are curtailed in periods of slow growth. Therefore, employees should be compensated for additional skills they acquire. In general, the evaluation and reward system must reward core workers and expedite dismissal of poor performers. In the coming decade, more work will need to be done by HRM to ensure that valued employees are retained and rewarded. Skill-based and team-based rewards will likely become more prevalent, and non-salary–based rewards (special perks, opportunities to represent the company at seminars, and so forth) will likely increase. Retraining existing workers to perform totally different jobs will continue to be a priority.

With the numerous pitfalls associated with involuntary termination, the early retirement option is a typical corporate downsizing measure implemented to try to encourage voluntary workforce reductions and prevent morale problems for surviving employees. Most companies offer an early retirement option for older, long-time employees. While early retirement is an important program, a key drawback often results from offering an enticing early retirement option to a large number of employees who qualify and decide to accept retirement. Prior to the downsizing, the company may not realize that the number of employees who will leave is far greater than anticipated. In addition, the firm may lose many valuable performers who may hold critical positions, especially in a company restructuring. For instance, one survey found that 90 percent of firms offering an early retirement option lost employees they valued as good performers (Boroughs, 1992).

DuPont is an example of a company that learned that lesson the hard way in the 1980s. In 1991, the company utilized a more successful approach to retirement options when it announced the need to reduce costs by $1 billion. When DuPont decided to outsource work that was not directly related to their products, the firm found that 6,500 employees were displaced. This time, however, DuPont developed a more selective retirement approach, designed to offer a more extensive package available only to this identified group. The package was modeled on a 50-year-old employee with 25 years of service who would normally receive a retirement pension of $7,512 each year based on actuarial analysis. DuPont agreed to eliminate the actuarial analysis for employees in this new downsizing group, raising the pension to $18,756 a year. All identified employees have agreed to leave the company voluntarily (Faltermayer, 1992).

In lieu of the above challenges, another important HRM challenge, therefore, is to visualize the long-term impact of downsizing on the workforce in order to implement strategies and techniques to circumvent the future consequences of current downsizing plans. For example, the entire organizational chart may need to be recreated to accommodate a smaller workforce with enhanced responsibilities. Whatever changes are necessary, the HRM department is challenged to be the link between management cost-cutting objectives and their effects on company employees. HRM's most important role in this process is to provide clear, consistent, and effective communication to all employees during the downsizing.

ORGANIZATIONAL RESPONSES TO DOWNSIZING

While there have been a number of successful organizational and HRM responses to downsizing a workforce, the number of inadequately conceived and poorly implemented programs appears to outweigh the success stories in the literature. Many successful downsizings have occurred in smaller companies or organizations that have historically been generous with their workforce. Given the dynamics of the recent economy, many firms have felt pressured to downsize quickly in the last few years. Many of these workforce layoffs have come from larger organizations within U.S. industries, such as the automobile and computer companies. The effects of their downsizing programs have just begun to be felt by the public. The long-term consequences of these downsizings will affect businesses into the next century.

In addition, there are predictions that other industries will jump on the downsizing bandwagon in the future. Analysts predict further downsizing within the airline, retail, and banking industries in the future (McGoldrick, 1992). In fact, many believe that "restructuring — reorganization, downsizing, acquisition and divestiture — has become a permanent feature of the corporate landscape as companies struggle to redefine what it means to be competitive, or merely survive, in a global economy" (McGoldrick, p. 76). With these predictions, a well-designed downsizing plan becomes critical to reduce the restructuring needed in the future.

One key factor that will influence the effectiveness of downsizing plans, and make some current plans inadequate for the future, is the changing U.S. workforce. With more women in the workforce, current plans may need to be adjusted to take into account different human resource needs. For example, recent research indicates that women have distinctive needs in the outplacement process, and may take up to 38 percent longer to place into another position (Phelphs & Mason, 1991). Similarly, women approach the outplacement process from a different perspective than men, sometimes looking for a recruiting firm that provides supportive services in addition to job placement responsibilities. With varying workforce needs, the concept of one comprehensive downsizing plan will not meet the need of the terminated employees. Many challenges will exist in this area for HRM in the future, with the development of appropriate placement services, with downsizing, as well as recognizing the needs of a diverse workforce at the beginning of the recruitment process.

Another dilemma facing many organizations and HRM departments that has not received enough attention in the past is the issue of ethical responsibility to employees versus the need to reduce overhead costs. As companies have focused on reducing short-term costs, some employees have begun to experience long-term psychological consequences. In addition to low employee morale, employees who are terminated without extensive outplacement support may experience great anxiety, despair, and even suicide after termination. One consultant outlines the causes behind a recent suicide:

The real story isn't the suicide, but what caused it. Corporate America is discarding its employees, especially their middle-aged, hard-to-find compar-able-job employees, without even blinking a corporate eyelash. Many men and women have become so despondent that nothing seems to deter them from choosing suicide. People who work beside these people day after day fail to recognize even one clue of their intentions. (Murphy, 1992, p. 30)

As corporate downsizing becomes prevalent, negative psychological effects of downsizing will increase unless top management and HRM develop adequate employee support mechanisms. Ironically, the suicide story Murphy discussed referred to a woman who was the head of counseling for an employee assistance program. Therefore, not only do the psychological problems of terminated and surviving employees need to be addressed differently in the future, so too, do the effects of implementing downsizing programs on the HRM staff.

What are the Optimas Awards about? They are about caring about people. They are about good business practices. Increasingly, in the 1990s, these two activities are converging. The *Personnel Journal*'s 1992 Optimas Award for Vision was bestowed on Household International for its program that found new positions elsewhere within the company for employees who were downsizing casualties. By becoming a strategic partner with management, HRM was able to provide the foresight and implement the program coincident with the downsizing process. Accomplished through an external hiring freeze and through the HRM efforts of a displaced employee committee, the net worker loss associated with the downsizing was minimized (Stuart, 1992).

Recently, to avoid involuntary layoffs, DuPont initiated a downsizing effort to reduce its 80,000 workforce by 5,500 through early retirement and work sharing. Early retirement incentive options to attract voluntary separation represents another HRM alternative strategy to manage workforce reduction. However, this strategy must be balanced against the cost of such incentive programs and the danger of losing some of the organization's top performers.

One corporate success story is Gannett Company's decision to base downsizing on attrition by not filling vacated positions and 3M's voluntary termination packages. While 3M has focused on employee downsizing since the late 1980s by reducing hiring significantly, the company has not lost sight of the value of continued college recruiting efforts. According to 3M's Senior Vice President, the "young technologists . . . [are] the lifeblood of a company that gets 30% of its revenue from products introduced within the past five years" (Faltermayer, 1992, p. 85). 3M does, however, stress the idea of long-term employment with the new recruits.

Two other creative approaches implemented by Worthington Industries and Baldor Electric are based on the shared downsizing responsibility between the company and employees. Worthington Industries, a steel cutter, found that layoffs could be avoided by linking an employee's wages closely to company profits. Costs have been kept lower during the recession automatically because of pay reductions. Even though Worthington experienced a 16 percent reduction in profits in 1991, no employees were terminated. Instead, average employee wages fell by 5 percent, with top management experiencing an 11 percent cut (Faltermayer, 1992). Baldor Electric's employees proposed a company downsizing program involving the idea of work sharing. The company realized that it did not want its most valuable resource walking out the door, so factory workers agreed to help cut costs by working a total of seven four-day weeks. The work sharing program is effective, because Baldor will not have to hire new employees when demand increases; the employees will already be trained and in place. Baldor, however, did not resort to work sharing before implementing other cost-cutting measures first.

In reality, a majority of the questions that need to be answered regarding downsizing present important challenges for HRM professionals in the coming years. The following list summarizes other questions raised in the current literature.

What is the most effective role for HRM to play in the strategic decision by top management to downsize?

How can HRM become the critical link between cost-cutting and the effects on employees?

How can HRM convince corporate decision makers of the need to invest significant resources into downsizing in terms of support systems, staffing, and monetary resources to gain the maximum positive long-term effects?

How should an organization determine the appropriate balance between termination and survivor plans?

What is a corporation's ethical responsibility to its employees in downsizing?

Does downsizing always need to include workforce layoffs? Are there more cost-effective, positive corporate responses?

Much of the current literature has begun to address human resources challenges by proposing solutions to some previously unanswered questions on downsizing. The role of HRM during periods of slower growth in organizations involves many facets. First and foremost, HRM must be aligned with corporate strategic objectives. Manning levels should be established to support these objectives with a core of permanent employees supplemented by temporaries as required to suit business-up cycles. Corporate objectives and financial position need to be communicated to all levels of the organization.

A key recommendation relates to the macro issue of the change process and avoiding resistance to change. HRM professionals need to consider behavioral reactions to change in designing their downsizing programs, for example, understanding the importance of employee participation in the change process so that the changes are more readily accepted. The key to effective employee participation in downsizing is through constant and consistent communication on all levels of the corporation. By communicating with employees, the uncertainty of the process is reduced, thereby eliminating typical resistance to change such as territorial or petty behavior. According to Kanter (1985), shock leads to resistance. Time and information are the keys to reducing the shock factor. Kanter's specific recommendations are based on the idea that "information counts in building commitment to change, especially step-by-step scenarios with timetables and milestones. Dividing a big change into a number of small steps can help make it seem less risky and threatening" (p. 53). Senior management and HRM professionals must be committed to the change process and demonstrate their commitment to the success of the organization by investing in their employees, especially during a period of workforce layoffs.

A second recommendation related to the overall change process involves the attitude conveyed by many corporations that past corporate actions were wrong. According to Kanter (1985), when employees hear this, their reaction involves embarrassment and defensiveness that leads to employee resistance to change. Kanter emphasizes that past actions should remain in the past as appropriate ideas for a particular time period. Senior management must also realize the advantage of leaving in place as many familiar sights and sounds as possible to reduce employee fear of large changes. The focus for management must be on implementing the required changes for the future by determining what strategies will lead to profitability and success.

Although the link between HRM and senior company officials has been mentioned, a critical link must be established between human resources and line management. These managers are much closer to lower level employees and can help reinforce key programs and reduce negative employee reactions like lawsuits. Human resources effectiveness is reliant, to a great extent, on bridging the gap between the top and bottom levels of the organization in the downsizing efforts.

Strategies to deal with slow growth and the accompanying downsizing need to be developed and clearly communicated to employees, and lower-level personnel should be included in the formation of these policies. Policies, such as job retraining and reassignment, and flexible workforce concepts need to be developed to eliminate or minimize layoffs. Layoffs and downsizings, where unavoidable, must be planned well in advance and effectively communicated to the employees to avoid the low morale and risk aversion paralysis that often accompany layoffs. Evaluation strategies must be developed to ensure that continued employment of poor performers is discouraged, and that core personnel are retained in periods of retrenchment. Good employees must be compensated and rewarded for their efforts. These efforts may involve recognition, involvement on task teams, and other non-monetary rewards. If layoffs or other reductions in force are unavoidable, severance plans should be formally established, and discharged employees should be treated equitably and with dignity. All policies and decisions must fully comply with EEOC and other legal guidelines and should be carefully reviewed by HRM prior to implementation. Early retirements and other grenade approaches should be avoided, if possible, because it is impossible to predict which employees will be lost.

In addition to the above recommendations, management development paths must be carefully planned because previous hierarchical development channels may not exist, and the impact of additional responsibilities on managers must be considered. Time and stress management training for the remaining managers would be beneficial to lessen the potential for overstress and burnout. Lower level managers should be rotated through a variety of lateral assignments, and outside educational training should be provided to prepare them for eventual upper management positions. Measures should also be taken to reinforce the corporate vision continually to ensure that tendencies to reestablish old hierarchical structures do not re-emerge. In essence, slower growth and corporate restructuring involve all aspects of HRM, and a multi-faceted HRM program is needed to effectively manage resources in a period of slower economic growth.

Other specific recommendations for actions to be taken by HRM professionals can best be understood and developed from a survey taken by Retirement Advisors, Inc. Retirement Advisors, Inc. surveyed human resources executives from 27 clients who had implemented a downsizing plan within the last three years about what they would like to do differently if given the opportunity. The following responses were given most often (Wallfesh, 1991):

HRM should be involved from the beginning of the process, not when policies need to be executed.

In order to be the most helpful, HRM needs more time to plan for the downsizing.

Across-the-board workforce reductions are not the most effective downsizing choice.

Outside assistance is needed from specialized consultants in various HRM areas.

Skills inventories need to be conducted on all surviving employees to maximize their utilization in the new workforce.

HRM professionals regretted not taking advantage of early retirement options.

HRM should pay more attention to the surviving employees.

From these human resources responses, an overall theme for downsizing can be created by thinking in terms of what Brockner (1992) refers to as the substance and style of layoffs. Substance can be translated into doing the right things, and style can be equated to doing things the right way.

In organizational terms, this chapter recommends, as Brockner does, that the substance of downsizing be broken into three critical phases: before the layoffs, during the layoffs, and after the layoffs. Strategic thinking and action-oriented plans should be developed accordingly for each phase of downsizing. Prior to a reduction in the workforce, a firm must consider the change elements already mentioned, as well as possible alternatives to cutting costs. Senior management and HRM must consider the long-term consequences of their actions at this phase, prior to the implementation of any programs. At that time, it is necessary to discuss how large the workforce reduction must be and whether a rigid or flexible termination plan will be more effective. Numerous questions must be addressed focusing on the corporate culture and what type of downsizing is appropriate.

Another consideration for HRM professionals must be the need for further layoffs or hirings and how those plans will affect the current workforce. Again, the key strategies must be evaluated within a sufficient time frame and with ample employee and management feedback. It is also important to identify key employees within the organization who will be critical in the implementation phase of a workforce reduction by establishing employee support and relaying feedback. Overall, the style of all phases of downsizing must always be based on an ethical responsibility and concern for employees, their needs, and the long-term goals of the organization.

One recommendation for the actual workforce reduction phase of downsizing is that the organization overcommunicate with their employees. In other words, there can never be too much information provided by HRM and senior management to employees. Employees must also play a role in the development of the downsizing plans if success is to be assured. The actual downsizing plans will obviously vary according to a company's size, industry, and financial situation; however, several recommendations can be made as to the basic human resources issues to consider.

Early retirement options can be established to reduce the number of employees terminated; however, the financial impact of this option must be weighed carefully. A standardized severance package should be created for employees who will be involuntarily terminated. When establishing the severance packages, legal guidelines must also be examined. For example, if a company is planning to close a plant or is planning a large layoff, the firm must adhere to several 1990 laws including the Employee Retirement Income Security Act, the Worker Adjustment and Retraining Notification Act, and the Older Workers Benefit Protection Act (Louchheim, 1991/92).

In addition to the plans developed for workers who are leaving the organization, the need for a formal survivor plan cannot be underestimated. The remaining employees represent the future of the organization, and it is vital for them to understand how the corporation will operate after the downsizing. A recommendation, depending on the size of the organization, is to hold a formal employee orientation to introduce everyone to the new organization and clearly explain the roles employees will play in the new structure. It is also vital to implement a plan designed to outsource or restructure the work left by terminated employees. Surviving workers must not be made to feel that they are responsible for many other jobs in addition to their own. HRM, however, must take a proactive role with the surviving employees in terms of new training courses and cross-training opportunities. Some companies can even find new methods of efficiency based on department or division restructuring of job tasks and employees.

In looking over the ideas highlighted throughout this chapter, a key question for HRM is: how should it be managed. Before implementing layoffs, HRM must plan carefully, to minimize the shock, confusion, and anger that inevitably follow. HRM has key responsibilities (along with other organizational managers): to perform an internal assessment impact, to create policies and timetables, to plan for severance pay and relocation counseling — a complete package of services to help employees.

The following are some suggestions when downsizing is imminent and unavoidable:

1. Be prepared. HRM personnel should study past changes and their impacts on their organization and others. That is, they should identify the lessons learned and think through policies and procedures well before they are needed. Any collective bargaining agreement should be carefully checked. Plans to counteract any potential adverse effects — communication networks, quality of work life, employee

motivation and morale, and work team and individual productivity — should also be developed and introduced when needed.

2. Organize the downsizing process. HRM personnel should systematically identify which functions, jobs, and people are to be reduced or eliminated, in what order, and when. Decisions should also be made on how functions will be handled once cut-backs occur. Efforts should be made to avoid across-the-board cuts. Functions and jobs should be targeted based on the organization's strategic plan and the bottom-line results the organization is seeking to achieve. HRM personnel should work to build a supportive work climate, clarify the change, and identify the primary impact on people and the organization as a result of the downsizing.

3. Sensitive communication issues should be addressed. HRM personnel should spend considerable time determining what employees need and want to know, develop a communication plan to provide that information, and then implement the plan. Communications should be based on honesty and openness.

4. Options and assistance should be clearly communicated to employees. If employees are to be given choices of any kind, HRM personnel should ensure that employees have access to the information they need to make informed decisions. In addition, if loss of a job is involved, outplacement services to help people locate new jobs should be provided and offer any special help through employee assistance programs or professional counseling services. HRM professionals should also work to see that their organizations consider alternatives to layoffs — job sharing, performance-based pay, and early retirement incentives.

5. Use damage-control measures. HRM personnel should monitor events closely, identify glitches as early as possible, do something to minimize the damage they can cause to the organization and its people, and modify the downsizing plan when necessary.

In the end, the main consideration for HRM in any downsizing situation is to become a part of the downsizing strategy in the planning stages so that all HRM personnel and resources can be maximized. HRM must offer as many services as possible to employees to help them through a stressful transition. HRM professionals must consider taking advantage of some of their own counseling and other services offered because of the pressure they must endure throughout the downsizing process. If planned and implemented carefully, HRM can be the key link between management and work force in the successful use of workforce reductions in downsizing in order to accomplish a company's cost-cutting goals.

A GLIMPSE OF THE FUTURE

If the current trend continues, there is no doubt that organizations of the future will be significantly different from those of today, due to both technological and human factors. The trend toward reduction of middle management layers will continue, driven by the information explosion. As management support systems become more sophisticated and are integrated into the organization, fewer levels of management will be required for decision making and control. Human resources information systems will also be utilized in a variety of ways — to assess staffing needs, to analyze proper levels of permanent and temporary workers, and to locate temporaries quickly and efficiently when needed. Organizations will utilize smaller cadres of permanent workers who are highly trained, flexible, and less specialized than today's workers. Less specialization will be required because computer resources will provide a variety of expertises previously out of the realm of the individual worker. The workplace will be highly automated and many jobs will be eliminated or modified. All of these factors will reinforce a continuing downsizing of corporations, although payrolls will be reduced in a more planned manner.

With the increase in women in the workforce and the increased emphasis of workers on family and community interests, work hours will become more flexible. More voluntary unpaid or reduced pay leave will be utilized, and more work will be done at home via computer networking. The trend to highly specialized temporary employees will continue, aided by computer networking, and many temporaries will be self-employed and work out of their homes. Workers in general will be better trained, and training costs will decrease as computer simulated training is developed. On the negative side, increased technology may adversely affect human relations skills as the trend for machines to talk to machines versus people to talk to people continues.

The increased use of technology and automation will continue to exert a negative effect on employment levels, and will reinforce the trend to eliminate management layers. The workforce of the future will be highly flexible, less specialized, and well trained, and an increasing number of highly specialized temporaries will be utilized.

In the future, we will see much more downsizing, even with improvements in the economy. Many companies expanded rapidly throughout the 1980s and increased their workforces at an even greater rate. Some of the workforce reductions, especially in the area of middle management, may help companies to reduce costs and operate more efficiently. The numerous downsizings that have taken place have awakened the private sector to the difficult decisions to be made to remain competitive in a global marketplace. One technique, however, that will become more prevalent in downsizing is the concept of rightsizing. The technique involves analyzing personnel needs based on the long-term strategies and objectives of the company and utilizing a combination of permanent and temporary employees with the required skills to satisfy the needs of the organization (Messmer, 1992).

HRM will continue to play a major role in organizations during periods of slower growth. HRM will become much more active in the downsizing process, including implementing techniques such as rightsizing. Reductions in force and other downsizing issues related to slower growth will continue to present a variety of challenges to organizations and HRM professionals. These include aligning human resources needs with corporate strategy, severance and compensation issues, and motivation and reward of core employees. Alternatives to layoffs and early retirement type incentives should be pursued, where possible, to eliminate the negative impact of layoffs on employee motivation and productivity. Significant issues remain for HRM to address in the next decade and in the future. These include management development concerns and the impact of technological changes on organizations. All of these issues must be carefully addressed by HRM to ensure profitability and survival of companies during periods of slower growth in today's global economy.

CONCLUSION

The issue discussed in this chapter is the role of HRM in downsizing efforts by organizations. In today's economic climate, more companies need to reduce expenses, improve cash flow, or enhance shareholder's returns on investment; many executives are looking at downsizing as a quick fix. Corporate layoffs threaten to accelerate in the coming years, even if the economy picks up. Many industries have yet to finish reshaping themselves in the face of increasing global and domestic competition. Other companies are still attempting to eliminate unnecessary management layers. The movement toward slower growth is a long-term trend driven by several factors. Among these are the use of information technology in lieu of human resources, increased automation, flatter organizational structures, and redesigned, flexible workforces.

Traditionally, economists have talked about labor as a variable cost, but often, management has treated labor as a quasi-fixed cost. During the past decade, management has rediscovered labor as a prime variable cost. With the discovery of labor as a variable, the HRM role in the corporation has escalated. An example of this escalation can be seen in the increased responsibility that HRM has achieved in the area of downsizing.

While some employees can reap benefits from downsizing, these benefits often provide dire consequences for the average employee who may find that some form of job displacement ensues. How the organization manages the downsizing process can go a long way in maintaining a positive relationship between employees and the organization. The possibility of maintaining a positive relationship during downsizing is best accomplished when the organization keeps in mind one of the oldest theories of moral conduct based upon the assertion that a person's actions toward another should be considered in light of how that person would wish to be treated in the same situation. This perspective calls for HRM professionals and key organizational leaders to examine the effects from the vantage point of those impacted. For example, in a merger situation, those initiating the consolidation should seriously consider the effects on employees from the vantage point of the employees. Would the top managers want to be treated in this way? If the answer is negative, then a reexamination of the process may be in order. According to this model, the dignity and importance of employees must be preserved in the process of consolidation in order to maintain a positive employee-employer relationship. If this is not possible, the process must be questioned because the negative effects on employees impact the organization.

In conclusion, HRM professionals should spend considerable time during the downsizing process addressing questions like:

Are there ways to downsize that will not have negative consequences for employees?

Will each employee be treated with dignity and respect in the downsizing process?

If negative effects are unavoidable, are there mechanisms to alleviate or lessen the impact?

If there are negative consequences, can these be shared among various employee groups so that no individual group bears the full brunt of the consequences?

If any employees suffer loss, are there measures that can be taken to alleviate the loss?

REFERENCES

Boroughs, D. L. 1992, May 4. Amputating assets. *U.S. News & World Report 112*: 50–52.

Brockner, J. 1992, Winter. Managing the effects of layoffs on survivors. *California Management Review 34*: 9–27.

Cameron, K. 1991, July. Downsizing can be hazardous to your future. *HRMagazine*: 85, 96.

Faltermayer, E. 1992, June 1. Is this layoff necessary? *Fortune*: 71–86.

Fuchsberg, G. & Bennett, A. 1992, October 23. Recovery or not, more companies plan to cut work forces, new survey says. *The Wall Street Journal*: A2.

Heenan, D. O. 1991, September/October. The right way to downsize. *The Journal of Business Strategy 12*: 4–7.

Kanter, R. M. 1985, April. Managing the human side of change. *Management Review*: 52–56.

Louchheim, F. P. 1991/92, Winter. Four lessons from downsizing to build future productivity. *Employment Relations Today 18*: 467–75.

McGoldrick, B. 1992, June. The CFO as chief firing officer. *Institutional Investor 26*: 75–79.

Messmer, M. 1992, August 3. Rightsizing, not downsizing. *Industry Week 241*: 23–26.

Moskal, B. S. 1992, August 3. Managing survivors. *Industry Week 241*: 15–22.

Murphy, M. 1992, May. Desperation in corporate America. *Personnel Journal*: 30–31.

Overman, S. 1991, August. The layoff legacy. *HRMagazine*: 29–32.

Phelphs, S. & Mason, M. 1991, August. When women lose their jobs. *Personnel Journal*: 64–69.

Stuart, P. 1992, August. New internal jobs found for displaced employees. *Personnel Journal*: 21–23.

Wallfesh, H. M. 1991, Summer. Downsize by design to get the intended results. *Employment Relations Today 18*: 175–83.

Weinstein, H. P. & Leibman, M. L. 1991, August. Corporate scale down, what comes next? *HRMagazine*: 33–37.

9

Ethics and the Role of Human Resources Management

Unquestionably, managers in any organization have the responsibility to serve the stakeholders and the organization itself. However, more and more organizations are acknowledging that they also have responsibilities to employees, customers, the community within which the organization operates, and even the environment and society. Even if profit is the organization's primary or only goal, ethical standards for dealing with these various constituencies have become a new competitive arena for business. Businesses that deal fairly and ethically with employees and communities incur goodwill and attract the best employees and loyal customers, as well as avoiding the considerable legal costs of failing in the ethical arena. Profit can still be an organizational goal, but the bottom line cannot be served at the expense of ethical standards of behavior without leaving one's moral obligation unfulfilled or sacrificing long-term performance. MacAdam (1992) suggests that quality, service, and cash flow are direct results of people's character, competence, and commitment. With this perspective, organizational responsibility now goes far beyond traditional business concerns.

There are strong incentives for organizations to proactively take the high road when confronting their ethical obligations. In addition to enhancing the organization's reputation, credibility, goodwill, and social balance sheet, ethical conduct may improve bottom-line performance by reducing the firm's exposure to stiff fines, penalties, and the loss of contracts and customers. Moreover, an organization that is viewed as ethical and fair may have an important competitive advantage in the recruiting and retaining of top employees.

There are other compelling motivations for an organization to institutionalize an ethics strategy, however. Linking strategy with ethics has simply become more common. Competitive people want to know — in express terms — what their company, and themselves by extension, stand for. Hence, one virtuous goal of this process is to close the values gap by creating an environment with shared convictions and a shared sense of purpose that will build mutually binding pride and commitment.

A major theme of this book is that contemporary human resources management (HRM) is now being viewed as a wide and diverse set of functions designed to align the mutual goals of both the organization and all of its stakeholders — particularly its employees. And in more and more organizations, HRM is conventionally being viewed as a resource for bringing to reality the organization's objectives. In addition, the Society for Human Resource Management affirmatively acknowledges HRM's intermediary role between organizations and employees as manifested by its adoption of a written code of ethics established to guide the activities of HRM professionals.

As a strategic resource for management to achieve its organizational goals, HRM will play a pivotal role in the design and execution of an ethics strategy. From recruitment, to training and development, to compensation and benefits HRM professionals must be responsive to an increasingly wider set of constituencies, for example, employees, management, stockholders, the environment, and so forth, when designing ethically-balanced HRM strategies. This chapter is concerned with the challenges confronting HRM professionals in their efforts to help develop an ethically-oriented organization. The chapter will first discuss how ethics poses a challenge to HRM professionals in their mission to align specific HRM programs with the overall strategic goals of the organization. It will then provide some examples of how organizations have attempted to create more ethically-oriented work environments. The chapter will then offer a glimpse of future ethics issues that HRM professionals and their organizations will need to address if they are to decrease the likelihood of unethical behavior.

ETHICS CHALLENGES FOR
HUMAN RESOURCES MANAGEMENT

Many organizations, in their efforts to address the national and global challenges of unethical behavior, are relying more and more on their HRM department. As a result, HRM professionals are finding that they are increasingly becoming involved in, and must be especially sensitive to, ethical issues because of the key role HRM professionals play in the development of human resources or people policies and programs. Thus, policies and programs that often make a major difference in the extent to which employees exhibit ethical or unethical behavior and in the ethical climate developed and maintained in their organizations has become an important responsibility for HRM departments.

With increased responsibility in the area of ethics, HRM professionals are confronted with a number of issues and challenges. To effectively perform their role as intermediaries between the employee and the organization in the ethics arena, HRM professionals must recognize that the ethical challenges that they will encounter are often the complex function of the industry (public and private), regulatory environment, and the cultural environment specific to each organization. A critical assessment of some of the more important ethical issues and challenges (and some of the responses to date) confronting HRM in its mission to align specific HRM programs with the overall strategic goals of the organization is provided below.

Diversified Workforce

With an increasingly diversified workforce, for example, age, gender, race, ethnicity, the competition for highly skilled and motivated labor will become greater. In the face of this stiffer competition for scarcer labor resources, the incentive for unethical HRM practices will be magnified. In answer to these opportunities for unethical hiring, transfer, and dismissal options, HRM professionals will continue to be tested to design innovative and multi-dimensional HRM programs to retain and develop its human capital. Commitment to an ethical approach that provides internal development and promotion opportunities not only retains ethical virtues but also has a strong economic rationale, that is, the low-cost premise that is more expensive to pursue a premium hiring strategy.

Also, with an aging workforce, where, by 2010, 25 percent of the U.S. population will be at least 55 years of age and 14 percent will be at least 65 years of age, the HRM challenge will be to provide new training, upgraded skills, and cross-training to its workforce consistent with the technological environment.

Further, the increase of dual career marriages may require HRM to perform a renewed critical appraisal of traditional anti-nepotism policies for co-workers who marry or live together as co-dependents. Implementation of a no-supervision policy so that roles are not compromised has been a positive first step by HRM in many organizations.

Downsizing

At least in the near future, downsizing, or rightsizing, will be an important driving force confronting many U.S. businesses. The critical challenge to HRM professionals will be to design and implement an effective labor force reduction strategy consistent with the overall organizational goals that is as fair and equitable as possible. If carefully designed and reinforced through forthright communication — consistent with any prevailing statutory requirements, for example, the

Worker Adjustment and Retraining Act — this extremely anguishing process can be achieved with the loss of organizational and employee goodwill minimized. Further, if balanced equitably, it is more likely to withstand the test of legal challenges.

HRM professionals must be concerned about designing and executing a workforce reduction strategy that is ethically balanced. One common approach has been to base it on seniority. However rational this approach may appear, how will this strategy affect other vital HRM programs in place, for example, recently hired Affirmative Action (AA) (Whiteside, 1983)? The dilemma for HRM professionals is to design an equitable labor reduction strategy that preserves both the merits of seniority-based systems and other HRM programs, for example, AA.

Other ethical issues associated with downsizing include what ethical duty, if any, organizations owe laid off workers, for example, extended benefits, outplacement services. Also, HRM must be vigilant in responding to any dysfunctional organizational effects that an improperly managed reduction process may have created with the surviving workforce. For example, the residue of an improperly managed reduction process may create another set of ethical dilemmas for the surviving workforce, for example, the contradictory message that a self-proclaimed humanistic organization sends when its reduction strategy is callous in its design and brutal in its execution.

Recruitment

Consistent with the diversification of the workforce, substantial ethical challenges will result in the recruiting process. For example, motivated with blind ambition to obtain key personnel deemed vital to turn a struggling corporation around, HRM may be reluctant to properly disclose the true financial health of the organization. A recruiting strategy that is only effective to the extent that it unfairly describes the position or exaggerates the true virtues of the organization will yield pyrrhic success in the long term. Most interviews today are not a very effective way to make hiring or promotion decisions. Indeed, they never were. In an attempt to determine the existence — or lack — of mutual fit between the organization and the candidate, the interview does provide an important opportunity to candidly convey the realistic negatives associated with the position. Establishing false expectations usually will cause the organization to incur expenses — turnover, lost productivity — that otherwise may have been avoided (Brink, 1992). Full ethically-balanced disclosure must be the cornerstone to the HRM recruitment strategy.

There are other recruitment-related ethical issues to which HRM will need to respond. HRM professionals must be sensitive to the ethical dilemmas that may result from an internal or external recruitment strategy. With special skill, HRM professionals must carefully assess the ethical benefits of internal hiring, for example, promotion of employee morale, goodwill, development, weighed against the benefits of an external recruitment strategy, for example, unequalled credentials, interjection of a much needed fresh perspective, and so forth.

Job Analysis

Job analysis will continue to play a pivotal role within HRM, particularly as the courts continue to take a more expansive view of individual property rights, for example, employment. The legal dangers of departing from a careful and ethical job analysis were illustrated in *Griggs* vs. *Duke Power*. In that case, the Supreme Court held that requiring a high school diploma was illegal because the company provided no evidence that high school education was a valid predictor of job performance. Hence, there are not only ethical but also legal incentives for HRM to perform accurately detailed job analyses that are both thorough and fair.

Termination

Termination is another vital area of HRM that is fraught with unethical opportunities. Separation deals made out of convenience pose significant ethical dilemmas. A critical assessment must be made of the ethical trade-offs of allowing employees to go quietly in an effort to avoid the threat of lawsuit or adverse organizational publicity balanced against the message the decision sends to honorable employees who generally uphold the ethical principles of the organization.

References

Similarly, HRM is continually confronted by ethical tension in the area of references. Specifically, there are the competing HRM interests to give neutral references — to reduce the risk of defamation lawsuits — and the moral and perhaps legal duty to properly inform prospective employers where potential harm is reasonably foreseeable. Conversely, HRM must exercise ethical and legal due diligence in screening the references of potential candidates responsive to the risk that negligent hiring may expose the organization to significant loss and liability (Munchus, 1992).

Compensation

An organization's reward system is one of the most powerful forces that motivates employee conduct. Hence, HRM must be especially careful in designing and executing a compensation program that encourages employee performance consistent with the ethical expectations of the organization. For example, a strategy linking pay to performance compensation that is driven solely by bottom-line results may produce a cut-throat workforce mentality that may ultimately undermine the initial goal of the bottom-line strategy, for example, a productive workforce. In the case of H. J. Heinz, their management incentive plan was designed with the laudable objective of motivating sales performance. However, in effect, it created an unhealthy pressurized environment that led to an unethical consciousness that pervaded throughout the organization and extended to its vendors (Post, 1981a). Ultimately, this compensation strategy contributed to widespread practices involving improper income and expenditure recognition. As a consequence, in addition to public embarrassment, H. J. Heinz was exposed to Securities and Exchange Commission (SEC) and Internal Revenue Service criminal investigations (Post, 1981b).

The underlying purpose of a pay-level policy is to link compensation programs to an organization's human resources (mainly attraction and retention) and business needs (mainly ability to pay). Competitive demands and efforts to decentralize decision making are likely to continue to push organizations toward more differentiation in pay policies. One equitable model includes a group variable-compensation approach. Under this strategy, base compensation is set at below-market or at-market but provides for above-market total compensation when business results exceed planned targets or if specified productivity improvement goals are achieved (Hestwood, 1992). Again, as described above, caution must be exercised by HRM professionals to ensure that the performance incentives do not stimulate improper corporate conduct. Hence, linked prosperity on both economic and ethical dimensions, must be the force driving the HRM compensation strategy (Laabs, 1992a).

Executive compensation has pressured and will continue to pressure HRM in the area of compensation management. Rewarding executives with multi-million dollar salaries and options while the organization struggles through an economic downturn and is forced to incur anguishing layoffs to its workforce will remain an extremely controversial HRM issue. Responsive to this unethical, if not unconscionable, organizational behavior, the government has proposed legislation that would limit the deductibility of executive compensation for federal income tax purposes. This will only complicate the challenge to HRM. The HRM task now will be to design comparable executive compensation packages that will minimize the tax consequences to the executive and the organization — while restoring some ethical rationale to the reward system. This complex area, like many other HRM areas in the twenty-first century, provide prime examples where outsourcing for special HRM expertise will increase. These resources must be utilized where cost-effective to augment and build upon in-house HRM competencies.

Benefits

Recently, a Fortune 100 company reported a record increase in quarterly earnings. However, this record-setting bottom-line performance did not come without any collateral damage. Specifically, it was noted that a significant factor in the record earnings was attributed to a strategy that converted a vast number of workers to part-time status. The goal achieved by this strategy was that these part-time workers were no longer eligible for company benefits, for example, health, pension — hence, dramatically improving the organization's bottom line.

The ethical dimensions of this corporate strategy are extremely controversial. The debate surrounding such organizational strategies will no doubt increase particularly with the passage of FASB 106. This accounting standard requires all companies to report, as a balance-sheet liability, the actuarial determined cash value of future postretirement health benefits (Wilbert & Dakdduk, 1991). Whereas in the past organizations could recognize these costs when incurred (through off-balance sheet financing on a pay-as-you-go basis), the requirement now is to discount these future costs to present day dollars. This huge catch-up reserve, which may be amortized over a 20-year period, is estimated to cost larger U.S. organizations millions of dollars, potentially resulting in double digit percentage reductions in pre-tax profits. IBM reported in 1991 that it was taking a first-quarter charge of $2.3 billion as a result of the accounting requirement. In answer to this added cost, companies are looking elsewhere, that is, at benefits, to shore up their bottom line. Small businesses will be particularly hard pressed by these new requirements.

Although not solely an HRM decision, organizations will no doubt look to HRM to provide the benefit/cost analysis, present viable alternatives, and execute an implementation strategy of the eventual decision. Again, the challenge to HRM will be to assess the ethical trade-offs among constituencies, that is, promissory agreements with stockholders and psychological contracts with employees. In the future, organizations will be judged on how they treat their human resources in the hard times and the good times (Rogers, 1992).

Human Resources Management Policy on Integrity

Ethical principles must be the backbone of an effective HRM program. The integrity of the HRM function will be compromised if it yields to political pressure to hire strictly on the basis of a manager's preference, for example. More drastically, the bottom-line objectives of the organization will be compromised if HRM does not recognize — or worse, HRM recognizes but fails to intervene for fear of retribution — improper labor resource allocation motivations, for example, inflating hiring needs to build empires, increasing budget authority, puffing-up job descriptions in order to get subordinates raises.

An HRM policy that caves into exception after exception from forceful political powers within the organization will jeopardize the credibility of all HRM programs. Insistence on consistency, fairness, and internal equity, even at the sacrifice of personal advantage, may be politically unwise but essential for HRM to develop and maintain a viable leadership role within the organization.

Labor Resource Allocation

HRM must be vigilant to the detection and protection of improper hiring practices, for example, empire building. Likewise, the hoarding of top performers by managers at the expense of promotion or recommending poor performers for promotion or transfer in order to extricate them from their division are other bottom-line dangers HRM professionals must be ethically responsive to.

Employee Assistance Programs

The HRM ethical challenges associated with this issue are enormous with no clear remedies. What ethical duty, if any, does an organization have to rehabilitate or provide sensitivity training to its workforce (Davidson, 1982)? Assuming there are no guarantees that the investment in such programs will be cost-effective, what incentive does the organization have when assessed against its obligations to its stockholders. Balancing competing constituents' interests, for example, shareholders that profit vis-à-vis employee wellness, will pose a daunting challenge for HRM professionals.

Studies conducted by several large companies have provided some astonishing results. McDonnell Douglas tracked 25,000 employees over a four-year period and determined that the company's employee assistance program saved $4 million in health claims and absence for every dollar spent. General Motors attributed an annual savings of $37 million to its employee assistance program that covers 10,000 employees.

Hence, the trade-offs are real for both the organization and the employee. Here, as in most HRM issues related to ethics, it is incumbent upon HRM to demonstrate with competent calculus the measurable return on investment that these HRM intervention programs will yield toward the bottom-line goals of the organization.

Affirmative Action

During the past two decades, there has been an increasing societal trend toward viewing organizations as vehicles for achieving social and political objectives. The beginning of this trend was signaled by the passage of the 1964 Civil Rights Act by Congress. This legislation was landmark in that it compelled organizations to deal fairly with minorities and women in hiring and promotion. As AA programs expand to the higher management echelons, the so-called glass ceiling, HRM will be called on again to justify this strategy. The moral argument that HRM must continually answer is that if an organization is truly institutionally blind and hires strictly on qualifications and experience then employee classes do not need protection. HRM must refute these arguments by demonstrating the long-term economic virtues of such a strategy. Specifically, HRM must continually reinforce the message that while the avowed purpose of AA may sound purely altruistic, for example, redress past discrimination, it actually has important practical — and strategic — purposes. Within the next decade, females and minorities will comprise the majority of the U.S. workforce. Their percentage of the total workforce will continue to increase indefinitely. Unless leading corporations get more females and minorities in nontraditional occupations (including senior management, engineering, the sciences, and so forth), the United States will not have a workforce capable of competing in critical areas as early as the second decade of the twenty-first century. Despite these facts, AA will continue to remain steeped in ethical controversy.

Performance Appraisal

From an ethical perspective, the appraisal process provides many challenging opportunities. It allows both the supervisor and employee to convey their mutual expectations regarding ethical conduct. This meeting of the minds must not be viewed as a once-a-year event but rather as the culmination of a continuous feedback process conducted throughout the year. Hence, it is incumbent upon the supervisor and the employee to proactively communicate throughout the year and identify perceived and actual ethical risks. Once these risks are identified, the parties can confer on how they can be best managed. The challenge to each of these parties is to possess the necessary interpersonal skills to effectively communicate their respective frame of reference.

For the annual performance appraisal process to be effective two things must occur. First, the appraisal must be the culmination of a year long week-in, week-out continuous feedback process. This will eliminate any unfair surprises for both parties. Second, de-couple the appraisal from salary discussions. This will refocus both parties on the objective of the appraisal — performance measurement and improvement. Without these two conditions, the process does disservice to the employee, the appraiser, the organization, and its co-workers.

Traditionally, this de-coupling is achieved by conducting the performance appraisal first and then conveying salary increase information at a later date. The logic behind this process is that by excluding salary discussions during the appraisal process, the employee's attention is focused on the appraisal. The effectiveness of this strategy is questionable due to the direct correlation between appraisal results and salary, however.

One would think that there may be a more effective and ethical method of de-coupling these two events. By first conveying the salary information and then scheduling the appraisal at a later date, the opportunity for a more effective appraisal may be increased. The employee's typical emotive responses to the appraisal may be defused because the salary results have already been conferred. Hence, the employee may be more responsive to critical appraisal and, more importantly, may be more enthusiastically receptive to constructive two-way feedback on how to improve performance, for example, build on strengths, minimize weaknesses. How to convey salary results without immediately evoking an appraisal dialogue would be one HRM challenge associated with this strategy.

Management Development

The challenge for HRM in the area of management development is particularly compelling. How do they ingrain the necessary inter-personal skills to managers responsible for the continuous managing, motivating, and appraising of a staff of employees? Bill Walsh, former championship coach of the San Francisco Forty-Niners offered this sage advice:

Take a group of ten [employees]. The top two will be supermotivated. Superstars will usually take care of themselves. Anybody can [manage] them. The next four, with the right motivation and direction, will learn to live up to their potential. The next two will be marginal. With constant attention, they will be able to accomplish something of value to the [organization]. The last two will waste your time. They won't be with [your organization] for long. [A manager's] goal is to focus [their] organizational detail and coaching on the middle six. They are the ones who most need and benefit from a manager's direction, monitoring, and counsel (Rapaport, 1993, p. 113).

This strategy can certainly have application purposes for HRM when assessing the risks of ethical exposure. Although careful not to altogether ignore the perimeters, emphasis on ethical performance, for example, training, monitoring, and so forth, will have the greatest return on investment for the organization if concentrated on the critical middle six of the manager's staff.

Privacy

Many organizational and public policy issues will pose significant ethical challenges to HRM. Drug testing, surveillance monitoring, smoking, and confidentiality of information all represent significant privacy issues where the rights of the individual must be carefully balanced against the rights of the organization, for example, protecting co-workers and containing health care costs.

While legislation like the Privacy for Consumers and Workers Act: HR 1218, has renewed the debate over electronic monitoring, several companies are proving that, used effectively, it can be valuable in today's workplace. Although there is general consensus that monitoring performance is necessary and essential to running a business, the controversy is over what is acceptable performance to measure. Stress and related health disorders have been documented as adverse effects on the human condition from employee monitoring that is nothing more than an electronic whip. Yet, firms such as Toyota, AT&T, and Charles Schwab have designed effective monitoring programs that even employees recognize as useful when applied as a training and quality control tool. The key to effective monitoring programs is not one that is designed with the express purpose of weeding out inefficient workers who presumably have a disabling grip on their organizations. Rather, the goal of a performance measurement system should not be directed to monitoring behavior but to improving behavior (Laabs, 1992b). It is the constructive dialogue resulting from the audit that provides the vital opportunity for both the organization and employee to mutually improve and prosper.

As benefit plans continue to increase in complexity and options, their administration, for example, enrollment, renewals, changes, plan and benefit options communication to employees and other consumers (spouses), and so forth, will become increasingly dependent on electronic human resources information systems (HRIS). Hence, HRM will need to design, test, and manage technically complex HRIS merely to cope with and keep pace with changes in benefit plans and employee elections. The danger of this reliance will require new HRIS competencies to enhance security and insure privacy (Adams, 1992).

HRM must be diligent in its protection of this information. Traditionally, HRM has preserved the integrity of this confidential information with such measures as restricted access, periodic review by the employee, and certified authorization prior to release. Breathtaking advances in technology will likely force HRM to revitalize continually its information protection security strategy.

Health and Safety

Few, if any, believe that organizations should operate in a completely free and unrestricted manner. Protection from reckless tolerance of design defects in rocket boosters to falsifying test data on experimental drugs in order to gain market approval not only provokes ethical controversy but also exposes the firm to potentially grave bottom-line consequences. Hence, HRM intervention in the form of ethics training has continued to provide a legitimate — but at times controversial — role in U.S. business.

Organizational Exit

As introduced in the downsizing and termination sections above, organizational exit issues create many ethical controversies for HRM. Further, if not managed properly, voluntary and involuntary exits by employees may have severe bottom-line consequences, for example, workers compensation, civil suits for wrongful termination, and so forth. The mere defense of allegations for wrongful dismissal can have substantial economic (for example, attorneys fees, non-productive effort required to respond) and social (for example, tainted corporate image) costs for the organization.

The HRM challenge is to train supervisors to manage terminations that will protect the organization from both ethical and legal challenges. Founded on such inalienable constitutional rights as notice and due process, HRM must design and execute a termination process that minimizes the trauma and potential hostility for the employee and the organization. Also, however anguishing the process, HRM must recognize certain valuable opportunities that the termination process may yield. In some cases, the termination process may reveal certain intrinsic organizational deficiencies in vital HRM programs, for example, selection, training, appraisal, and employee assistance programs. Hence, it is essential that HRM critically assess this feedback and recognize it as an opportunity to improve both organizational and HRM performance.

There are other important ethical issues that need to be considered by HRM professionals. For example, although protection of whistle blowers from reprisal may uncover some early warning signals for the organization, deliberate caution must be exercised in the utilization of such programs. There is the danger that these programs may be utilized for purposes not contemplated, for example, disgruntled workers, with significant consequences for both the organization and employees involved. A weak or poorly administered complaint investigation process can become the Achilles heel of an otherwise effective human resources grievance resolution program, for example, sexual harassment (Longnick-Hall, 1992). Hence, HRM professionals must thoroughly investigate with due diligence all allegations of wrongdoing.

Contracts of employment also pose ethical challenges for HRM professionals. Some states have taken a more expansive view of what constitutes an employment contract. For instance, despite expressly stating that employment is at will, some courts have upheld that written personnel policies and procedures create a binding expectation covenant between the employer and employee. Hence, since all procedures described in these personnel policies potentially represent implied — if not expressed — rights and benefits to which each employee is entitled, HRM professionals must ensure that they are carefully designed and communicated.

Ethical issues, in connection with employee retirement, will grow in importance for HRM, particularly with the aging of the U.S. workforce. HRM professionals must ensure that the institutionalization of retirement planning in their organizations is based on an ethical duty to assist employees in this important, often traumatic, transition process. Some organizations have affirmed their ethical obligations to their retirees through the extension of various postretirement benefits, for example, assistance in the form of tuition reimbursement and a gradual phased-in retirement schedule at work to facilitate the transition to postretirement life.

The Global Marketplace

The forces of global competition and the emergence of regional free trade zones, for example, North American Free Trade Agreement, will thrust organizations into essential, but unfamiliar, transnational relationships, for example, multinational strategic alliances, joint ventures, free trade zones. HRM will play a pivotal role in determining the success of these strategic relationships. From coordinating recruitment and training to benefits and compensation, to discipline procedures and organizational exit, these alignments will place an uncommon burden not contemplated by traditional HRM professionals. As global boundaries fade, the geographic market landscape will create a complex set of transnational economic and social contracts and, hence, agency relationships. Ethical issues likely to be confronted in this transnational environment include protection of proprietary information, conflict of interest, and respect for cultural differences, for example, norms, customs. A prime example of this challenge can be illustrated by the Foreign Corrupt Practices Act. The Foreign Corrupt Practices Act had the alleged purpose to deter U.S. companies from bribing foreign officials — despite the fact that this practice was customary in foreign countries. Some shudder at the arrogance of the United States to impose its moral judgement with righteous indignation on the rest of the world. This intrusive moralizing may have complicated unenvisioned adverse effects, for example, choking off potentially prosperous global business relationships.

While some of the organizational and HRM department's specific responses to date outlined above appear effective and are on the right track, their success has generally been isolated. On overall balance, despite several potential economic and social ethical dangers confronting organizations and HRM, ethical issues are not universally perceived as a top priority within many organizations. Still, HRM professionals will be increasingly challenged to design and implement innovative strategies to protect the organization from these threats while responding to the constantly rising ethical expectations of society.

ORGANIZATIONAL RESPONSES TO ETHICAL ISSUES

Health care reform, emerging new classes of protected workers, income tax legislation, benefit accounting standard changes, executive compensation controversy, global competition, strategic alliances, trade pacts, family leave, and other sweeping social changes may place an undue burden on the traditional HRM role in organizations. Clearly, the fallout from all of these current and emerging issues remains unclear, except that they will have a dramatic impact on HRM professionals.

The challenge for HRM professionals is to identify these issues within the context of their organization, assess the cost and benefits consistent with overall organizational goals, and then demonstrate to management the wisdom of HRM recommendations. Unless observable and measurable cost savings can be demonstrated by implementing a comprehensive ethically-balanced HRM program, corporations may exercise their right to breach these social contracts and simply avoid their ethical obligations as an ordinary cost of doing business. It is unclear whether the penalties associated with unethical behavior, for example, employee turnover, poor quality, fines, penalties, and so forth, will actually exceed the costs of honoring ethical conduct, for example, costs of implementing, monitoring, and managing ethically-balanced programs. It should not be left unsaid that ultimately, the corporate overhead cost of all ethically-driven programs and/or fines and penalties will be burdened by the public.

Relatively speaking, little is known about the causes of ethical or unethical behavior or the best way to teach ethics. Adding to the problem is the fact that ethics is part of an individual's social, religious, and cultural heritage, so there is no one right set of ethics. Theoretical research on ethics has blossomed in the past decade concerning ethics. As a result, such theories are beneficial in posing a number of questions that HRM professionals and their organizations must work to find answers to if they are going to create ethically-oriented organizational cultures and employees. Some of the questions are:

What are the dimensions of ethical behavior (Reidenbach & Robin, 1990)?

What is the relationship between an individual's evaluative criteria and their moral development (Reidenbach & Robin, 1990)?

What are the causes/factors of ethical behavior?

How does ethical behavior vary by company size and industry (Daley, Murphy, & Smith, 1992)?

How can ethical behavior be predicted (Reidenbach & Robin, 1990)?

What are the best training/evaluation methods (Brenner, 1992)?

Many legal questions being heard in our courts today about corporate responsibilities have an ethical component that poses other questions that are in need of answers, such as:

What is the employee's right to privacy, both in and outside the workplace (Rifkin, 1991a)?

What is the public's right to privacy regarding personal information (Lacayo, 1991)?

What is the company's responsibility to the external environment (Frederick, Hoffman, & Petry, 1990)?

To date, in response to questions like these, HRM professionals have undertaken a number of initiatives. One such response has been in the area of corporate codes of ethics.

An organization's values statement and code of ethics represents its moral cornerstone for cultural development (Benson, 1989). More strategically, they provide a vital HRM opportunity to enable the company's chief executives to frame the corporate character and conscience of the organization. Hence, this black letter expression of the moral foundation should reflect personal values and ambitions of the organization's founding principals. Once established, these concepts, if oriented, managed, and monitored properly by HRM, will evolve — through action, inaction, and feedback — into norm-building standards. These norms can then provide the essential measurement standards for social interaction that are pivotal to minimizing agency monitoring costs (Axelrod, 1986).

Deeds add credibility to words. By proactively defining and then conveying the moral and ethical expectations for its organization, HRM has taken an important initiative to visibly frame its principles for conduct to its agents, that is managers and employees. These ethical guidelines will then provide a valuable form of moral measurement for individual decisions. Like ideas, decisions have consequences. By biopolitical design, the human nature of every individual is constantly fighting the tension between self and social interest. However, when employees are confronted with conflicting interests, this code will hopefully provoke them to consciously consult these principles and then weigh carefully the consequences of their decisions from each constituent's viewpoint. This code will provide incentives — through positive and negative reinforcement from social interaction — that employees not only accrue the wealth effects of good decisions but must also be accountable and bear the burden of poorly motivated decisions. Mindful of the careful assessment of foreseeable outcomes and consequences of their actions, employees then — with competent calculus — can strike a rational, objective, and equitable balance among all alternatives in rendering their decision.

There is no argument that there are real dangers that may result from publication of such a document. Some individuals may inappropriately apply this code, while others may seek to use this code for personal advantage. However, not unlike how an organization establishes strict performance and conformance standards for material and technology, or physical capital, HRM professionals cannot neglect their corporate duty to define their expectations for their human capital. The code represents a strategic opportunity to diffuse efficiently — and hence manage better — risk-bearing within the organization. This code acknowledges the vital fact that every organization thrives on agency relationships where the company and its employees have correlative rights (Brooks, 1989). The code expressly clarifies to all of their employees that they are not merely isolated individuals. Every employee has been elevated to become a responsible risk-bearing agent within the organization. There is no way for management to completely shed all risk-bearing within an organization full of maximizing agents motivated by a complex set of explicit and implicit contracts, (for example, employment, psychological, socials contracts) each motivated by differential horizons and diverse and conflicting objectives. However, this code can represent one important HRM strategy to minimize the cost and bottom-line exposure associated with a vast and complex set of agency contracts (Pratt & Zeckerhauser, 1985).

From the ideals conferred in the code and values statement, HRM must emerge to provide form and shape to the company culture. For example, at Levi Strauss, HRM designed a set of ideals by which the management team and employees could weave the corporate mission into the organization — in the form of an aspirations statement. For the innovation and vision that the company has demonstrated in virtually every area of its operations, Levi Strauss earned the 1992 *Personnel Journal*'s Optimas award in the general excellence category. One driving force behind the company's new goals was to place a strong emphasis on valuing its employees. However, it was not until Levi Strauss' management embraced the vital fact that people can give you the competitive advantage that these goals were institutionalized. Now, senior managers from Levi Strauss' many facilities come to a retreat center in the Santa Cruz mountains near San Francisco for a week of training that centers on the aspirations statement. Valuing diversity, leadership, and ethics are the topics of discussion. Values and diversity lasts three days. The three days that are devoted exclusively to ethics demonstrates that Levi Strauss is serious about its values. Levi Strauss' chief executive officer, Bob Hass, feels strongly that "In the long run, these are the right [HRM] strategies for our company's success and the well-being of our people" (Laabs, 1992c).

Hence, with the same vigor that HRM aligns its programs with the overall organization's economic goals, HRM must equally inculcate the organization, through HRM programs, with the overall social and ethical goals of the organization. HRM must carefully assess the ethical consequences among all stakeholders throughout the design and implementation processes of HRM strategy. Further, affirmation of this HRM commitment should be manifested through reinforced communication and ethics training. This process should commence at orientation, where most new employees' attention and enthusiasm is high. HRM must capitalize on this opportunity by providing specific information about the organization's culture and establishing mutual expectations for effective performance and conduct.

Deeds add credibility to words. Corporate due process must be the backbone of all HRM ethical principles. Productivity is directly related to corporate due process when that efficiency is an acknowledged function of the organization's quality of life. A good due process system boosts morale. It can foster an atmosphere of trust and confidence in management and co-workers. Several leading companies proactively embrace this philosophy. Bank of America has instituted a three-step "let's talk" procedure. Federal Express ensures the integrity of its philosophy through its Guaranteed Fair Treatment Procedure. These programs not only provide a climate of mutual trust but also represent a significant competitive advantage in recruiting and retaining human resources, explains Walter Kimbaugh Jr., Federal Express's managing director of human resources.

People are more sophisticated today, and expect more from the job. Even what the church and extended family used to do are coming into the workplace. Companies that start to understand this reality will survive. One way to ensure your company will survive is to listen to employees, so management and employees can work towards the same goals. Without that, you're open to third-party intervention, e.g., unions, regulation, or employees will not give you more than what's required. (Seeley, 1992, p. 46)

Similarly, a position paper at Control Data stated: "any concept of employee justice is incomplete without the presence of some mechanism to challenge the power system" (p. 48). Hence, HRM professionals should see due process as an essential requirement to keep the corporate ego in check.

A GLIMPSE OF THE FUTURE

As we approach the twenty-first century, it is evident that HRM has a special role to play in ensuring that organizations deal fairly and ethically with their employees and that the employees deal fairly with each other, the organization, and clients. Despite efforts to date to address ethical issues in organizations, several issues will still provide ongoing challenges for HRM professionals. A number of these issues are briefly discussed below.

Diverse Workforce

As companies adopt more and more diverse workforces, those employees will bring with them different social, cultural, religious, and personal values. For the HRM department, this means that these employees will all have different perspectives on what is right and wrong, and what is ethical. The challenge for HRM professionals will be not only to teach the employee the company's way but also, in some cases, to adapt the company's view to changing beliefs about ethics (Rundles, 1991).

Employee Rights

As the workforce becomes more diverse, HRM professionals will have to deal with a greater variety of lifestyles, family structures, religions, cultures, and backgrounds. In addition, HRM professionals must comply with anti-discrimination, equal opportunity, and the Americans with Disabilities legislation. This means that HRM professionals can expect to face even more complex ethical issues when hiring, firing, promoting, compensating, and appraising performance. For instance, AIDS has raised a new set of ethical dilemmas about what rights the victim has to privacy, to continue working while sick, and to continue to receive company health coverage. HRM professionals will have to be well informed about issues like terminal illness, alternative lifestyles, and alternative family structures so that they can advise and help set company policies to deal with the ethical dilemmas that accompany these issues.

International Competition

As U.S. companies become more involved in international commerce, employees abroad will certainly face circumstances under which their ethical beliefs about proper behavior are challenged by the cultural beliefs in that country. Part of the HRM professional's job in the future will be to define for those employees what is acceptable, and what is not.

Examples of practices that would be considered unethical in the United States, but acceptable in other countries, are blatant sex or race discrimination in hiring, job assignment, or compensation; use of child labor; or failing to provide safe working conditions. In Singapore, it is common to see help wanted ads for "Chinese women, age 21–28." This type of advertisement violates U.S. laws and ethics regarding age and sex discrimination (Fisher, Schoenfeldt, & Shaw, 1993).

New Technologies

The advent of new technologies, especially those that allow the collection and storage of information, will pose serious challenges to HRMs. The key question will be: What is rightly private and what is within the company's domain?

Alana Shoars, former E-mail administrator at Epson, America, Incorporated, was fired for questioning the company's alleged monitoring of employee messages. Shoars filed a $75 million class-action suit against Epson in a California court; there is also a similar lawsuit filed against Nissan Motor Company. The growing availability of low-cost network monitoring software, as well as personal computers, is raising new ethics-related questions about privacy, integrity, influence, and impact. Unfortunately, codes of ethics in many companies are seldom detailed enough to adequately cover information and technology systems (Rifkin, 1991b).

Legal Issues

While the public sector grapples with ethical issues, it is likely that Congress, the FASB, and the SEC will also create significant legal or reporting requirements for companies in the future. These requirements will further define for the company what is ethical, and will challenge HRM professionals to ensure training and compliance within the organization to these new rules.

The SEC has recently taken steps to increase disclosure of financial information for domestic companies that would reveal corrupt foreign practices and insider trading (Skousen, 1991). In addition, the United States Sentencing Commission has created tough new guidelines to ensure that almost every domestic law applicable to corporations — including antitrust, workplace health and safety, government contracting, and insider trading rules — will be enforced with more muscle. Fines and penalties for such infractions have been increased, and in some cases, criminal penalties are being pursued in cases where they previously would not have been held accountable for corporate misdeeds. Corporate liability for an employee's actions is also being expanded, opening the door to more civil suits, greater penalties, and fines (Friedman, 1991).

HUMAN RESOURCES MANAGEMENT POLICY: A KEY TO ETHICAL BEHAVIOR

HRM cannot be all things to all people all of the time. However, like each company's board of directors, HRM does have an affirmative ethical and legal duty to act in the best interests of all its constituents — its employees, shareholders, suppliers, communities, and the environment. HRM goals and objectives can only be successfully achieved by the assurance that their actions are aligned equitably with each stakeholder's expectations. Hence, the best that can be expected is for HRM to put forth balanced policies — made with competent rationale — that minimize or diffuse equitably the collateral damage associated with tough choices.

Good HRM policy analysis is not about choosing between the employee and the stockholder. Sound policy analysis is about understanding the context of the corporate promissory agreement and all of its derivative contracts. It is essential that HRM policies be ethically flexible in their construction and agile in their doctrine to respond to — and efficiently meet — changing internal and external forces that will affect the organizational environment. Expectations of consumers, co-workers, and society for corporate performance are constantly bursting through new dimensions. People in organizations have not suddenly become immoral. What has changed are the contexts in which corporate decisions are made, the demands that are being made on business and the nature of what is considered proper corporate conduct. In the context of a rapidly changing social and global environment, HRM policy must be viewed as a long-term set of central conceptions marked by a perpetual series of amendments, each with its own unique HRM policy life cycle. Admittedly, these concepts, however noble, fly in the face of precedence, consistency, and equitable application, — each a cornerstone of the conventional U.S. worker expectation.

Likewise, to be effective, HRM policy must be ethically balanced in its construction. If the HRM policy sets ethical standards too low, it is likely to face stiff substantive due process challenges such as failing to meet stakeholders' interests, for example, employee rights, shareholder protection. Conversely, if the HRM policy sets ethical standards too high, the burden imposed on the organization and its employees may have a dangerous chilling effect that chokes off entrepreneurial risk-taking and innovation. To thwart this risk, employees may retreat to an anticipatory defense whose strategy is to do nothing.

Trust in organizational policy alone is misplaced. HRM traditionally has not been very effective in ensuring socially desirable behavior in an institutional environment. It is difficult to legislate a consensus of values through the policymaking process where property rights are polarized, for example, employee privacy rights (smoking) versus organizational rights to contain health care costs. Generally the only significant measurement that organizations receive positive feedback from is for good earnings. The capital markets are very efficient at providing feedback on corporations' economic contracts. However, feedback on industry's social contracts, for example, ethical performance, are largely ignored except in a negative context, for example, employee scandal, public corruption, environmental disasters. It is revitalizing to note that some progress is being advanced to change the payoffs in the areas of social contracts. Quality awards, for example, Malcolm Baldridge, are receiving increased attention — despite their controversial merit. Environmental programs are also beginning to receive positive acknowledgements. As vigorously as legislation reinforces the non-conformist's conduct, society must continue to develop positive incentive systems for the conformist in the area of ethical conduct. For HRM, by designing a positive incentive system, for example, Optimas awards, that motivates organizations to champion causes in the area of ethical behavior and to covet their rewards, normalization of these ethical contracts will be hastened.

CONCLUSION

Ethical issues will pose major challenges to organizations in the twenty-first century. The ethical challenges that HRM will likely encounter will be a complex function of the industry, regulatory, and cultural environment specific to that organization. Hence, HRM must be prepared to design and execute innovative solutions consistent with the complex set of diverse and competing stakeholder interests. The mission continually confronting HRM is how to align best specific HRM programs with the overall strategic goals of the organization in order to maximize the mutual benefits of all stakeholders. More importantly, now and in the future, HRM must recognize these challenges as vital opportunities. HRM has the formidable, but unique, opportunity to translate its historical role in the organization from being an overhead cost center burden to becoming a strategic profit center. By converting ethical issues — or any HRM issue for that matter — into a decision process that is linked to cost savings, cost reduction, cost avoidance, or boosted production and quality, HRM has not only added value to the organization in a moralistic sense but also has made a positive, observable, and measurable contribution to the bottomline.

The payoffs for an HRM strategy that is ethically responsive to all of the organization's stakeholders can be substantial. An HRM strategy, one that holds contemplated organizational policy decisions in abeyance until the reasonably foreseeable outcomes among all constituents is carefully considered, may protect the firm from exposure to significant legal, economic, and social costs. Perhaps the most salient feature of an HRM strategy that is ethically-balanced is that it may provide an important competitive advantage to the organization in recruiting and retaining its most vital resource — labor. Today, and in the twenty-first century, the HRM challenges, rewards, and risks will be great. To be effective, HRM will need the entrepreneurial courage, vision, skill, and ability to challenge conventional assumptions and test new HRM programs not contemplated within the traditional organizational role of HRM.

REFERENCES

Adams, L. E. 1992, February. Securing your HRIS in a microcomputer environment. *HRMagazine*: 56–61.

Axelrod, R. 1986, December. An evolutionary approach to norms. *American Political Science Review 80*(4): 1096–1111.

Benson, G.C.S. 1989. Codes of ethics. *Journal of Business Ethics 8*: 305–19.

Brenner, S. N. 1992, May. Ethics programs and their dimensions. *Journal of Business Ethics 5*: 391–99.

Brink, T. L. 1992, December. A discouraging word improves your interviews. *HRMagazine*: 49, 50, 52.

Brooks, L. J. 1989. Corporate codes of ethics. *Journal of Business Ethics 8*: 117–29.

Daley, J. M., Murphy, P. R., & Smith, J. E. 1992, January. Executive attitudes, organizational size and ethical issues: Perspectives on a service industry. *Journal of Business Ethics 1*: 11–19.

Davidson, D. L. 1982. *Jim Sawyer (A) (Harvard Business School Case Series)*. Boston, MA: The President and Fellows of Harvard College.

Fisher, C., Schoenfeldt, L. F., & Shaw, J. B. 1993. *Human resource management* (2nd ed.). Boston: Houghton Mifflin.

Frederick, R., Hoffman, W. M., & Petry, E. S., Jr. 1990. *Business, ethics, and the environment*. New York: Quorum Books.

Friedman, R. A. 1991. *The balanced workforce at Xerox corporation (Harvard Business School Case Series)*. Boston, MA: The President and Fellows of Harvard College.

Hestwood, T. M. 1992, January. Setting fair pay policy. *HRMagazine*: 75–76, 78.

Laabs, J. J. 1992a, June. Surveillance: Tool or trap? *Personnel Journal*: 96–104.

Laabs, J. J. 1992b, November. Ben & Jerry's caring capitalism. *Personnel Journal*: 50–57.

Laabs, J. J. 1992c, December. HR's vital role at Levi Strauss. *Personnel Journal*: 34–46.

Lacayo, R. 1991, November 11. Nowhere to hide. *Time*: 34–40.

Longnick-Hall, M. L. 1992, March. Checking out sexual harassment claims. *HRMagazine*: 17–21.

MacAdam, M. N. 1992, March. The earnestly ethical executive. *Executive Excellence*: 12.

Munchus III, G. 1992, June. Check references for safer selection. *HRMagazine*: 75–77.

Post, R. J. 1981a. *H.J. Heinz Company (A) (Harvard Business School Case Series)*. Boston, MA: The President and Fellows of Harvard College.

Post, R. J. 1981b. *H.J. Heinz Company (B) (Harvard Business School Case Series)*. Boston, MA: The President and Fellows of Harvard College.

Pratt, J. W. & Zeckerhauser, R. J. 1985. *Principals and agents: The structure of business*. Boston, MA: Harvard University Press.

Rapaport, R. 1993, January/February. To build a winning team: An interview with head coach Bill Walsh. *Harvard Business Review*: 111–20.

Reidenbach, R. E. & Robin, D. P. 1990, August. Toward the development of a multidimensional scale for improving evaluations of business ethics. *Journal of*

Business Ethics: 639–53.

Rifkin, G. 1991a, October 14. Are corporate codes enough? Maybe not. *Computerworld*: 87.

Rifkin, G. 1991b, October 14. The ethics gap: Despite growing attention, Many IS managers say, "It's not my job". *ComputerWorld*: 83–85.

Rogers, B. 1992, May. Companies develop benefits for part timers. *HRMagazine*: 89–90.

Rundles, J. 1991, July. U.S. West drives progressive human resource policies from the top down. *Colorado Corporate Business Magazine*: 22.

Seeley, R. S. 1992, July. Corporate due process. *HRMagazine*: 46–49.

Skousen, K. F. 1991. *An introduction to the SEC*: Cincinnati, OH: South-Western Publishing Company.

Wilbert, J. R. & Dakdduk, K. E., 1991, August. The new FASB 106. *Journal of Accountancy*: 36–41.

Whiteside, D. E. 1983. *Duke Power Company (Harvard Business School Case Series)*. Boston, MA: The Presidents and Fellows of Harvard College.

10

Human Resources Management: A Review and Preview

The management of people at work is one of the primary keys to organizational success. Yet, a backlog of problems has caused too little attention to the management of human resources in the past. Finance, general management, marketing, production, and research and development all received much more attention than human resources management (HRM). Awareness of inadequacies of HRM has come as we compared our success in this area with that of organizations in other countries where human resources were considered critical to success. Organizations in the United States have considerable catching up to do.

In efforts to catch up, it is not enough to stay on top of the latest developments within a rapidly changing discipline. Increasingly, managers in some organizations recognize that people are human resources to be managed effectively, just like money and other organizational resources. In addition, these same organizations and managers have discovered that better management of human resources can be a major source of productivity improvement and growth. These companies' corporate public relations documents often refer to people as the most important or valuable resource in an organization.

In response to the recognition given to human resources, organizations have recently elevated the importance of their HRM function as a major organizational component in their efforts to be successful and remain competitive. Despite the elevation of the HRM function, many organizations and their HRM functions operate as if they are still facing the problems and challenges of the 1970s. These same organizations and their HRM functions fail to recognize that their environment is changing faster and becoming more complex, more competitive, and more global than ever. Such changes pose new challenges and issues that organizations and their HRM functions must respond to if they are to compete and survive in the coming decades.

In light of the ideas presented throughout this book, this chapter first discusses the HRM mission and activities. It then highlights the importance of HRM as a strategic partner in today's and tomorrow's organizations. Next, the discussion turns to the importance of evaluating the value added by HRM. The chapter then turns to a discussion of the role of HRM in developing future managers and leaders and offers a framework (individual management development plan) as one tool that HRM professionals and their organizations can use to increase the effectiveness and success of their management development efforts.

The chapter concludes with a look at some of the current and future changes and challenges for HRM professionals.

DEFINING THE HUMAN RESOURCES MANAGEMENT MISSION AND ACTIVITIES

In the years to come, when an organization is genuinely concerned about people, its total organizational philosophy, climate, and tone will reflect this belief. In this book, HRM has been used to describe the function that is concerned with people — employees. HRM is the function performed in organizations that facilitates the most effective use of people (employees) to achieve organizational and individual goals. HRM reflects the increased concern both society and organizations have for people. Today employees — the human resource — demand more of their jobs and respond favorably to management activities that give them greater control of their lives.

HRM consists of numerous activities, including: job analysis, equal employment opportunity compliance, human resources planning, employee recruitment, selection, and orientation, performance evaluation and compensation, training and development, safety, health, and quality of work life, and labor relations.

These activities are accepted functions of HRM. It should be emphasized that in our view effective value-added HRM is:

Action Oriented — Effective HRM focuses on action rather than on record-keeping, written procedures, or rules. Certainly HRM uses rules, records, and policies, but it stresses action. HRM emphasizes the solution of employment problems to help achieve organizational objectives and facilitate employee development and satisfaction.

Individual Oriented — Whenever possible, HRM treats each employee as an individual and offers services and programs to meet the individual's needs.

Worldwide Oriented — HRM is not only a U.S. function or activity; when it is adding value to an international organization, it is being practiced efficiently and continuously in each component of the organization, regardless of whether the component is in Hong Kong, Poland, or Mexico.

Future Oriented — Effective HRM is concerned with helping an organization achieve its objectives in the future by providing HRM activities that are clearly contributing to the organizational success (for example, by providing for competent, well-motivated employees).

In order to effectively carry out its responsibilities in the future, an HRM department should reflect several design and organization factors. First, regardless of the changes in ways that organizations are organizing, the design and structure must allow the HRM department to carry out its primary responsibilities of delivering HRM services, advising line management, and supporting the organization's strategic objectives.

While the specific structure and organization of an HRM department will vary from organization to organization in the coming years, all HRM departments will share functional, managerial, and strategic purposes. That is, regardless of the particular organization or marketplace in which an HRM department will operate, it must carry out the following activities:

Design and deliver HRM programs, practices, and processes that meet the needs of the organization and its employees (effectively manage the psychological contract).

Support line supervisors' efforts to achieve business goals through effective management of employees.

Contribute to the development of the organization and strategic planning by developing HRM practices that enhance overall competitiveness.

In recent years, the last point of contributing to the organization's strategic objectives has been increasingly accepted as an important part of HRM's role in different organizations. However, despite growing emphasis on strategic HRM, an HRM department's effectiveness will still ride upon how well it carries out traditional HRM functions. These activities are likely to remain important since traditional HRM programs, policies, and practices have the most direct and universal impact on an organization's workforce. As a result, effective HRM departments will need to address customer needs in the following areas: recruitment, selection, placement, compensation and benefits, employee development, employee productivity and morale, legal compliance, and retention.

The success of HRM professionals will depend on effective implementation of HRM programs and policies by line managers. As a result, developing, educating, and influencing managers to motivate, manage, and discipline employees effectively will remain an essential HRM function. Besides educating managers about company HRM policies and relevant legal requirements, HRM professionals will also need to understand the unique challenges facing particular managers.

To serve as a strategic contributor to the organization, HRM professionals must fully understand the organization's business, its
competitors, and the internal and external factors affecting short- and
long-term organizational planning. In the future, such knowledge will
be essential not only to develop HRM plans that are consistent with the
overall organizational strategy but also to establish HRM as a value-
added component in organizational planning. In the coming decade, top
management will more likely value input from HRM professionals who
can foster organizational development, be out in the forefront of future
legislation and regulations, and recommend proactive responses to a
variety of problems or issues. When HRM professionals are able to add
value to their organizations (that is, help build competitive advantage)
they will be strategic partners in helping to accomplish the organization's strategic goals and objectives.

STRATEGIC ROLE OF HUMAN
RESOURCES MANAGEMENT

The task of building competitive advantage demands that all functions within an organization play an integral part in the development of
strategic plans. This new, strategic role of HRM will require that HRM
professionals take on new roles and accept new responsibilities. As the
core responsibilities of HRM professionals become integrated in the
actual organizational functions, the measurement of the value added to
the organization by HRM will become increasingly important as HRM
will have a direct and quantifiable bottom-line impact.

Wilhelm (1990) has recently noted that the "critically important task
of guiding line management in achieving superior organizational
capability" is a future responsibility for HRM professionals (p. 130).
Wilhelm further suggests that HRM professionals will

Contribute up front to strategy, set goals, choose the means for accomplishing
goals, measure results, and develop mechanisms for corrective action . . . managerial confidence and the capability to sense, articulate, and implement
major changes in business strategy, structure, culture, and people have
become essential requirements of business survival and success. (p. 130)

This suggests that there may be a vacuum of needed skills among HRM
professionals (especially in the area of leadership) who will be expected
to take on increasingly complex roles in their organizations. Selective
staffing at high levels with leader-experts who possess the requisite
skills needed to transform HRM and recruiting persons with a Master's
in Business Administration for entry-level positions in order to benefit
from their general business knowledge may be viable ways of filling the
vacuum of needed skills among HRM professionals. In addition, by
bringing in individuals at the bottom level who are oriented toward

broad business issues, organizations will be able to develop a new breed of HRM professional. These individuals will accomplish business goals through HRM practices, resulting in a closer link between HRM programs and bottom-line outcomes.

Kydd and Oppenheim (1990) have identified several firms that have already closely related HRM to strategic planning. These firms have tied selection, appraisal, rewards, and development to business goals. The practices exhibited by the organizations provided evidence of the feasibility of tying HRM procedures to business strategy in order to build competitive advantage.

Colgate-Palmolive Company

The programs carried out by the HRM department at Colgate-Palmolive provide an example of the increasing role HRM will play in strategy development and implementation. Colgate-Palmolive is a global manufacturing company with sales of over $5 billion, which recently received new marching orders. After assuming the presidency several years ago, the new chief executive officer developed and communicated a new strategic direction for the company based on what he called his corporate initiatives (Burg & Smith, 1987; Dessler, 1994). Among other things, the new strategy emphasized concentrating on new products, being the low-cost producer, simplifying businesses and structures, pushing decision making down, promoting entrepreneurial action, and improving morale and motivation. The new strategy aimed at making Colgate-Palmolive a leaner, more responsive competitor in its global markets and in focusing the company more clearly on health-related products.

Consistent with this new strategy, several major steps were made at once. Four major businesses were divested, including two sports and recreation companies. A major reorganization took place that eliminated one level of senior management. Additional resources were diverted to new product development and research and development. And the human resources programs at Colgate-Palmolive got a new mandate to help Colgate-Palmolive achieve its new goals.

The programs laid out for Colgate-Palmolive's HRM provide a glimpse of how HRM today is, and will continue to be, pressed to get involved in strategic management. At Colgate-Palmolive, HRM was directed by the president to develop and execute programs designed to create a company culture that would achieve the following:

Encourage a spirit of teamwork and cooperation within and among business units in working toward common objectives, with an emphasis on identifying, acknowledging, and rewarding personal and unit excellence.

Foster entrepreneurial attitudes among the managers and innovative thinking among all employees.

Emphasize the commonality of interest between the employees and shareholders (Burg & Smith, 1987, p. 17).

To that end, numerous HRM programs had to be designed. For example, the company's executive incentive compensation plan was redesigned to place more emphasis on individual performance and achieving operating targets. Employee benefits were redesigned to make them more flexible and responsive to employees' needs. At the same time, cost controls and employee variable pay costs were instituted, two changes that were accomplished by effectively communicating both the changes and the reasons for them. The bottom line was that by implementing a number of programs (including those aimed at redesigning compensation and benefits) HRM was able to contribute to a refocusing of Colgate-Palmolive employees' efforts in a manner that contributed to the execution of Colgate-Palmolive's strategic plan.

Through recruitment, selection, training, and other HRM practices, organizations will rely more and more on HRM departments to obtain a pool of human resources capable of implementing a given strategy. The recent experience of Allied Signal on developing a pool of human capital as a means of increasing its competitive advantage provides another example of HRM's role in the strategic process. Allied Signal, under the leadership of chief executive officer Larry Bossidy, has implemented a total housecleaning and cultural change in which HRM has played an important role.

Allied Signal

First, Bossidy developed a statement of corporate vision ("one of the world's premier companies, distinctive and successful") and values (for example, customer satisfaction, integrity, teamwork, and speed). Although this statement seems to be standard fare for corporate vision/value statements, it has galvanized people (Stewart, 1992).

Second, he immersed the company in total quality management (TQM) as a means of turning the vision and values into reality. For example, to implement the TQM program, all 90,000 employees are expected to attend four-day courses in TQM concepts, procedures, and applications.

Finally, he implemented a top-to-bottom change in HRM. In the quest to increase the quality of their human resources pool, teams of top managers developed detailed plans for revamping college recruiting, staffing, career development, and training and education. These teams studied top companies such as Corning, Bechtel, Hewlett-Packard, and Johnson & Johnson using them as benchmarks. In addition, they held focus groups with employees to identify how HRM could better serve the needs of employees. Their master plan is to develop a deeper pool of human capital through career pathing, rotating managers across businesses, and management education. Bossidy believes that this investment in people will help Allied Signal achieve its ambitious growth goals.

As organizations like Colgate-Palmolive and Allied Signal continue to change strategies to gain competitive advantage, the strategic role of HRM, in the process, will continue to rise in importance. This will be the case especially as organizations continue to recognize that change strategies often require changes in the types, levels, and mixes of skills for their employees. Thus, helping their organization's employees develop or acquire strategy-related skills, which are essential elements of the implementation strategy, will be but one of the value-added roles HRM professionals will play in the coming years.

As HRM increasingly takes on the role of a strategic partner, it will have more and more input into the formulation of the organization's strategy that develops and aligns HRM programs to help implement the strategy. However, for the HRM function to become truly strategic in its orientation, it must double its efforts in ensuring that HRM activities are continuously evaluated on the degree to which they help the organization accomplish its strategic objectives. The following section discusses the evaluation of HRM as a key component that will contribute to the increased value of HRM in the organizational success equation in future years.

EVALUATING THE HUMAN RESOURCES MANAGEMENT DEPARTMENT

The success of HRM in the future will depend not only on the formulation and execution of superb HRM strategic plans but also on the continuous evaluation of progress toward accomplishment of specified objectives. While evaluation of other components of the organization may be performed in terms of profitability ratios, sales increases, and so forth, traditionally, the evaluation of the HRM department has been more difficult. For example, some of the perceived obstacles to evaluating the effectiveness of HRM departments are (Cashman & McElroy, 1991): difficulty in conducting scientific evaluation, difficulty in quantifying HRM's return on investment, difficulty in assessing impact of HRM, difficulty in identifying effectiveness criteria, lack of time — HRM staff, design problems, objectives not defined, evaluation not valued by top management, evaluation costs too much, evaluation not required, evaluation anxiety on the part of HRM staff, lack of management support, and misuse of evaluation results. In spite of these perceived obstacles, HRM professionals need to make a stronger effort to convince top management of the value of their units to the overall mission of the organization.

The strategic management of human capital to create competitive advantage is dependent upon key assumptions about the workforce.

In order to support the investment in people, one must accept the proposition that people want to be productive, and that they will become engrossed in their jobs when they are presented with the right incentives and the correct work environment. This conviction must be held at all levels of the organization in order for HRM to be evaluated and to fully accomplish its strategic goals. In organizations where top management is not convinced of the importance of the human component, HRM professionals are bound to be stymied in their attempts to increase their impact on employees and frustrated by the lack of respect they must endure.

Capitalization on employees as assets is a long-term process, with little immediate feedback about the effectiveness of HRM programs available. Trying to measure the effects of a program after a short period will only lead to misinterpretation of the results. Additionally, the subjectivity of many of the characteristics that HRM programs affect makes measurement problematic.

The difficulty of objectively measuring the success of HRM programs is compounded by the complexity of connecting employee attitudes and knowledge to measurable factors, such as productivity. While productivity is clearly quantifiable, dissecting the components of productivity to discover elements that are the result of individual differences, which depend on luck and which are connected to training, is perplexing. This inability to determine concrete connections has resulted in underutilization of HRM as an effective resource.

How should an organization go about evaluating its HRM function? Are there particular measures or indicators that reveal how well this function is meeting its responsibilities and supporting the organization's efforts to reach organizational objectives? HRM evaluations can be approached from a number of angles. Qualitative evaluations (for example, checklists) examine the types of programs and services an HRM function is providing, how well it delivers those programs and services, and which HRM areas or customers could benefit from new programs or improved processes. Quantitative evaluations calculate the cost-benefit value of different HRM activities and compare these other statistical measures at the program, departmental, or organizational level.

The checklist approach poses a number of questions that can be answered either yes or no. This method is concerned with whether important activities have been recognized and, if so, whether they are being performed. Essentially, the checklist is an evaluation in terms of what should be done and the extent to which it is being done. Some typical HRM checklist questions are:

Are all legally mandated reports submitted to requiring agencies on time?
Are human resource requirements forecasts made at least annually?

Are all employees appraised at least annually?

Are career opportunities communicated clearly to all employees?

The more yes answers there are, the better the evaluation; no answers indicate areas or activities where follow-up or additional work is needed to increase HRM's effectiveness.

The quantitative method of evaluating the performance of HRM activities relies on the accumulation of numerical data and the calculation of averages, ratios, or cost-benefit values for different HRM activities. These measures can be tracked over time and compared to internal or external norms. Although quantitative data may be somewhat useful for external comparisons with similar organizations, they are probably most helpful in establishing internal baselines (frames of reference) and showing the direction of movement from those baselines (Caruth, Noe, & Mondy, 1990). Some examples of quantitative measures for HRM are (Mondy & Noe, 1994): women and minorities selection ratio, women and minorities promotion ratio, women and minorities termination ratio, average recruiting cost per applicant, average recruiting cost per employee hired, turnover percentage, new hire retention percentage, andpercentage of new hires lost.

Before conducting an evaluation, HRM professionals must first decide what aspects of the HRM function to assess. Making the decision prior to conducting the evaluation is essential to ensure that appropriate data are available for conducting the evaluation. HRM evaluations can take place at any of the following levels:

Program Level. Program evaluations measure the impact of HRM activities or services. Examples of this type of evaluation include:
> calculating the cost savings associated with a change in benefit options;
> collecting employee ratings of a training program;
> tracking absenteeism rates before and after instituting a program to reward good attendance; and
> tallying the costs of a change in salary structure against the associated savings in terms of employee retention, reduced recruitment costs, and so forth.

Department Level. This type of HRM evaluation focuses on the overall effectiveness of the HRM function. Approaches to evaluating the effectiveness of HRM departments include:
> tracking annual HRM department costs, staffing levels, and activities to evaluate HRM productivity over time and in comparison to industry norms;
> polling employees and managers regarding their satisfaction with the quantity and quality of HRM programs and services; and
> auditing HRM processes to determine if better HRM staff training or different methods of performing these activities would improve efficiency or quality.

Organizational Level. HRM evaluations at the organizational level involve looking at the overall organizational norms, goals, or issues that HRM could address. Examples of organizational HRM evaluation include:

determining the number of HRM plans to facilitate organizational strategic goals and assessing the impact of these HRM plans;

surveying employees to determine areas in which managerial training could improve HRM policy implementation; and

tracking the number of consultations with employees and managers to assess HRM staff impact on the workforce.

To evaluate effectively the HRM function in the future, HRM professionals must recognize that a variety of sources can provide information regarding the effectiveness of the HRM function. Some of these sources are: interviewing HRM customers (that is, obtain customer feedback using individual interviews, focus group discussions, or written surveys); reviewing documents (that is, review company documents in at least seven areas: employment, salary administration, termination practices, equal employment opportunity, training, employee communication, and employee relations); observing HRM operations and activities (that is, use observations to evaluate how well a particular process for completing an HRM activity works or to monitor the quality of interactions and services provided by HRM staff); and compiling benchmark data (that is, compare the organization's quantitative HRM measures to published norms found in surveys and databases).

Cascio (1992) has noted that it has been said many times that if HRM professionals are to make meaningful contributions to an enterprise they must think and act like businesspeople. To promote this sort of outlook, it is useful to ask: "How much profit must a profit center make to keep an HRM department going?" The point of answering this question is to recognize that there is an important connection between HRM and profits.

A second important question that management should ask and that HRM professionals should be prepared to answer is "How much more product can be sold because of your services?" While many HRM contributions are not related directly to the bottom line, it is important to promote increased awareness of how HRM activities relate to the purposes of the organization. Here are some possible HRM department responses in six key areas (Bellman, 1986):

1. Here's what we did for you (in recruiting), here's what it cost, and here's what you would have done without us and what it would have cost you.

2. Here's how much money we saved you by changing insurers in our benefits package.

3. Here's an idea that workers developed in a training program we were leading. It's now working and saving you $50,000 per year.

4. If you had not asked us to do this executive search, you would have had to go outside, at a cost of $30,000. We did it for $5000.

5. You used to have an unhappy person doing this job for $40,000 per year. As a result of our job redesign, you now have a motivated person doing the same work for $20,000.

6. In working with the union on a new contract, we found a new way to deduce grievances by 30 percent, saving the company 6,429 hours per year in management time.

Even though precise bottom-line numbers might continue to be hard to obtain in the future for many HRM activities, it is important to encourage HRM professionals to think in these terms. In reality, for the HRM function to be effectively evaluated in the future, HRM must be truly strategic in its orientation and engage in strategic management in an effort to effectively serve the various internal customers.

In this respect, one recent trend within the field of HRM, consistent with the TQM philosophy, is for HRM professionals to take a customer-oriented approach to implementing the function. In more progressive companies, this means that the HRM function is defined in terms of its customer base, its customers' needs, and the technologies required to satisfy customers' needs. For example, Weyerhauser Corporation's HRM department identified 11 characteristics that would describe a quality HRM organization; they are:

1. Human resources products and service are linked to customer requirements.

2. Customer requirements are translated into internal service applications.

3. Processes for producing products and services are documented with cost/value relationships understood.

4. Reliable methods and standardized processes are in place.

5. Waste and inefficiency is eliminated.

6. Problem solving and decision making are based on facts and data.

7. Critical success variables are tracked, displayed, and maintained.

8. Human resources employees are trained and educated in total quality tools and principles.

9. Human resources systems have been aligned to total quality implementation strategies.

10. Human resources managers provide leadership and support to organizations on large-scale organizational change.

11. Human resources professionals function as strategic partners in managing the business and implementing total quality principles.

A customer orientation increases the organization's ability to evaluate the HRM function and enhances HRM as a strategic partner. In all likelihood, the customer-service orientation will be the trend of the future. It provides a means for HRM to be effectively evaluated and to identify who its customers are, what customers' needs are being met, and how well those needs are being met. IBM's HRM function has actually become a business and may provide an example for what the future holds for HRM professionals and their departments.

When work units seek to implement TQM in their function, these efforts require that the unit begins to think of itself as a business. This entails defining who the customers are, what the customers' needs are, and what products the unit is producing to meet those needs. When the work unit is a staff function, this process presents some problems because it is sometimes difficult to treat the unit as a business itself. However, IBM's HRM department has gone beyond thinking about the function as a business to actually making it one (Thornburg, 1993).

IBM is developing a subsidiary company called Workforce Solutions that is made up of much of what used to be known as IBM's personnel function. The division is now a professional services firm that provides what amounts to human resources consulting services to line managers. The newly expanded role presents a unique set of problems and issues.

First, Workforce Solutions, in line with TQM principles, must identify its customers, recognize the customers' needs, and define the product and service offerings to meet those needs. Because the new division will be a profit center within the organization, increased attention must be paid to identifying the costs of the various products and services and developing systems for billing clients within IBM. These needs have repercussions on the appraisal and training systems within the division. Workforce Solutions' employees will be appraised by how well they obtain certain profit figures. The new appraisal requires training the traditional HRM managers in accounting and financial techniques.

Because Workforce Solutions is in its infant stages, it is too early to tell how effective this new structure is. If it turns out to be successful, the subsidiary may begin to offer its products and services to firms other than IBM. Thus, this extensive restructuring, consistent with the principles of TQM, may turn out to be the model for the HRM organization of the future. This is a mind-set that will have to become instilled in today's and tomorrow's HRM professionals who hope to demonstrate the value that the function adds to the organization.

HUMAN RESOURCES MANAGEMENT'S ROLE IN DEVELOPING FUTURE MANAGERS AND LEADERS

Throughout this book, we have discussed many of the challenges and changes facing organizations and their HRM departments as they approach the twenty-first century. Because of changes such as these, HRM professionals will have to help their organizations' managers and leaders change their approaches to their jobs if they are to succeed in meeting the new challenges. In fact, their profiles should look some-what different than they often do today. Consider a prediction from *The Wall Street Journal* concerning what successful executives will be like in the year 2000 compared to what they are like today. For the past several decades, executive profiles have typically looked like this:

He started out as a finance man with an undergraduate degree in accounting. He methodically worked his way up through the company from the controller's office in a division, to running that division, to the top job. His military back-ground shows. He is used to giving orders — and to having them obeyed. As head of the United Way drive, he is a big man in his community. However, the first time he travelled overseas on business was as chief executive. Computers make him nervous. (Bennett, 1989, p. A-4)

Now compare this with predictions about what a twenty-first century executive will look like:

His [or her] undergraduate degree is in French literature, but he also has a joint MBA/engineering degree. He started in research and was quickly picked out as a potential CEO. He zigzagged from research to marketing to finance. He proved valuable in Brazil by turning around a failing joint venture. He speaks Portuguese and French and is on a first-name basis with commerce ministers in half a dozen countries. Unlike his predecessor's predecessor, he isn't a drill sergeant. He is first among equals in a five-person Office of the Chief Executive. (Bennett, 1989, p. A-4)

Clearly, the future holds considerable excitement and promise for managers and leaders who are properly prepared to meet the challenges. How do HRM departments and their organizations prepare them? One study suggested that the manager of the future must be able to fill at least the following four roles (Ehrlich, 1989):

1. Global Strategist — Executives of the future must understand world markets and think internationally. They must have a capacity to identify unique business opportunities and then move quickly to exploit them.
2. Master of Technology — Executives and managers of the future must be able to get the most out of emerging technologies, whether these technolo-gies are in manufacturing, communications, or marketing.
3. Politician Par Excellence — The successful executive of the future will understand how to cut through red tape to get a job done, how to build bridges with key people from highly divergent backgrounds and points of view, and how to make coalitions and joint ventures work.
4. Leader-motivator — Finally, the executive of tomorrow must understand group dynamics and how to counsel, coach, and command work teams and individuals so they perform at their best. Future organizations will place greater emphasis on teams and coordinated efforts, requiring managers to understand participative management techniques.

To this list we would add that managers of the future must be great communicators. They must be able to communicate effectively with an increasingly diverse set of employees as well as customers, suppliers, community, and government leaders.

Whether these predictions and others like them are accurate is difficult to know. Suffice it to say that most futurists agree that the organizational world of the twenty-first century will likely resemble, to some extent, the portrait described here. The task for future HRM professionals, then, is to help develop these requisite skills in their organization's managers and leaders to the extent possible so they will be ready for the challenges of the next decade.

A SUMMARY GLIMPSE OF THE FUTURE: CHALLENGES AND CHANGES FOR HUMAN RESOURCES MANAGEMENT PROFESSIONALS

As we move through the final decade of the twentieth century and on to the twenty-first, there can be little doubt that HRM faces some of the greatest challenges since its definition as a separate staff function almost a century ago. This renewed vigor stems from numerous influences, such as the changing nature of the economy and government-legal influences, new organizational forms, global competition, and the increased feeling that organizations are vehicles for fulfilling societal goals. In conclusion, some of the factors that will continue to force HRM to be transformed from a narrowly defined specialty into a more strategic function are presented below.

The HRM function is undergoing a number of changes in terms of its importance to the organization as well as in the way it operates. Among the major current and future changes in the operational aspects of the HRM function are the following (Harvey, 1986; Herren, 1989; Leap & Crino, 1993; Dessler, 1994):

The influence of the HRM function will continue to increase. Most top management teams realize that the management of human resources is a vital organizational function. A survey of HRM managers indicates that the HRM function has gained influence and has the potential to continue doing so in the near future. HRM managers are becoming more involved in general business decisions and more aware of the impact HRM programs have on organizational goals (McDonough, 1986).

HRM's traditional role as consultant to the organization should increase in the years ahead. In fact, top HRM jobs are increasingly demanding a proven track record in providing top-notch consulting services on previous jobs. Because organizations must cope with shorter product life cycles, increased competition, and a more sophisticated workforce, HRM's expert advice in areas like redesigning organizations, monitoring attitudes, instituting, quality improvement teams, and molding company culture will be in high demand.

While HRM's consultative/staff role will expand, its line role will expand as well. In fact, there are already quite a few precedents for HRM being a line function. It has always been so in the largest Japanese firms and in the military, where HRM might make staffing decisions more or less unilaterally. And the Vatican's HRM department, which picks and appoints the bishops of the Catholic church, is strictly a line department. Today, even the most prestigious and influential U.S. HRM departments generally only advise and assist line managers. To make the jump to a more line-oriented role, the way these departments are staffed will probably change, too. For example, the vice president for HRM may increasingly have a top-level operating background and come up through the ranks before assuming the HRM role.

HRM policies will be centrally formulated, but implemented on a decentralized basis. The legal and economic complexity of many HRM policies requires that they be centrally formulated by HRM professionals at the corporate level. However, improvements in management information systems will allow these policies to be applied on a decentralized basis. Management development programs will also be required to enable line managers to acquire the background and skills needed to implement HRM policies.

The use of automation and human resources information systems will increase. As is the case of nearly all organizational functions, such as accounting, finance, marketing, and production, computer technology will continue to permeate the personnel/HRM function. Software programs for microcomputers have been developed to plan, monitor, and evaluate HRM programs (King, 1985). Human resources information systems are being used to manage recruitment, selection, training, performance appraisal, compensation, and other HRM programs. However, this means that organizations must deal with the problem of computer anxiety among employees (Faerstein, 1986).

HRM departments will be more accountable for their contributions to the organization's mission, goals, and objectives. As noted earlier, there is a trend toward integrating HRM strategies with global organizational strategies. As corporations in the United States attempt to compete with Japanese and other foreign producers, the HRM function will be expected to make greater contributions to productivity and efficiency (Mischkind, 1987; Nienstedt, & Wintermantel, 1985). HRM managers use hard quantitative measures to monitor absenteeism rates, employee turnover, and on-the-job accidents and injuries. In addition, HRM managers use reliability and validity coefficients, base rates, and percentage of correct decisions to assess the utility of employment selection predictors. Training and development programs can be evaluated by using either simple or sophisticated research designs that provide assessments of learning, retention, and behavioral changes among trainees. Initially, some of the hard measures of the HRM department's effectiveness were precipitated by legal requirements, such as the record-keeping requirements of the Occupational Safety and Health Administration and the Equal Employment Opportunity laws. Additional measures were devised to determine the cost effectiveness of HRM programs, and these efforts will undoubtedly be expanded to examine the impact of the HRM function on the organization's strategies and contributions to bottom-line financial and market measures.

HRM professionals must be increasingly cognizant of the attitudes of employees and their desire to be creative. The education levels and knowledge of the labor force have increased. This trend is attributable to additional formal schooling, as well as the greater individual awareness that comes with constant exposure to the news media. As a result, employees are often more critical about the manner in which business is conducted in the workplace, and, in many instances, they also want a chance to demonstrate their creativity. HRM professionals must help the organization maintain a pulse on current employee attitudes in order to eliminate problems before they escalate into serious matters. Thus, HRM professionals must be able to use employee attitude surveys skillfully (Wright, 1986; Smallwood & Folkman, 1987). Encouraging and channeling employee creativity is important for two reasons. First, employees may have suggestions for improving productivity, cutting costs, or implementing new products and services. Second, employees who are allowed to demonstrate their intelligence and ingenuity are more likely to be satisfied and fulfilled in their jobs. Quality circles and participative management techniques have helped in this respect. In addition, suggestion systems and patent policies should be integrated into compensation programs (Meehan, 1986). Finally, HRM managers must help devise methods for fostering employee creativity, especially when group norms are stifling (Blake & Mouton, 1985).

HRM is a pervasive function that requires cooperation and efforts of supervisory employees at all levels. Even when HRM policies are created on a centralized basis, they are applied in a decentralized manner. Middle-level managers and first-line supervisors are all responsible for understanding and implementing a variety of selection, training, performance appraisal, compensation, employee discipline, health and safety, and other HRM policies. Supervisors, for example, often make the final decisions on which employees are hired, how and when they will be trained, the quality of their performance appraisals, and the amount of their pay raises. Unlike organizational decisions affecting production facilities, finances, or marketing, HRM decisions are often widely shared. It is, therefore, important that all supervisory employees appreciate the importance of HRM and its various functional areas.

Increased calls for responding to the demands of a more diverse workforce. HRM professionals must be aware of the changing nature of the workforce and anticipate its probable impact on the quality, quantity, and demand for human resources. They must plan recruitment, selection, and training programs appropriate to the labor force of the future and the business and legal environments that are likely to exist. Each diversity dimension and trend (increases in the number of women, minorities, aged, and disabled, for example) can be examined as an isolated aspect of the challenge to HRM; however, it is the interconnectedness and the dynamic interaction of these forces that will continue to help reshape organizations and how they relate to the workforce.

While past efforts to assimilate a culturally diverse workforce have sprung from legal pressure or moral concerns over fairness, those efforts must now be viewed in light of bottom-line issues. In addition, the challenge of assembling and managing a workforce that reflects the population it serves — in terms of age, race, gender, education, and experience — is complex now, and will become more so, as the nation diversifies further. HRM professionals in the private sector will feel the mounting pressure to design and implement policies and programs that draw diverse people to their organization, motivate them to excel, and pull them into the highest reaches of management.

Changing demographics and a changing workforce will demand changes in employee benefits. For instance, elder care — direct or indirect care provided to aging relatives — will become more popular as employees and their relatives get older. Furthermore, the tendency toward earlier retirement seems to have bottomed out. The expectation for the coming years is for a very gradual increase in the retirement age, for example, the average retirement age is expected to increase for salaried employees in 40 percent of the organizations recently surveyed and for union employees in about one-third of them. Less than 20 percent of the respondents expect a decrease in this average age (Paine, 1988). The United States has already adopted a gradual increase in the normal retirement age for Social Security purposes.

Consistent with the gradually rising retirement age, about one-third of the organizations surveyed expected early retirement windows to be used less frequently than in the past. In turn, the organization's gradually aging workforce will trigger other HRM changes, as employers have to cope with elder care, motivate plateaued workers, upgrade employees' skills, and institute more flexible work hours.

HRM professionals must continue to find ways to help their organizations reconcile the conflicting needs of women, work, and families. HRM policies that were designed for a traditional family consisting of a male breadwinner and female homemaker are out of date.

Restructuring career ladders and compensation. The shift to knowledge work and knowledge workers also creates a need to rethink and restructure career ladders, compensation, and recognition (Drucker, 1988). The traditional career ladder in most businesses has only managerial rungs. But for most knowledge workers, a promotion to a management job is a wrong reward. The good ones often prefer to keep on doing professional or technical work. In the knowledge-based organization, knowledge workers are the bosses, and the manager is in a supporting role as their planner and coordinator. But this means that jobs — their responsibilities, relationships, and rewards — have to be thought through and redesigned, again, probably by the HRM function.

As organizations continue their efforts to remain union-free, HRM professionals will need to work toward creating an atmosphere in which workers do not feel the need for union representation. HRM professionals will serve as the catalyst for developing and maintaining nonunion attitudes. Remaining union-free requires a strong commitment by management at all levels, open communication, and trust. In many ways, the commitment necessary to maintain a union-free environment requires a much more demanding effort by the HRM professional. Some organizations will not maintain that commitment and, therefore, will become vulnerable to organizing efforts. HRM professionals, therefore, must ensure that an employee relations system is created whereby employees are treated in a positive manner, allowing each individual to maintain his or her self-esteem and advance individually as the organization advances.

Slower growth in the labor force. The number of workers available to the labor force is expected to grow much more slowly over the next ten years than it has in the past. This will make recruitment more difficult. As one expert puts it: "In a scarce labor market, the HRM department needs to differentiate itself and the company from the competition so that they can attract the desirable, highly qualified job seekers who are in demand" (Herren, 1989, p. 20). Recruiting top-notch candidates during the next ten years will, therefore, be a very challenging task for HRM professionals.

The training function will take on added importance in the coming years as increasingly complex knowledge jobs must be filled in part by a workforce that is often ill prepared educationally to meet the new challenges. Increasingly, HRM will be called upon to implement a growing range of training programs, from basic skills and literacy training up through computer skills training and training interpersonal communications and leadership. Thus, in this area, too, the role of HRM will have to expand in the next few years.

But perhaps the most striking change in HRM will be its growing role in developing and implementing corporate strategy. Strategies increasingly involve merging employees from different organizations. This means that companies must face demographic and workforce changes discussed earlier in this book. It will increasingly be necessary to involve HRM in the earliest stages of developing the organization's strategic plan. HRM will move from reactor to developer and implementer of strategy.

International human resources management will increasingly be recognized as a major determinant of success or failure in international business. Thus, HRM will need to become more global in nature. HRM practices in one country will need to be adopted and adapted to meet the needs of another country. To compete in the world economy, U.S. companies with the assistance of their HRM professionals will need to put greater effort into selecting and retraining talented employees, employee training and development, and dismantling the traditional company structure, which limits employees' ability to be innovative and creative (Hitt, Hoskisson, & Harrison, 1991). Besides taking steps to ensure that employees are better used, HRM professionals must ensure that their organizations do a better job of preparing employees and their families for overseas assignment. Additionally, HRM professionals will be required to put more time into training and developing foreign employees.

CONCLUSION

As highlighted throughout this book, a review of the recent HRM literature illustrates the rapidly shifting nature of the HRM landscape. Some of the more prominent trends present complex and often perplexing problems or challenges with which HRM practitioners must deal as we move closer to the twenty-first century. As noted earlier in this book, some of these challenges are:

planning for downsizing, streamlining, and restructuring;

dealing with corporate mergers and acquisitions, along with the deregulation of some industries;

linking HRM goals, objectives, plans, and programs to the company's strategic plans;

getting top management to realize that human resources are as critical to the success of the organization as financial resources;

helping the organization to remain competitive on a global basis;

cultivating ethical behavior, trust, and teamwork;

responding to increasing diversity in the workforce;

dealing sensitively, compassionately, and successfully with employee performance problems;

appreciating, understanding and responding to changing employee expectations;

accepting the role of computers and HRM; and

accepting the changing operational aspects of the HRM.

Several shifts also characterize the new organizational requirements and challenge the assumptions that have traditionally dominated HRM activities. These and other shifts have resulted from a redefined focus within many U.S. organizations. In many instances this is a focus away from the internal (the way we've always done it) to the external (what the customer values). Such a fundamental change in focus has forced corollary changes that make the continuous improvement of work just as important as the work itself. Listed below are the three major shifts that pose challenges to traditional HRM activities:

1. Organization structure. The first shift can be found in the very shape and structure of the organization. The shift is from the classic hierarchical form, which requires a vertical/functional orientation, to a process-flow orientation that orients people horizontally along the service/product delivery chain.
2. Nature of jobs. The second shift can be found in the very nature of jobs. No longer defined as a set of narrow, discrete tasks performed by individuals, jobs are now being thought of as work performed by self-managed teams. These teams, largely cross-functional, perform whole activities related to customer products or services. Implicit in this new definition is the need for workers to have more complete information about how the business works and the way the business functions in its markets. Control now comes from information, feedback, and measurement rather than from close scrutiny by a boss.
3. Psychological contract. The third shift is the psychological contract between the organization and its employees. This company-centered contract initially regarded employees as interchangeable parts and later as assets. The contract is now viewed as more partnership centered. Employees are viewed as internal customers and important sources of competitive advantage.

As a result of challenges and shifts like those presented above, the bedrock assumptions on which HRM policies and practices were built have turned to shifting sand. Thus, traditional HRM processes (that is, employee training, compensation systems, and so forth) demand reconstruction and alignment with new organizational premises. It has been the premise of this book that HRM professionals must be more proactive if they are to effectively address a continuously changing set of challenges and issues. It is our hope that the ideas expressed in this book will, in some way, help HRM professionals address the inevitable challenges and changes.

REFERENCES

Bellman, G. M. 1986. Doing more with less. *Personnel Administrator 31*: 46–52.
Bennett, A. 1989. February 27. Going global: The chief executives in the year 2000 are likely to have had much foreign experience. *The Wall Street Journal*: A-4.

Blake, R. R. & Mouton, J. S. 1985, August. Don't let group norms stifle productivity. *Personnel*: 28–33.

Burg, R. & Smith, B. 1987. November/December. Restructuring compensation and benefits to support strategy, Part I, Executive compensation. *Compensation and Benefits Review*: 15–22.

Caruth, D. L., Noe III, R. M., & Mondy, R. W. 1990. *Staffing the contemporary organization*. New York: Praeger Publishers.

Cascio, W. F. 1992. *Managing human resources*. New York: McGraw-Hill.

Cashman, M. E. & McElroy, J. C. 1991, January. Evaluating the HR function. *HRMagazine 36*: 70–73.

Dessler, G. 1994. *Human resource management* (6th ed.). Englewood Cliffs, NJ: Prentice Hall.

Drucker, P. 1988, January 20. *The Wall Street Journal*: B2.

Ehrlich, E. 1989, September 25. How the next decade will differ. *Business Week*: 142–56.

Faerstein, P. H. 1986, January. Fighting computer anxiety. *Personnel*: 12–17.

Harvey, L. J. 1986, November. Nine major trends in HRM. *Personnel Administrator*, 102–5, 108–9.

Herren, L. 1989, June. The new game of HR: Playing to win. *Personnel*: 19–22.

Hitt, M. A., Hoskisson, R. E., & Harrison, J. S. 1991. Strategic competitiveness in the 1990's: Challenges and opportunities for U.S. executives. *Academy of Management Executive 5*(2): 7–22.

King, A. S. 1985, May. How "micros" are changing HR information management. *Personnel*, 49–56.

Kydd, C. T. & Oppenheim, L. 1990. Using human resource management to enhance competitiveness. *HRMagazine 29*(2): 145–66.

Leap, T. L. & Crino, M. D. 1993. *Personnel/Human resource management* (2nd ed.). New York: Macmillan.

McDonough, E. F. 1986, January. How much power does HR have, and what can it do to win more? *Personnel*, 18–25.

Meehan, R. H. 1986, February. Programs that foster creativity and innovation. *Personnel*: 31–35.

Mischkind, L. A. 1987, July. Seven steps to productivity improvement. *Personnel*: 30.

Mondy, R. W. & Noe III, R. M. 1994. *Human resource management* (5th ed.). Boston, MA: Allyn & Bacon.

Nienstedt, P. & Wintermantel, R. 1985, August. Restructuring organizations to improve productivity. *Personnel*: 34–40.

Paine, T. 1988. Benefits in the 1990's. *Personnel Journal*. 82.

Smallwood, N. & Folkman, J. 1987, August. Why employee surveys don't always work. *Personnel*: 20–28.

Software Magazine. 1989, January. How the government created HR systems. *Software Magazine*: 3.

Stewart, T. 1992, November 30. Allied Signal's turnaround blitz. *Fortune*: 72–76.

Thornburg, L. 1993, February. IBM's agents of influence. *HRMagazine*: 80–84.

Wilhelm, W. R. 1990. Revitalizing the human resource management function in a mature, large corporation. *HRMagazine 29*(2): 129–44.

Wright, M. 1986, September. Helping employees speak out about their jobs and workplace. *Personnel*: 56–60.

Index

ABOUT THE AUTHORS

Ronald R. Sims is Professor of Business Administration at the College of William and Mary, where he teaches courses in organizational behavior and human resource management. His research focuses on experiential learning, employee training and development, and other human resource management issues.

Serbrenia J. Sims received her Ed.D. from the College of William and Mary in higher education administration. Her research focuses on higher education policy, diversity, and human resource management issues in the public and not-for-profit areas.

ISBN 0-89930-885-6

EAN

9 780899 308852

HARDCOVER BAR CODE